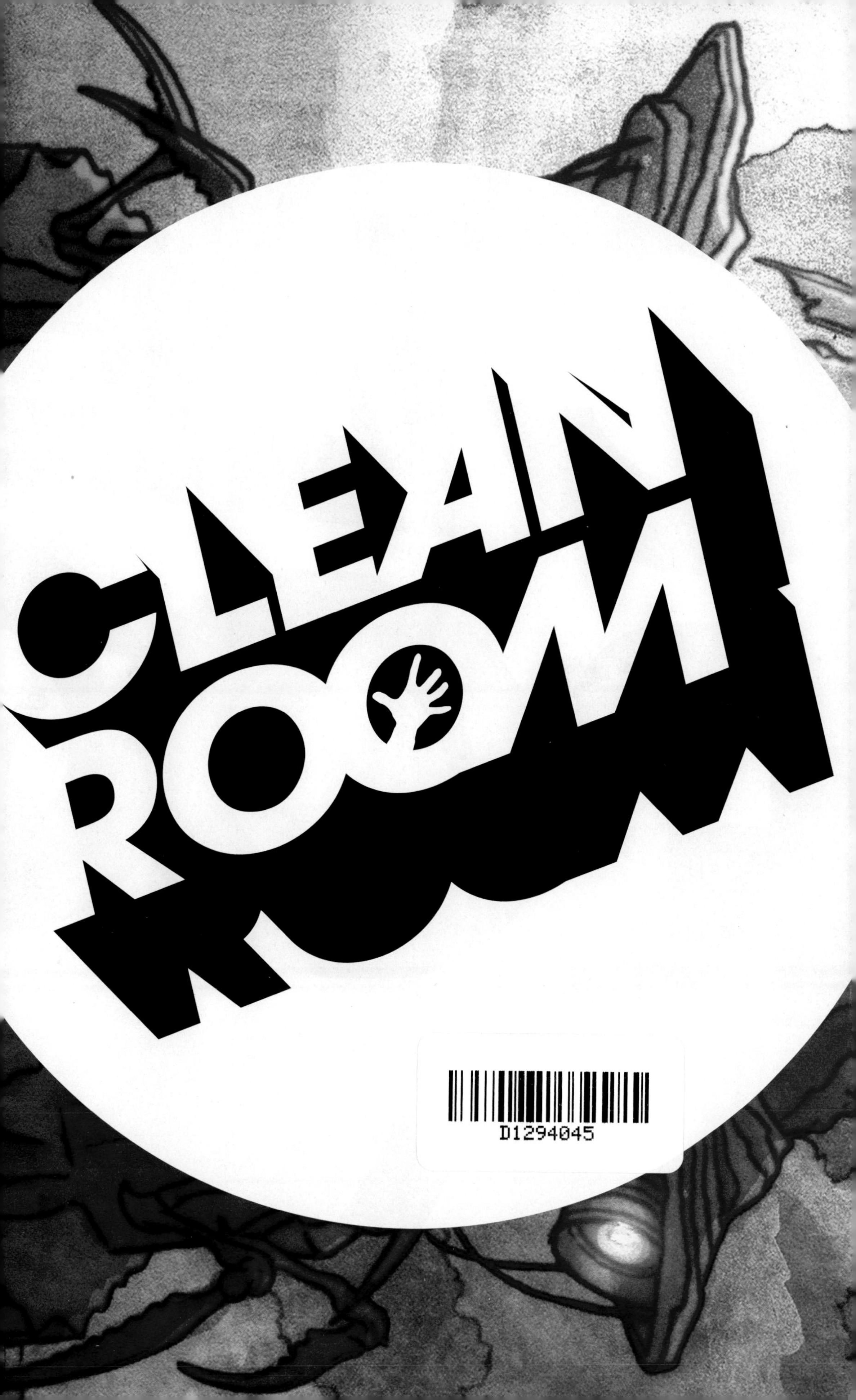
CLEAN
ROOM

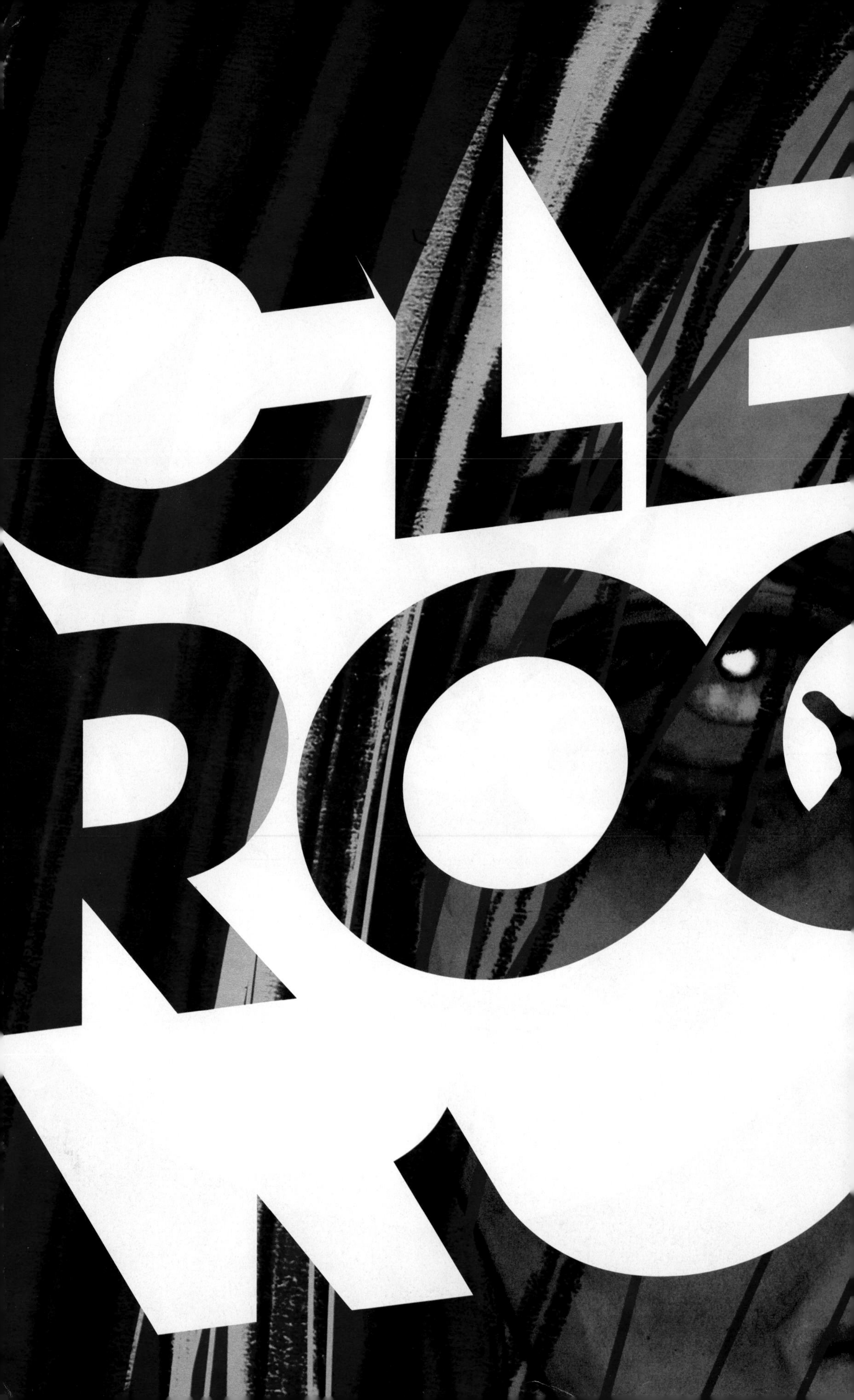

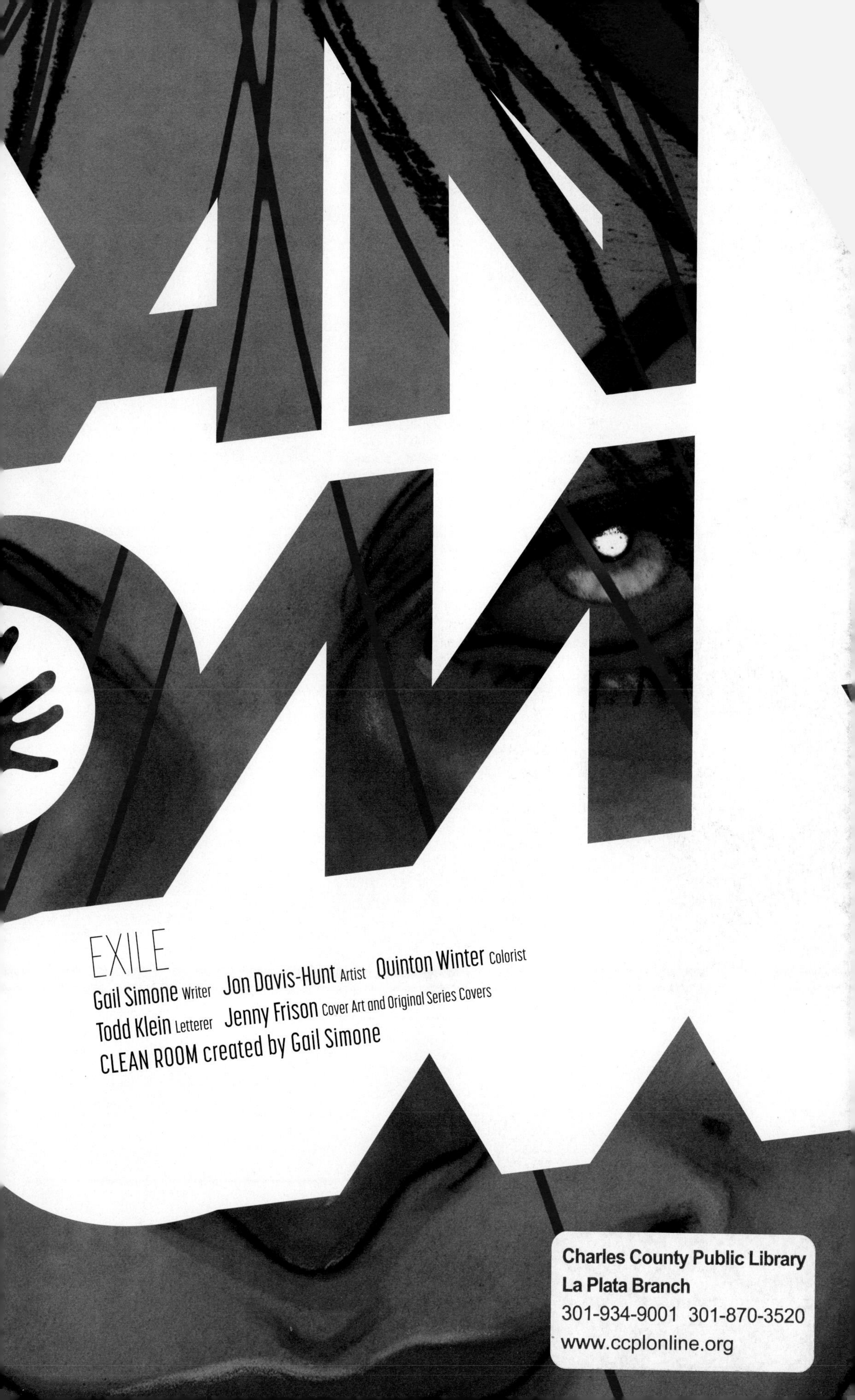

EXILE

Gail Simone Writer Jon Davis-Hunt Artist Quinton Winter Colorist
Todd Klein Letterer Jenny Frison Cover Art and Original Series Covers
CLEAN ROOM created by Gail Simone

SHELLY BOND MOLLY MAHAN Editors - Original Series
ROWENA YOW Associate Editor - Original Series
MAGGIE HOWELL Assistant Editor - Original Series
JAMIE S. RICH Group Editor - Vertigo Comics
JEB WOODARD Group Editor - Collected Editions
SCOTT NYBAKKEN Editor - Collected Edition
STEVE COOK Design Director - Books
LOUIS PRANDI Publication Design

DIANE NELSON President
DAN DiDIO Publisher
JIM LEE Publisher
GEOFF JOHNS President & Chief Creative Officer
AMIT DESAI Executive VP - Business & Marketing Strategy,
Direct to Consumer & Global Franchise Management
SAM ADES Senior VP - Direct to Consumer
BOBBIE CHASE VP - Talent Development
MARK CHIARELLO Senior VP - Art, Design & Collected Editions
JOHN CUNNINGHAM Senior VP - Sales & Trade Marketing
ANNE DePIES Senior VP - Business Strategy, Finance & Administration
DON FALLETTI VP - Manufacturing Operations
LAWRENCE GANEM VP - Editorial Administration & Talent Relations
ALISON GILL Senior VP - Manufacturing & Operations
HANK KANALZ Senior VP - Editorial Strategy & Administration
JAY KOGAN VP - Legal Affairs
THOMAS LOFTUS VP - Business Affairs
JACK MAHAN VP - Business Affairs
NICK J. NAPOLITANO VP - Manufacturing Administration
EDDIE SCANNELL VP - Consumer Marketing
COURTNEY SIMMONS Senior VP - Publicity & Communications
JIM (SKI) SOKOLOWSKI VP - Comic Book Specialty Sales & Trade Marketing
NANCY SPEARS VP - Mass, Book, Digital Sales & Trade Marketing

CLEAN ROOM: EXILE

DC Comics
2900 West Alameda Avenue
Burbank, CA 91505
Printed in the USA. First Printing.
ISBN: 978-1-4012-6740-7

Logo design by STEVE COOK

Library of Congress Cataloging-in-Publication Data

Names: Simone, Gail, author. | Davis-Hunt, Jon, artist,
colorist. | Winter, Quinton, colorist. | Klein, Todd, letterer. |
Frison, Jenny, artist.
Title: Clean room. Volume 2, Exile / Gail Simone, writer ;
Jon Davis-Hunt, artist ; Quinton Winter, Jon Davis-Hunt,
colorists ; Todd Klein, letterer ; Jenny Frison, cover art
and original series covers.
Other titles: Exile.
Description: Burbank, CA : DC Comics/Vertigo, [2017]
| "Clean Room created by Gail Simone" | "Originally
published in single magazine form as CLEAN ROOM 7-12"
Identifiers: LCCN 2016038918 | ISBN 9781401267407
(paperback)
Subjects: LCSH: Comic books, strips, etc. | BISAC: COMICS
& GRAPHIC NOVELS / Superheroes.
Classification: LCC PN6727.S51579 C58 2017 | DDC
741.5/973–dc23
LC record available at https://lccn.loc.gov/2016038918

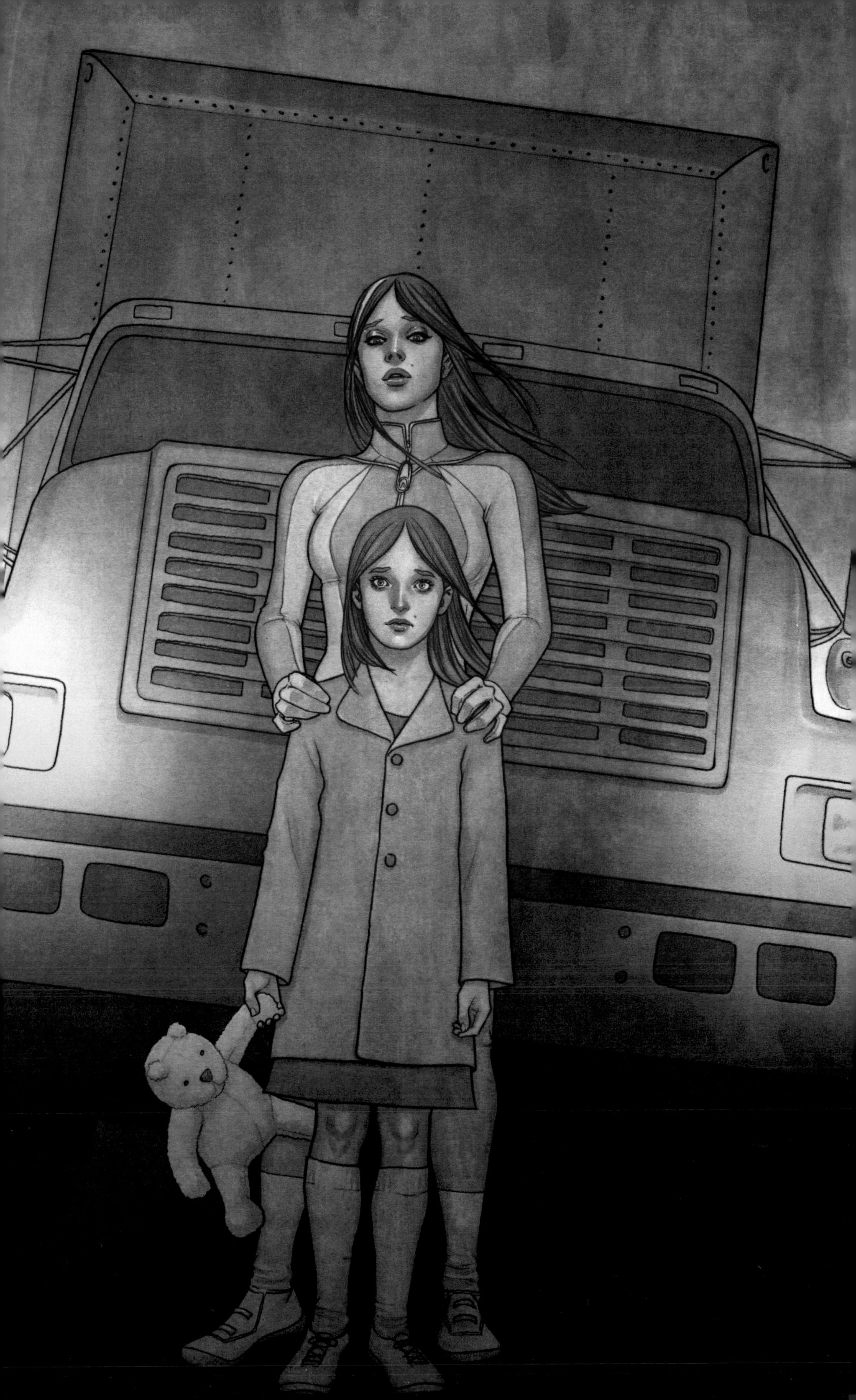

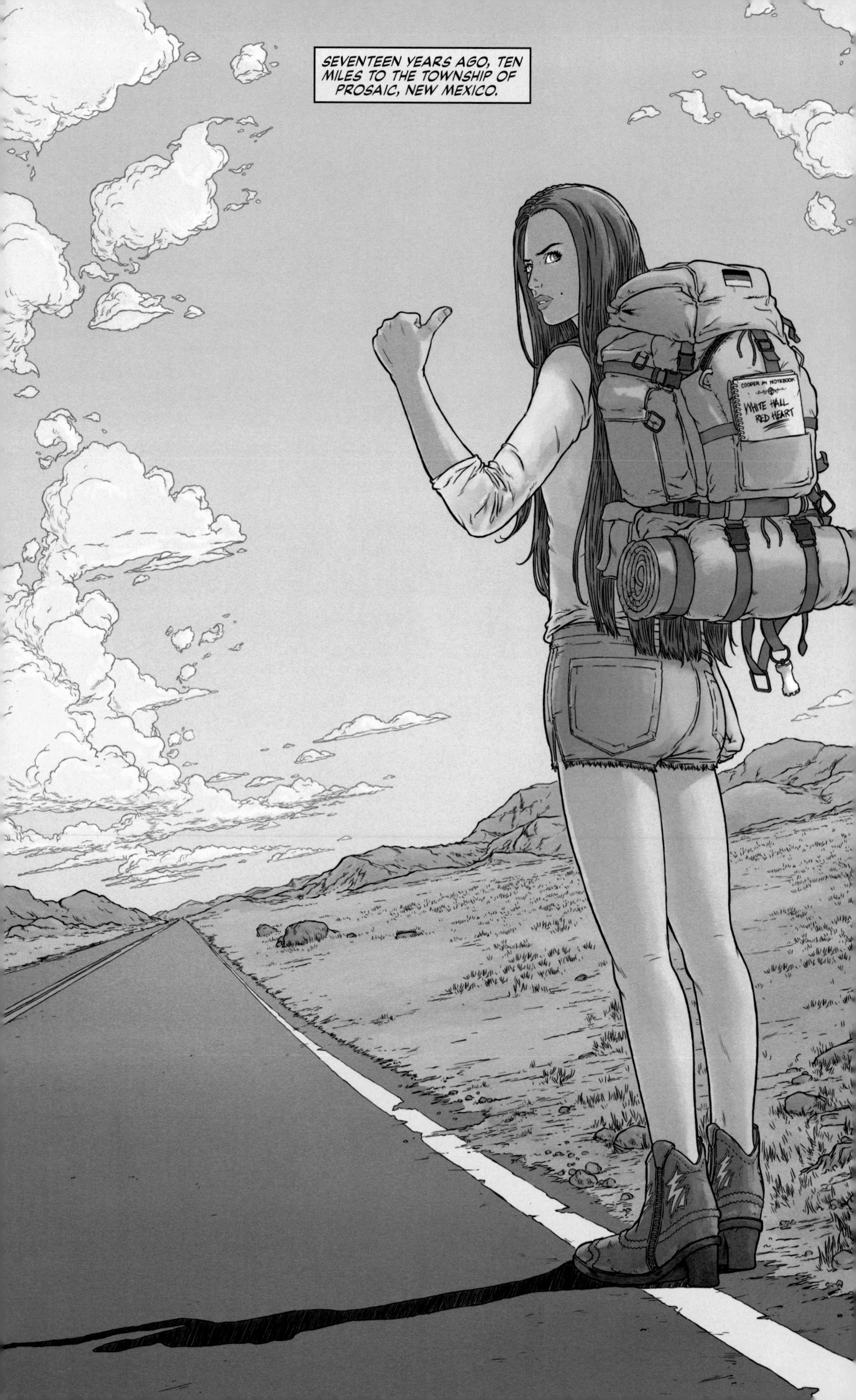
SEVENTEEN YEARS AGO, TEN MILES TO THE TOWNSHIP OF PROSAIC, NEW MEXICO.
COOPER A4 NOTEBOOK
WHITE HALL RED HEART

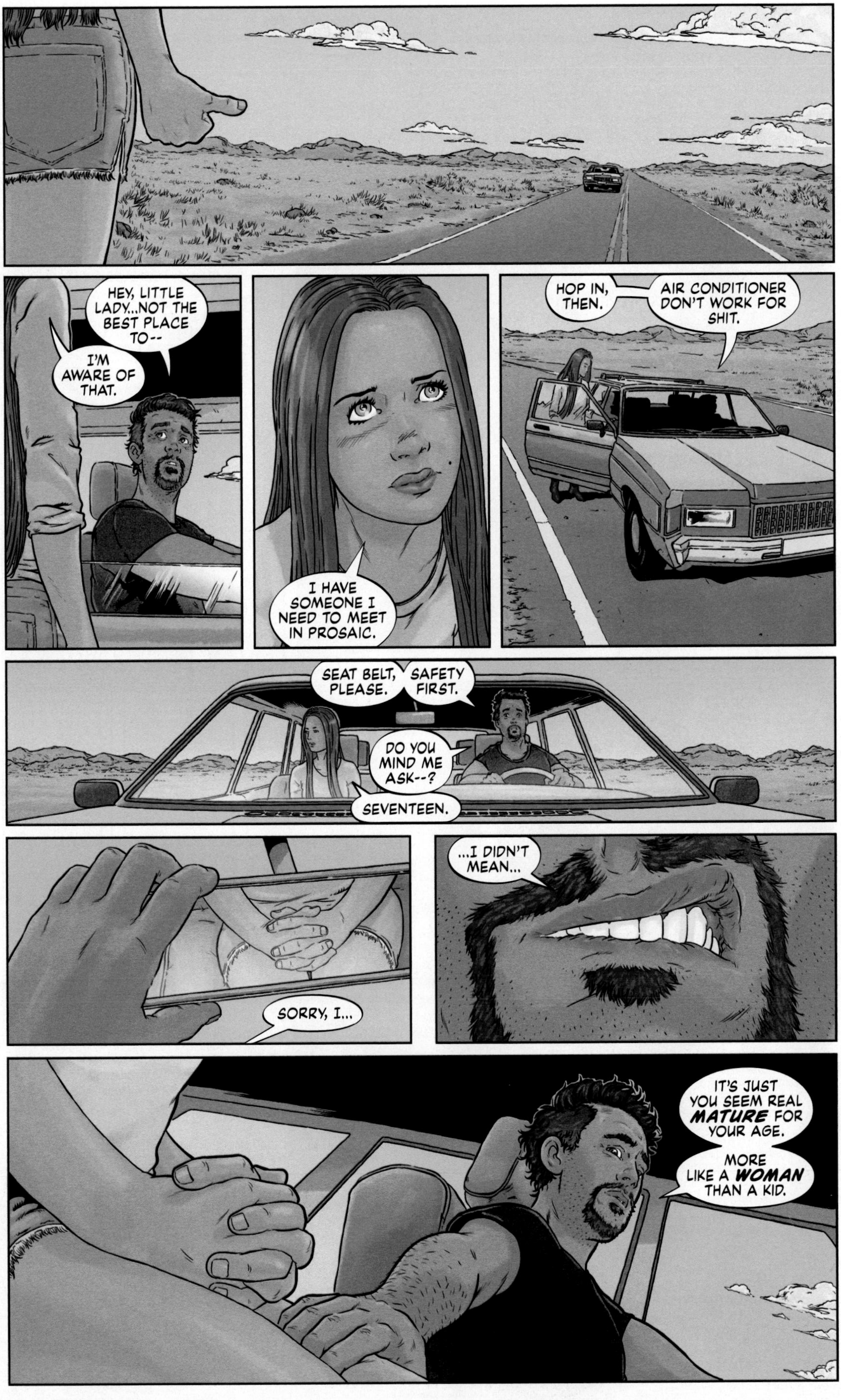
HEY, LITTLE LADY...NOT THE BEST PLACE TO--
I'M AWARE OF THAT.
I HAVE SOMEONE I NEED TO MEET IN PROSAIC.
HOP IN, THEN.
AIR CONDITIONER DON'T WORK FOR SHIT.
SEAT BELT, PLEASE.
SAFETY FIRST.
DO YOU MIND ME ASK--?
SEVENTEEN.
SORRY, I...
...I DIDN'T MEAN...
IT'S JUST YOU SEEM REAL **MATURE** FOR YOUR AGE.
MORE LIKE A **WOMAN** THAN A KID.

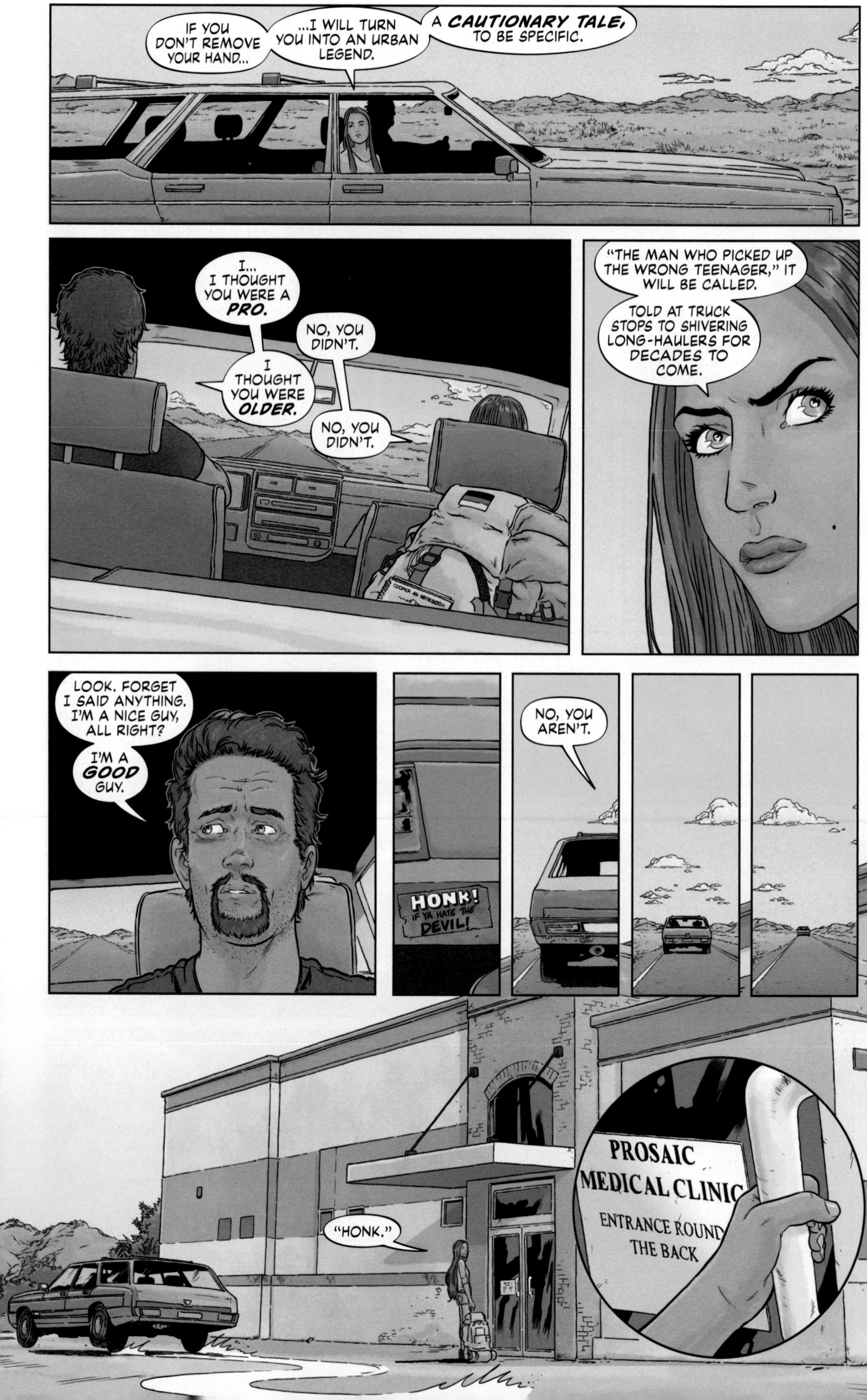
IF YOU DON'T REMOVE YOUR HAND...
...I WILL TURN YOU INTO AN URBAN LEGEND.
A CAUTIONARY TALE, TO BE SPECIFIC.
I... I THOUGHT YOU WERE A PRO.
NO, YOU DIDN'T.
I THOUGHT YOU WERE OLDER.
NO, YOU DIDN'T.
"THE MAN WHO PICKED UP THE WRONG TEENAGER," IT WILL BE CALLED.
TOLD AT TRUCK STOPS TO SHIVERING LONG-HAULERS FOR DECADES TO COME.
LOOK. FORGET I SAID ANYTHING. I'M A NICE GUY, ALL RIGHT?
I'M A GOOD GUY.
HONK! IF YA HATE THE DEVIL!
NO, YOU AREN'T.
"HONK."
PROSAIC MEDICAL CLINIC
ENTRANCE ROUND THE BACK

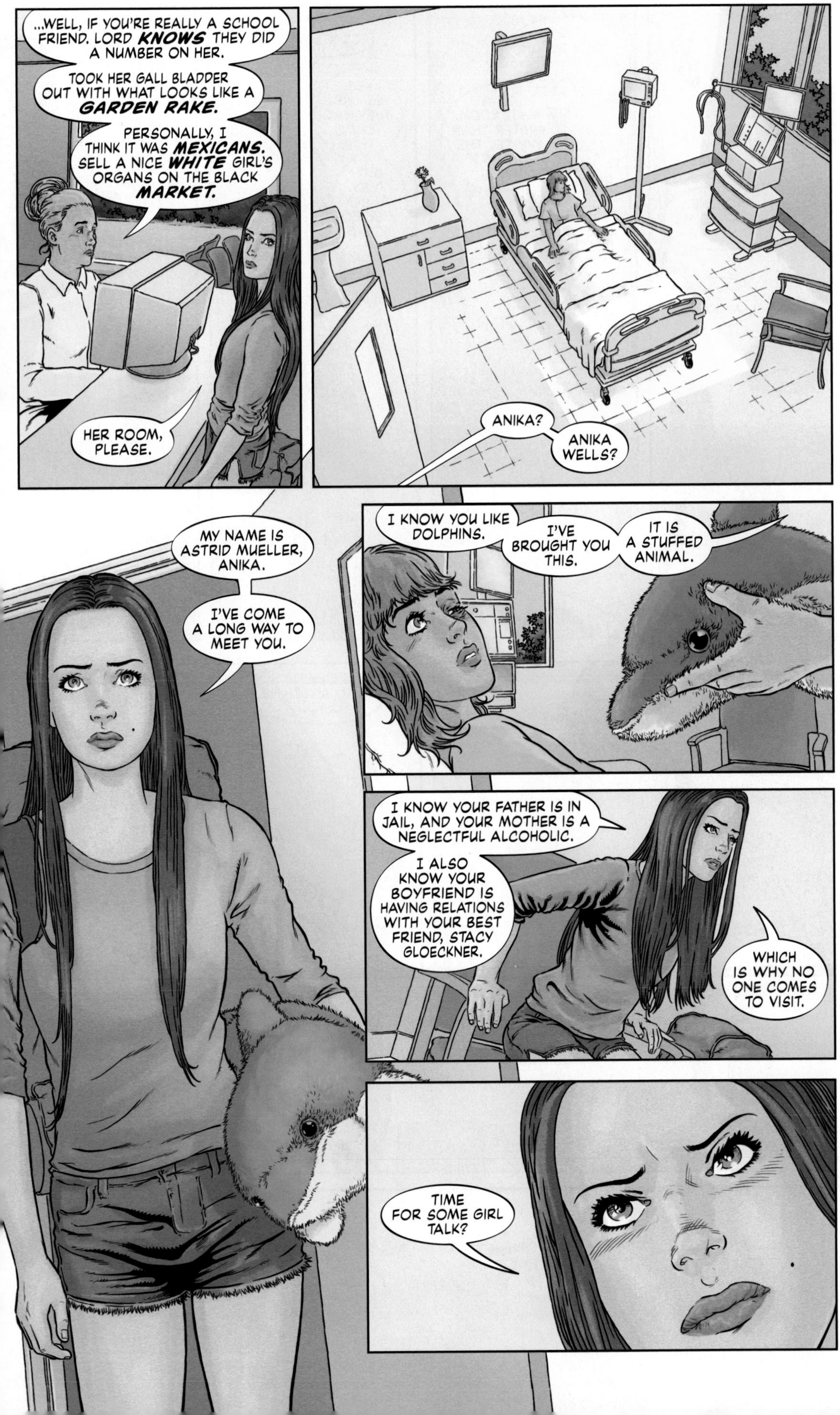
...WELL, IF YOU'RE REALLY A SCHOOL FRIEND. LORD **KNOWS** THEY DID A NUMBER ON HER.
TOOK HER GALL BLADDER OUT WITH WHAT LOOKS LIKE A **GARDEN RAKE.**
PERSONALLY, I THINK IT WAS **MEXICANS.** SELL A NICE **WHITE** GIRL'S ORGANS ON THE BLACK **MARKET.**
HER ROOM, PLEASE.
ANIKA?
ANIKA WELLS?
MY NAME IS ASTRID MUELLER, ANIKA.
I'VE COME A LONG WAY TO MEET YOU.
I KNOW YOU LIKE DOLPHINS.
I'VE BROUGHT YOU THIS.
IT IS A STUFFED ANIMAL.
I KNOW YOUR FATHER IS IN JAIL, AND YOUR MOTHER IS A NEGLECTFUL ALCOHOLIC.
I ALSO KNOW YOUR BOYFRIEND IS HAVING RELATIONS WITH YOUR BEST FRIEND, STACY GLOECKNER.
WHICH IS WHY NO ONE COMES TO VISIT.
TIME FOR SOME GIRL TALK?

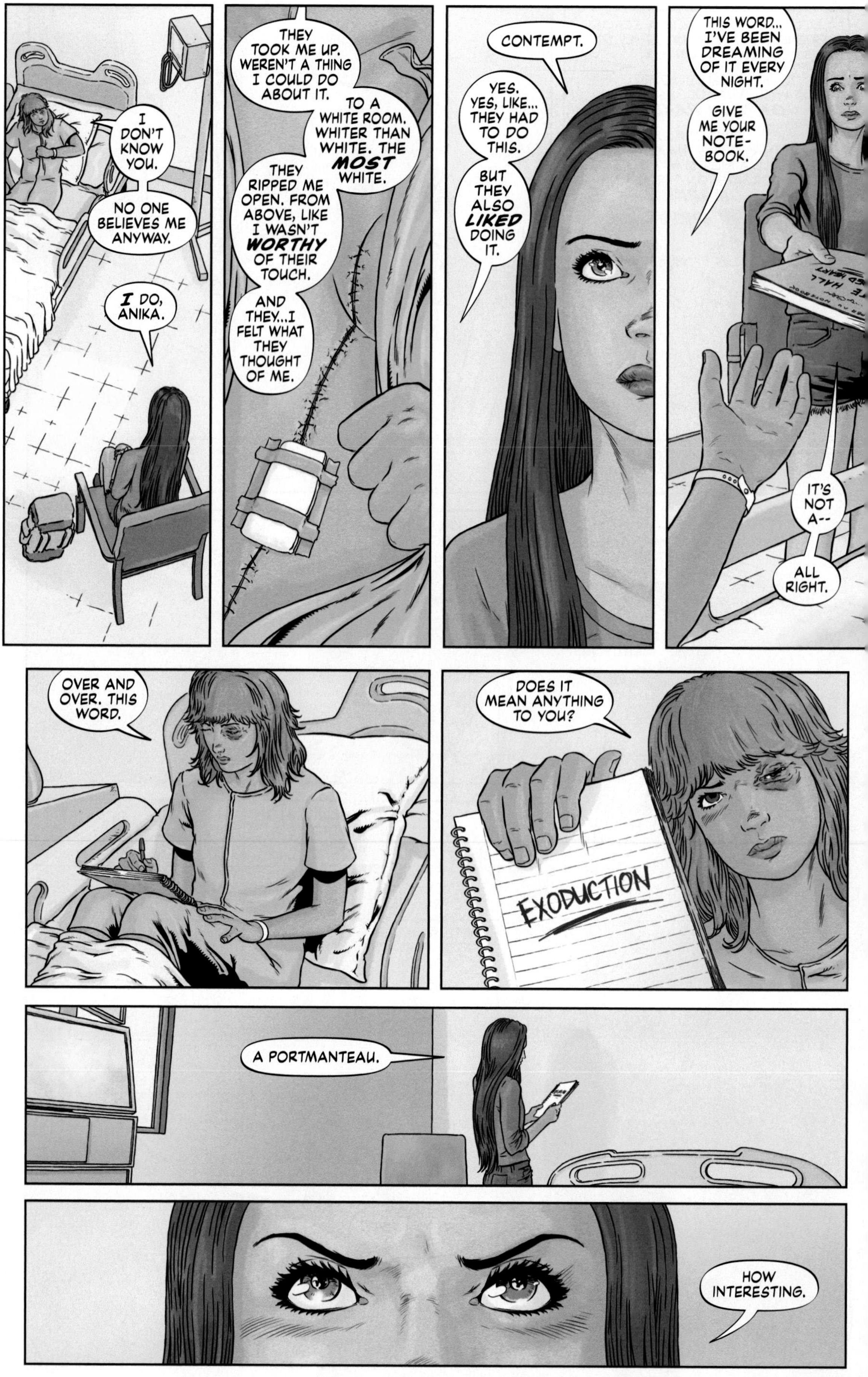
I DON'T KNOW YOU.
NO ONE BELIEVES ME ANYWAY.
I DO, ANIKA.
THEY TOOK ME UP. WEREN'T A THING I COULD DO ABOUT IT.
TO A WHITE ROOM. WHITER THAN WHITE. THE MOST WHITE.
THEY RIPPED ME OPEN. FROM ABOVE, LIKE I WASN'T WORTHY OF THEIR TOUCH.
AND THEY...I FELT WHAT THEY THOUGHT OF ME.
CONTEMPT.
YES. YES, LIKE... THEY HAD TO DO THIS.
BUT THEY ALSO LIKED DOING IT.
THIS WORD... I'VE BEEN DREAMING OF IT EVERY NIGHT.
GIVE ME YOUR NOTE-BOOK.
IT'S NOT A--
ALL RIGHT.
OVER AND OVER. THIS WORD.
DOES IT MEAN ANYTHING TO YOU?
EXODUCTION
A PORTMANTEAU.
HOW INTERESTING.

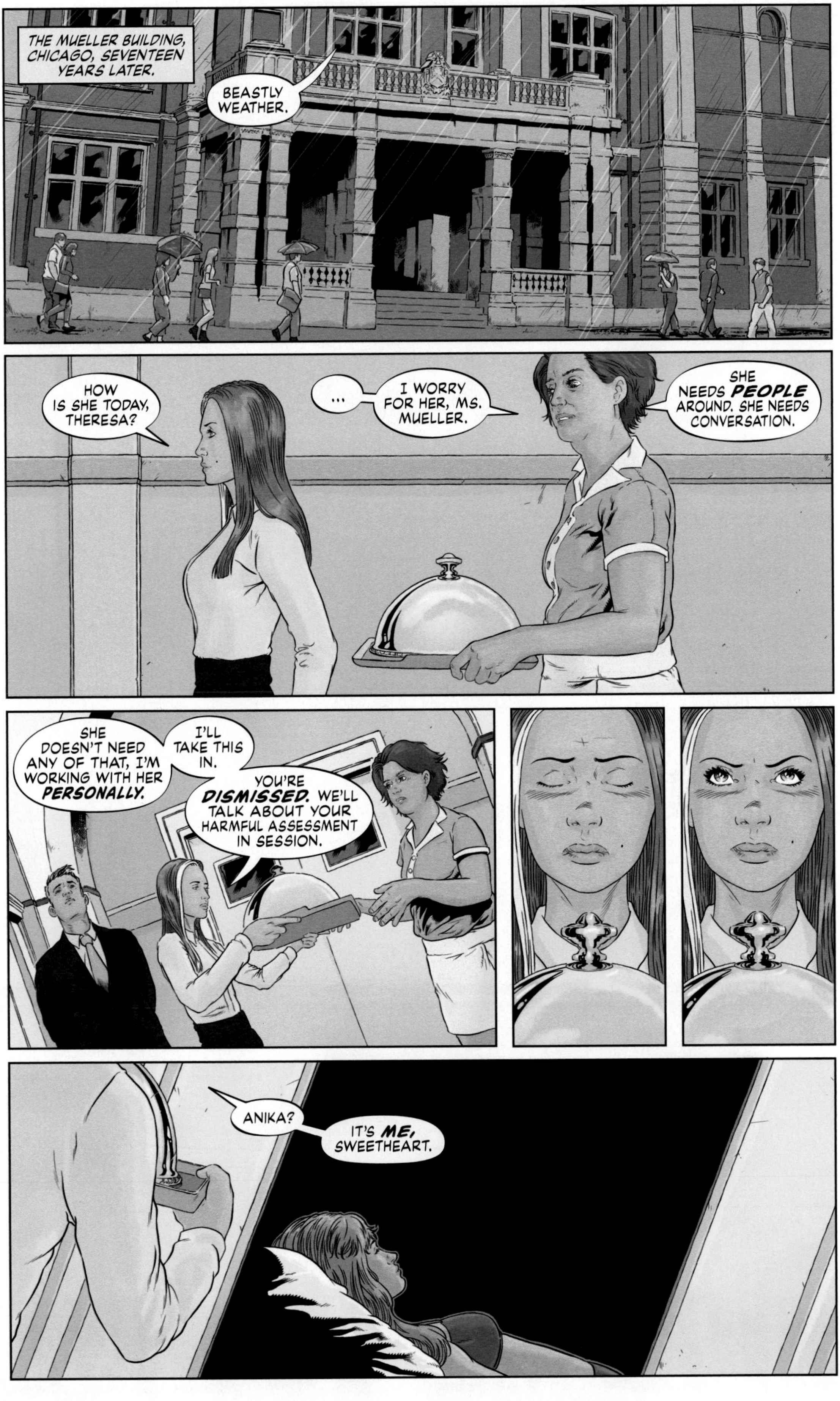
THE MUELLER BUILDING, CHICAGO, SEVENTEEN YEARS LATER.
BEASTLY WEATHER.
HOW IS SHE TODAY, THERESA?
...
I WORRY FOR HER, MS. MUELLER.
SHE NEEDS PEOPLE AROUND. SHE NEEDS CONVERSATION.
SHE DOESN'T NEED ANY OF THAT, I'M WORKING WITH HER PERSONALLY.
I'LL TAKE THIS IN.
YOU'RE DISMISSED. WE'LL TALK ABOUT YOUR HARMFUL ASSESSMENT IN SESSION.
ANIKA?
IT'S ME, SWEETHEART.

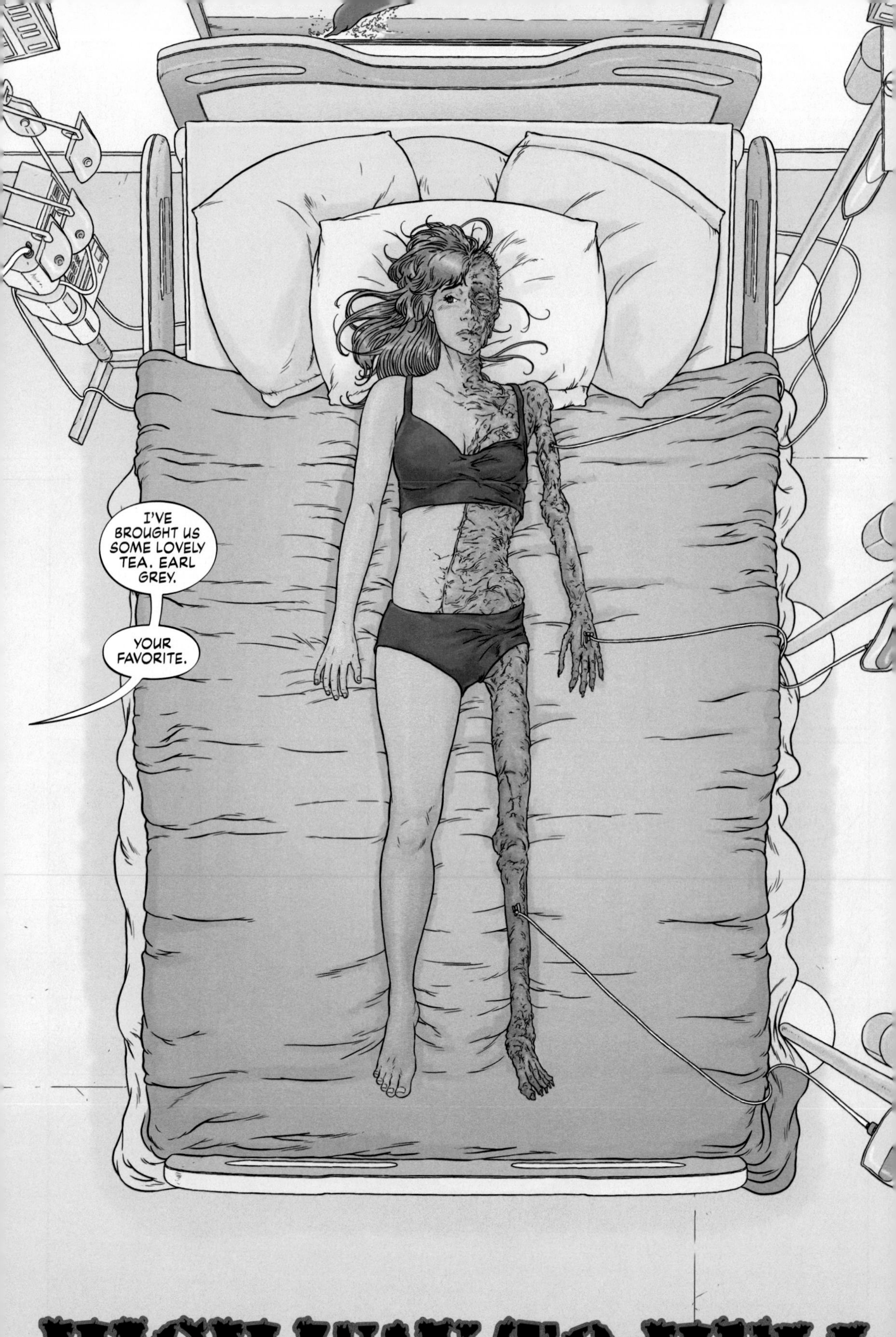
I'VE BROUGHT US SOME LOVELY TEA. EARL GREY.
YOUR FAVORITE.

HIGH WAY TO HELL

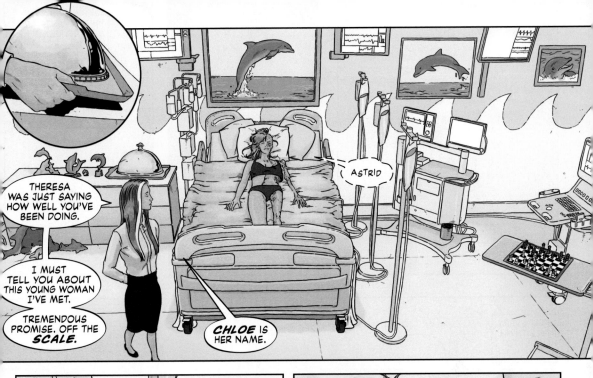

THERESA WAS JUST SAYING HOW WELL YOU'VE BEEN DOING.

I MUST TELL YOU ABOUT THIS YOUNG WOMAN I'VE MET.

TREMENDOUS PROMISE. OFF THE *SCALE*.

CHLOE IS HER NAME.

ASTRID

WE CAN FINISH OUR GAME.

I BELIEVE IT WAS MY MOVE?

ASTRID

ASTRID

YOU HAVE TO LET ME GO

WHAT THEY DID TO ME

YOU HAVE TO LET ME GO

...

I CAN'T.

I'M SORRY.

I CAN'T DO THIS WITHOUT YOU.

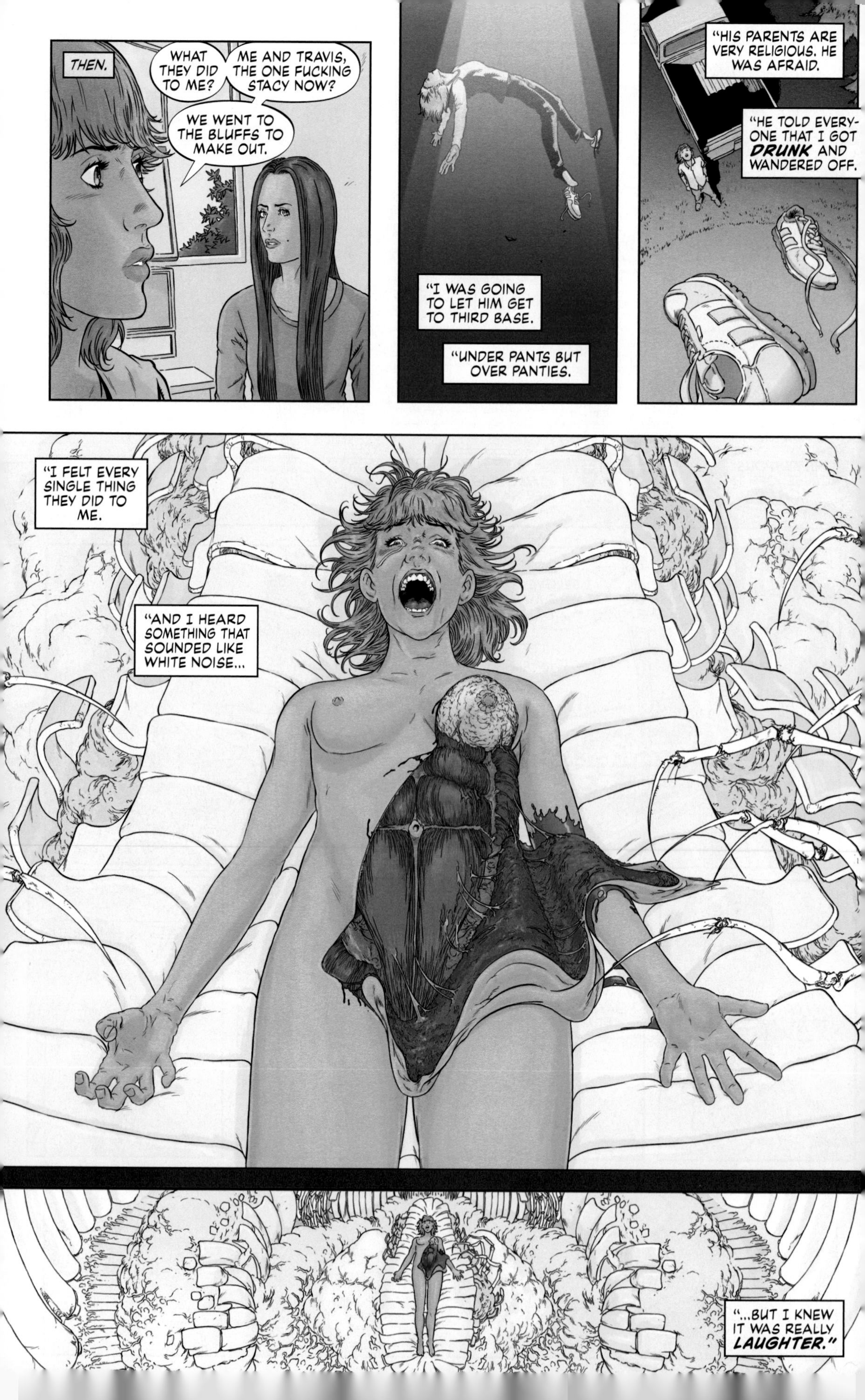
THEN.
WHAT THEY DID TO ME?
ME AND TRAVIS, THE ONE FUCKING STACY NOW?
WE WENT TO THE BLUFFS TO MAKE OUT.
"I WAS GOING TO LET HIM GET TO THIRD BASE.
"UNDER PANTS BUT OVER PANTIES.
"HIS PARENTS ARE VERY RELIGIOUS. HE WAS AFRAID.
"HE TOLD EVERY-ONE THAT I GOT DRUNK AND WANDERED OFF.
"I FELT EVERY SINGLE THING THEY DID TO ME.
"AND I HEARD SOMETHING THAT SOUNDED LIKE WHITE NOISE...
"...BUT I KNEW IT WAS REALLY LAUGHTER."

YOUR MOVE.

...

WHEN I WAS SIX YEARS OLD, I WAS COMING HOME FROM CHURCH WITH MY FAMILY.

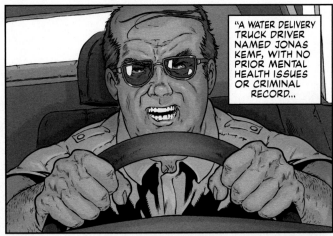

"A WATER DELIVERY TRUCK DRIVER NAMED JONAS KEMF, WITH NO PRIOR MENTAL HEALTH ISSUES OR CRIMINAL RECORD...

"...RAN OVER ME, DELIBERATELY. RIGHT IN THE STREET.

"THEN HE BACKED UP TO DO IT AGAIN."

SINCE THAT DAY, I'VE BEEN ABLE TO SEE THINGS OTHERS CANNOT.

SPECIFICALLY, A RACE OF...

WELL, I THINK YOU MET THEM, ANIKA.

I BELIEVE THESE... ENTITIES...MEAN TO DO US HARM.

I BELIEVE THEY CAN HIDE INSIDE OF US. DO THINGS TO OUR FLESH.

AND I'VE BEEN TRACKING THEM, ANIKA.

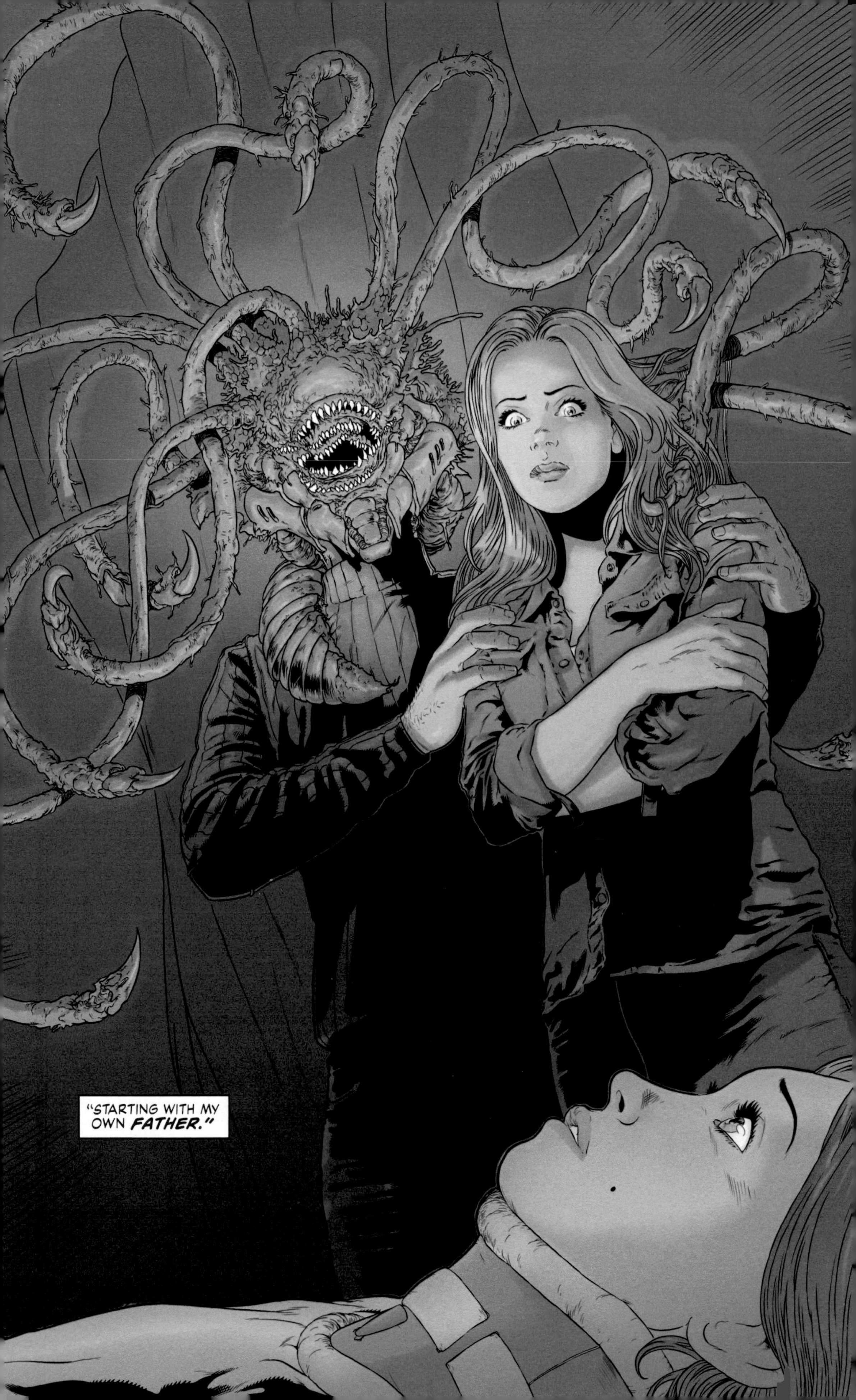
"STARTING WITH MY OWN FATHER."

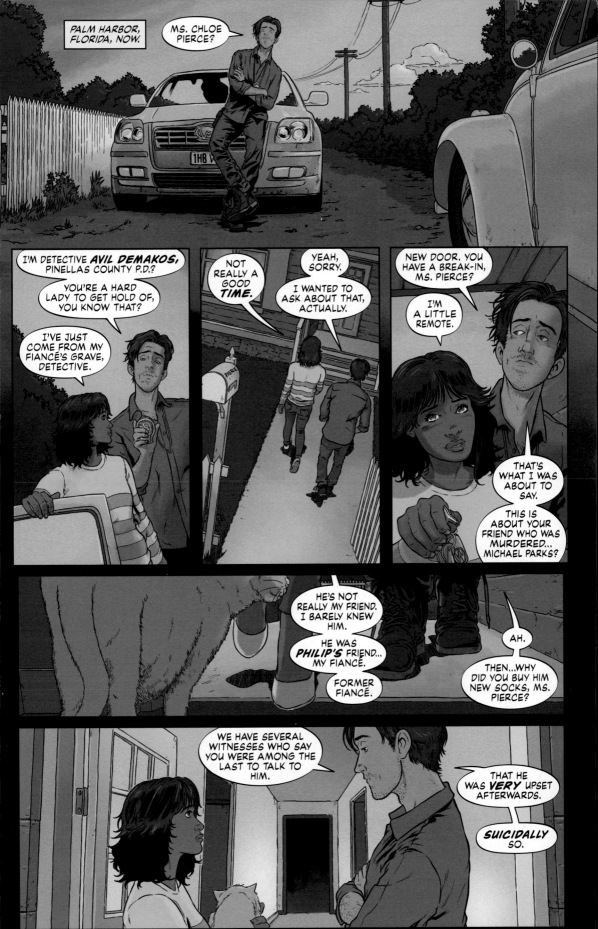

PALM HARBOR, FLORIDA, NOW.

MS. CHLOE PIERCE?

I'M DETECTIVE **AVIL DEMAKOS**, PINELLAS COUNTY P.D.?

YOU'RE A HARD LADY TO GET HOLD OF, YOU KNOW THAT?

I'VE JUST COME FROM MY FIANCÉ'S GRAVE, DETECTIVE.

NOT REALLY A GOOD **TIME**.

YEAH, SORRY.

I WANTED TO ASK ABOUT THAT, ACTUALLY.

NEW DOOR. YOU HAVE A BREAK-IN, MS. PIERCE?

I'M A LITTLE REMOTE.

THAT'S WHAT I WAS ABOUT TO SAY.

THIS IS ABOUT YOUR FRIEND WHO WAS MURDERED... MICHAEL PARKS?

HE'S NOT REALLY MY FRIEND. I BARELY KNEW HIM.

HE WAS **PHILIP'S** FRIEND... MY FIANCÉ.

FORMER FIANCÉ.

AH.

THEN...WHY DID YOU BUY HIM NEW SOCKS, MS. PIERCE?

WE HAVE SEVERAL WITNESSES WHO SAY YOU WERE AMONG THE LAST TO TALK TO HIM.

THAT HE WAS **VERY** UPSET AFTERWARDS.

SUICIDALLY SO.

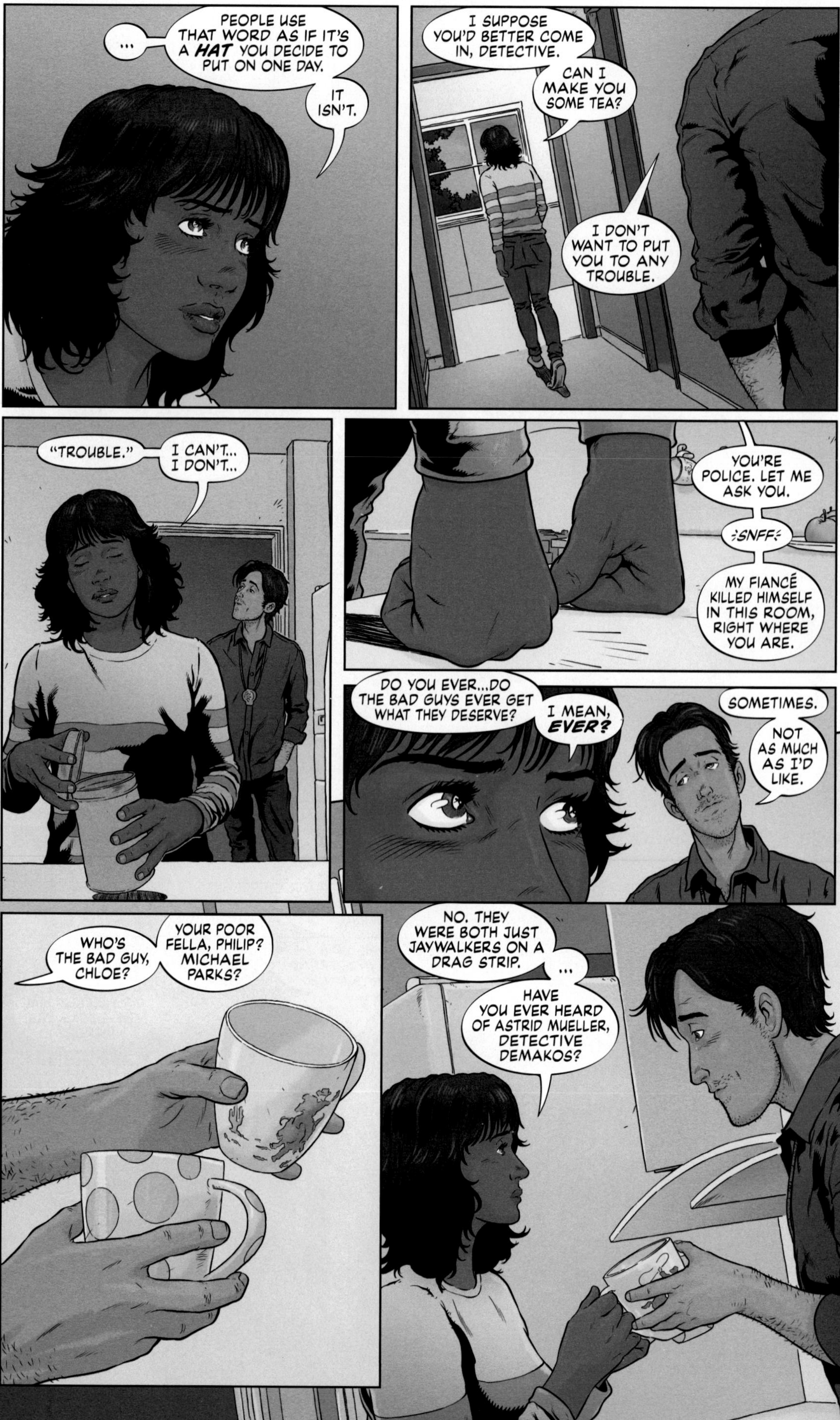
...
PEOPLE USE THAT WORD AS IF IT'S A HAT YOU DECIDE TO PUT ON ONE DAY.
IT ISN'T.
I SUPPOSE YOU'D BETTER COME IN, DETECTIVE.
CAN I MAKE YOU SOME TEA?
I DON'T WANT TO PUT YOU TO ANY TROUBLE.
"TROUBLE."
I CAN'T... I DON'T...
YOU'RE POLICE. LET ME ASK YOU.
SNFF
MY FIANCÉ KILLED HIMSELF IN THIS ROOM, RIGHT WHERE YOU ARE.
DO YOU EVER...DO THE BAD GUYS EVER GET WHAT THEY DESERVE?
I MEAN, EVER?
SOMETIMES.
NOT AS MUCH AS I'D LIKE.
WHO'S THE BAD GUY, CHLOE?
YOUR POOR FELLA, PHILIP? MICHAEL PARKS?
NO. THEY WERE BOTH JUST JAYWALKERS ON A DRAG STRIP.
...
HAVE YOU EVER HEARD OF ASTRID MUELLER, DETECTIVE DEMAKOS?

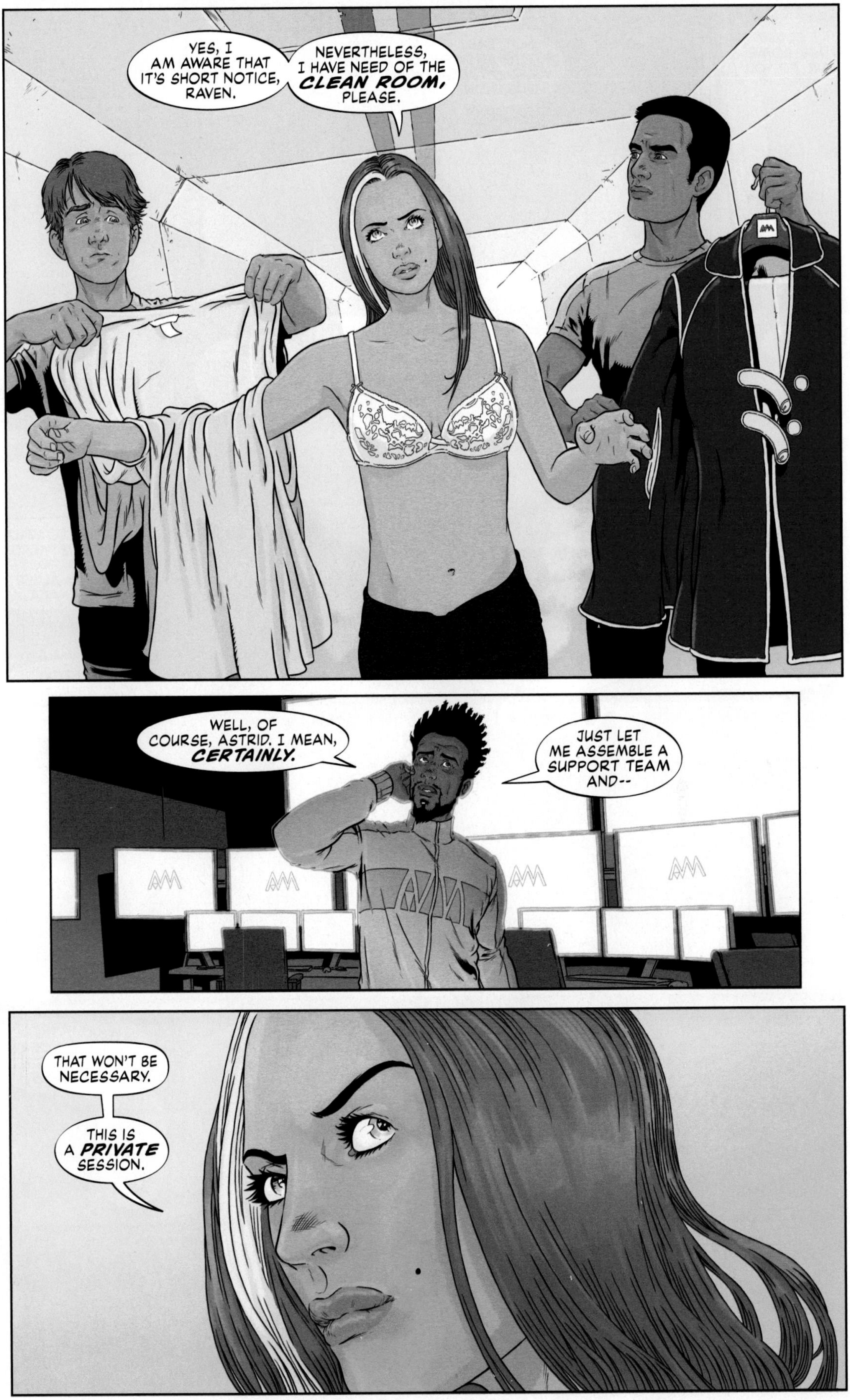
YES, I AM AWARE THAT IT'S SHORT NOTICE, RAVEN.
NEVERTHELESS, I HAVE NEED OF THE *CLEAN ROOM,* PLEASE.
WELL, OF COURSE, ASTRID. I MEAN, *CERTAINLY.*
JUST LET ME ASSEMBLE A SUPPORT TEAM AND--
THAT WON'T BE NECESSARY.
THIS IS A *PRIVATE* SESSION.

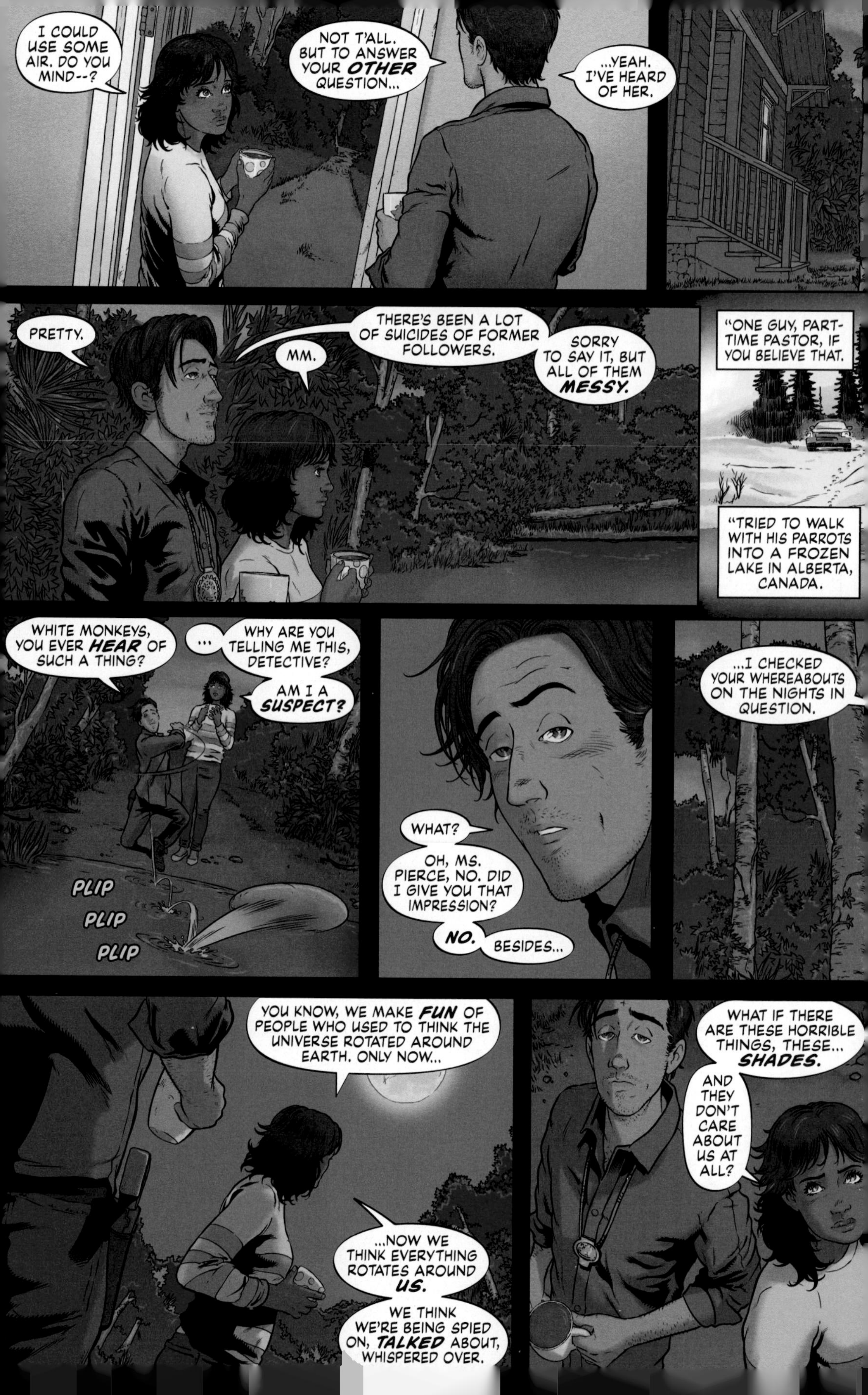
I COULD USE SOME AIR. DO YOU MIND--?
NOT T'ALL. BUT TO ANSWER YOUR OTHER QUESTION...
...YEAH. I'VE HEARD OF HER.
PRETTY.
MM.
THERE'S BEEN A LOT OF SUICIDES OF FORMER FOLLOWERS.
SORRY TO SAY IT, BUT ALL OF THEM MESSY.
"ONE GUY, PART-TIME PASTOR, IF YOU BELIEVE THAT.
"TRIED TO WALK WITH HIS PARROTS INTO A FROZEN LAKE IN ALBERTA, CANADA.
WHITE MONKEYS, YOU EVER HEAR OF SUCH A THING?
...
WHY ARE YOU TELLING ME THIS, DETECTIVE?
AM I A SUSPECT?
PLIP
PLIP
PLIP
WHAT?
OH, MS. PIERCE, NO. DID I GIVE YOU THAT IMPRESSION?
NO.
BESIDES...
...I CHECKED YOUR WHEREABOUTS ON THE NIGHTS IN QUESTION.
YOU KNOW, WE MAKE FUN OF PEOPLE WHO USED TO THINK THE UNIVERSE ROTATED AROUND EARTH. ONLY NOW...
...NOW WE THINK EVERYTHING ROTATES AROUND US.
WE THINK WE'RE BEING SPIED ON, TALKED ABOUT, WHISPERED OVER.
WHAT IF THERE ARE THESE HORRIBLE THINGS, THESE... SHADES.
AND THEY DON'T CARE ABOUT US AT ALL?

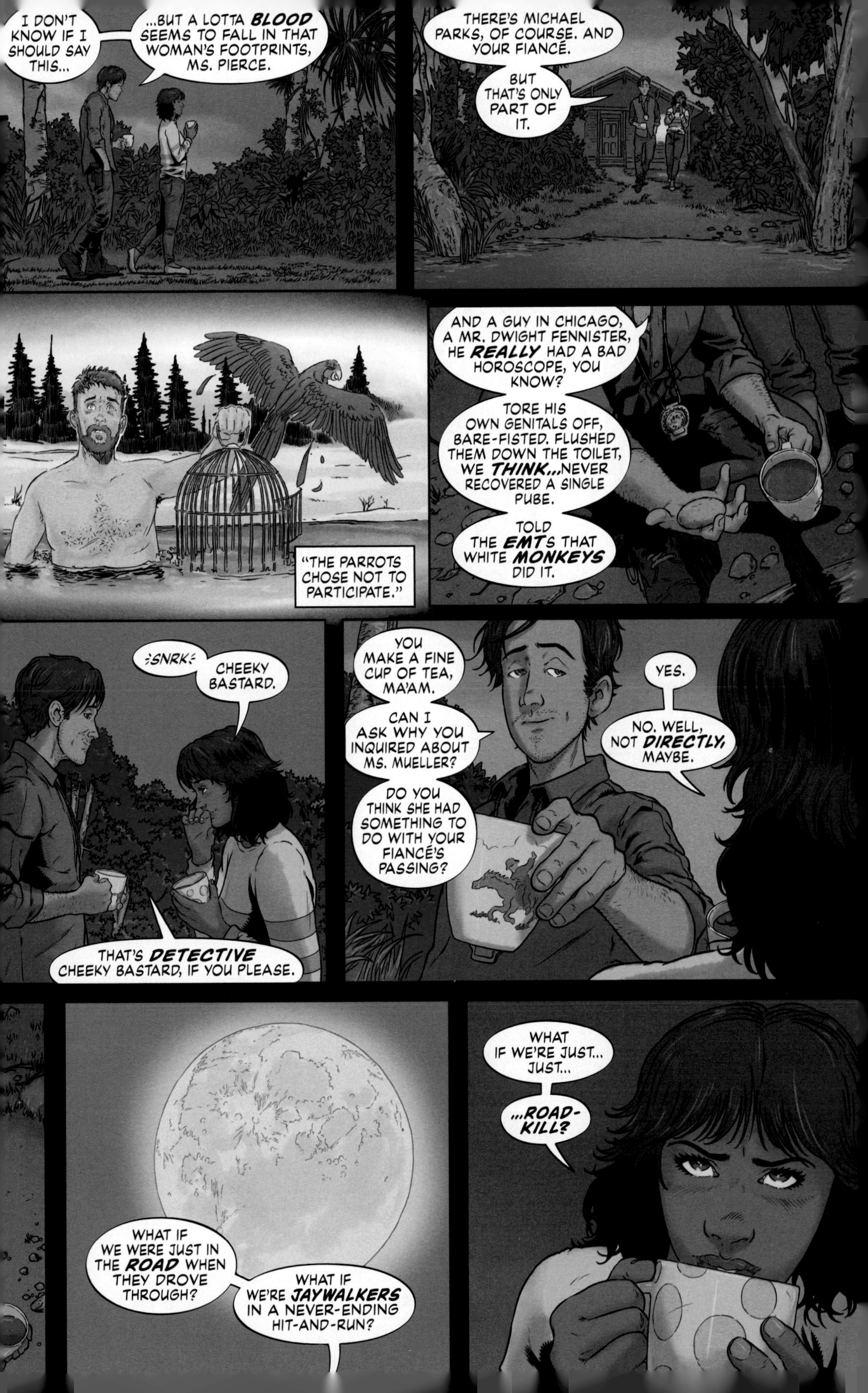
I DON'T KNOW IF I SHOULD SAY THIS...
...BUT A LOTTA BLOOD SEEMS TO FALL IN THAT WOMAN'S FOOTPRINTS, MS. PIERCE.
THERE'S MICHAEL PARKS, OF COURSE. AND YOUR FIANCÉ.
BUT THAT'S ONLY PART OF IT.
"THE PARROTS CHOSE NOT TO PARTICIPATE."
AND A GUY IN CHICAGO, A MR. DWIGHT FENNISTER, HE REALLY HAD A BAD HOROSCOPE, YOU KNOW?
TORE HIS OWN GENITALS OFF, BARE-FISTED. FLUSHED THEM DOWN THE TOILET, WE THINK...NEVER RECOVERED A SINGLE PUBE.
TOLD THE EMTs THAT WHITE MONKEYS DID IT.
SNRK
CHEEKY BASTARD.
THAT'S DETECTIVE CHEEKY BASTARD, IF YOU PLEASE.
YOU MAKE A FINE CUP OF TEA, MA'AM.
CAN I ASK WHY YOU INQUIRED ABOUT MS. MUELLER?
DO YOU THINK SHE HAD SOMETHING TO DO WITH YOUR FIANCÉ'S PASSING?
YES.
NO. WELL, NOT DIRECTLY, MAYBE.
WHAT IF WE WERE JUST IN THE ROAD WHEN THEY DROVE THROUGH?
WHAT IF WE'RE JAYWALKERS IN A NEVER-ENDING HIT-AND-RUN?
WHAT IF WE'RE JUST... JUST...
...ROAD-KILL?

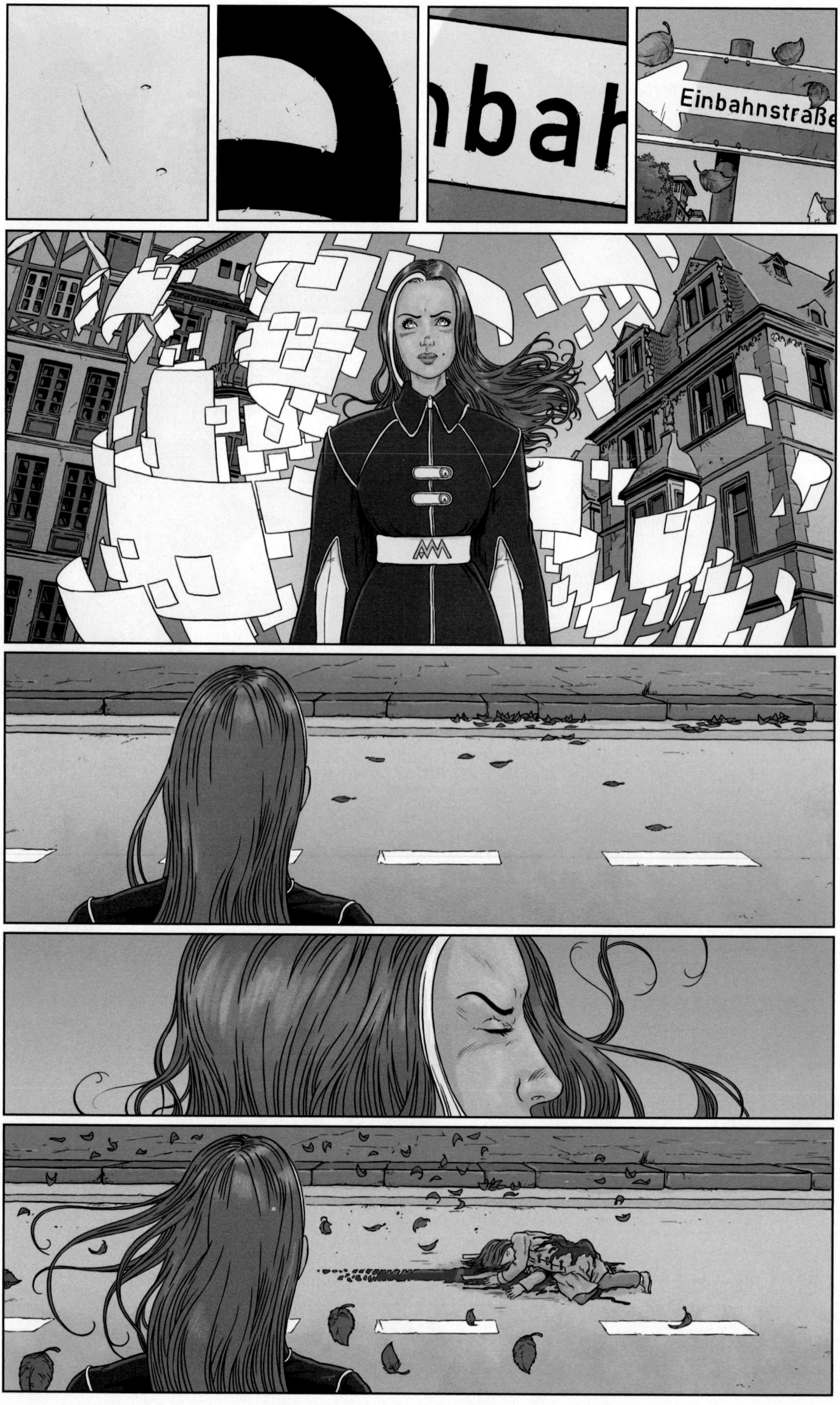

nbah
Einbahnstraße

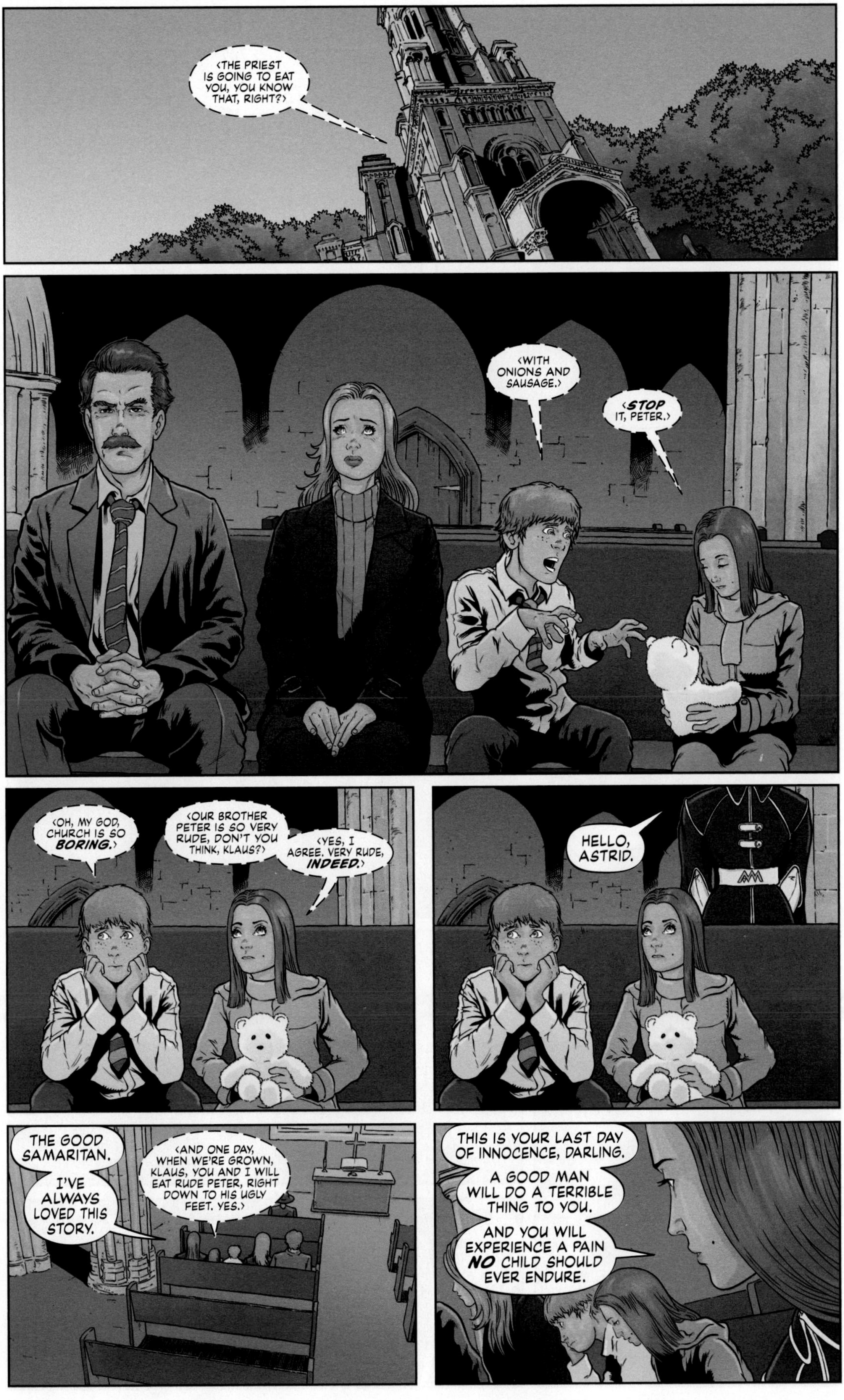
‹THE PRIEST IS GOING TO EAT YOU, YOU KNOW THAT, RIGHT?›
‹WITH ONIONS AND SAUSAGE.›
‹STOP IT, PETER.›
‹OH, MY GOD, CHURCH IS SO BORING.›
‹OUR BROTHER PETER IS SO VERY RUDE, DON'T YOU THINK, KLAUS?›
‹YES, I AGREE. VERY RUDE, INDEED.›
HELLO, ASTRID.
THE GOOD SAMARITAN.
I'VE ALWAYS LOVED THIS STORY.
‹AND ONE DAY, WHEN WE'RE GROWN, KLAUS, YOU AND I WILL EAT RUDE PETER, RIGHT DOWN TO HIS UGLY FEET. YES.›
THIS IS YOUR LAST DAY OF INNOCENCE, DARLING.
A GOOD MAN WILL DO A TERRIBLE THING TO YOU.
AND YOU WILL EXPERIENCE A PAIN NO CHILD SHOULD EVER ENDURE.

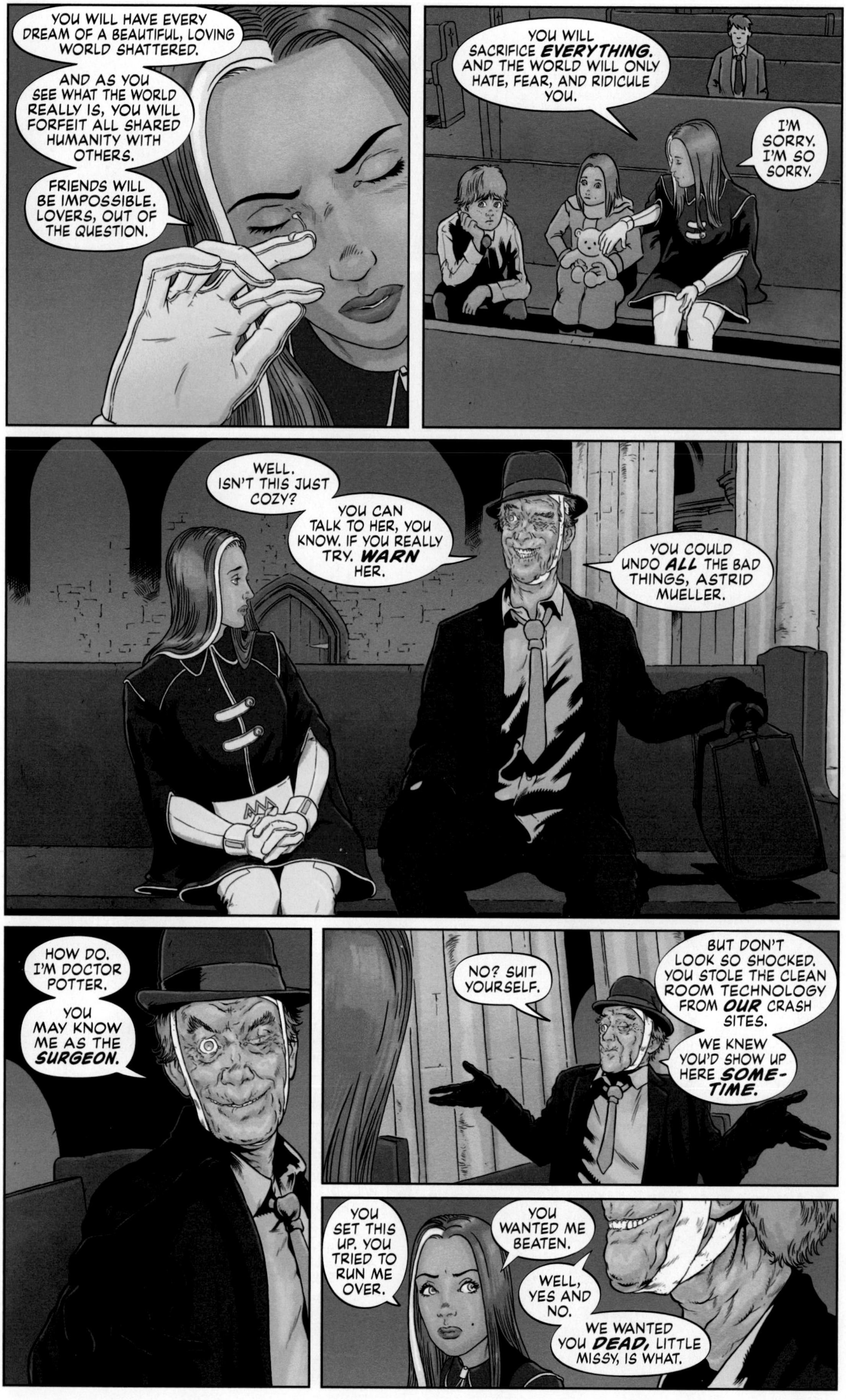
YOU WILL HAVE EVERY DREAM OF A BEAUTIFUL, LOVING WORLD SHATTERED.
AND AS YOU SEE WHAT THE WORLD REALLY IS, YOU WILL FORFEIT ALL SHARED HUMANITY WITH OTHERS.
FRIENDS WILL BE IMPOSSIBLE. LOVERS, OUT OF THE QUESTION.
YOU WILL SACRIFICE EVERYTHING. AND THE WORLD WILL ONLY HATE, FEAR, AND RIDICULE YOU.
I'M SORRY. I'M SO SORRY.
WELL. ISN'T THIS JUST COZY?
YOU CAN TALK TO HER, YOU KNOW. IF YOU REALLY TRY. WARN HER.
YOU COULD UNDO ALL THE BAD THINGS, ASTRID MUELLER.
HOW DO. I'M DOCTOR POTTER.
YOU MAY KNOW ME AS THE SURGEON.
NO? SUIT YOURSELF.
BUT DON'T LOOK SO SHOCKED. YOU STOLE THE CLEAN ROOM TECHNOLOGY FROM OUR CRASH SITES.
WE KNEW YOU'D SHOW UP HERE SOME-TIME.
YOU SET THIS UP. YOU TRIED TO RUN ME OVER.
YOU WANTED ME BEATEN.
WELL, YES AND NO.
WE WANTED YOU DEAD, LITTLE MISSY, IS WHAT.

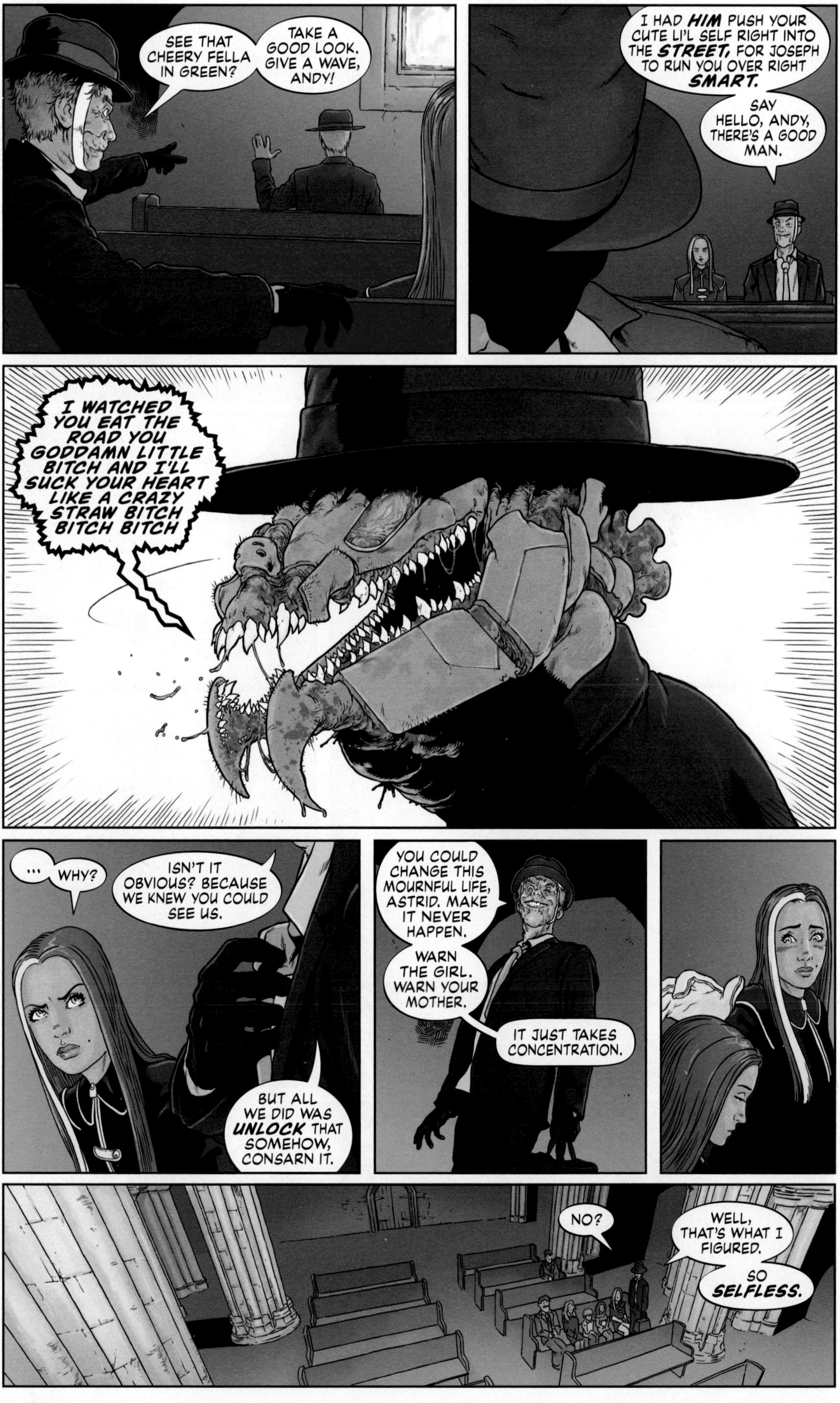
SEE THAT CHEERY FELLA IN GREEN?
TAKE A GOOD LOOK. GIVE A WAVE, ANDY!
I HAD HIM PUSH YOUR CUTE LI'L SELF RIGHT INTO THE STREET, FOR JOSEPH TO RUN YOU OVER RIGHT SMART.
SAY HELLO, ANDY, THERE'S A GOOD MAN.
I WATCHED YOU EAT THE ROAD YOU GODDAMN LITTLE BITCH AND I'LL SUCK YOUR HEART LIKE A CRAZY STRAW BITCH BITCH BITCH
...
WHY?
ISN'T IT OBVIOUS? BECAUSE WE KNEW YOU COULD SEE US.
BUT ALL WE DID WAS UNLOCK THAT SOMEHOW, CONSARN IT.
YOU COULD CHANGE THIS MOURNFUL LIFE, ASTRID. MAKE IT NEVER HAPPEN.
WARN THE GIRL. WARN YOUR MOTHER.
IT JUST TAKES CONCENTRATION.
NO?
WELL, THAT'S WHAT I FIGURED.
SO SELFLESS.

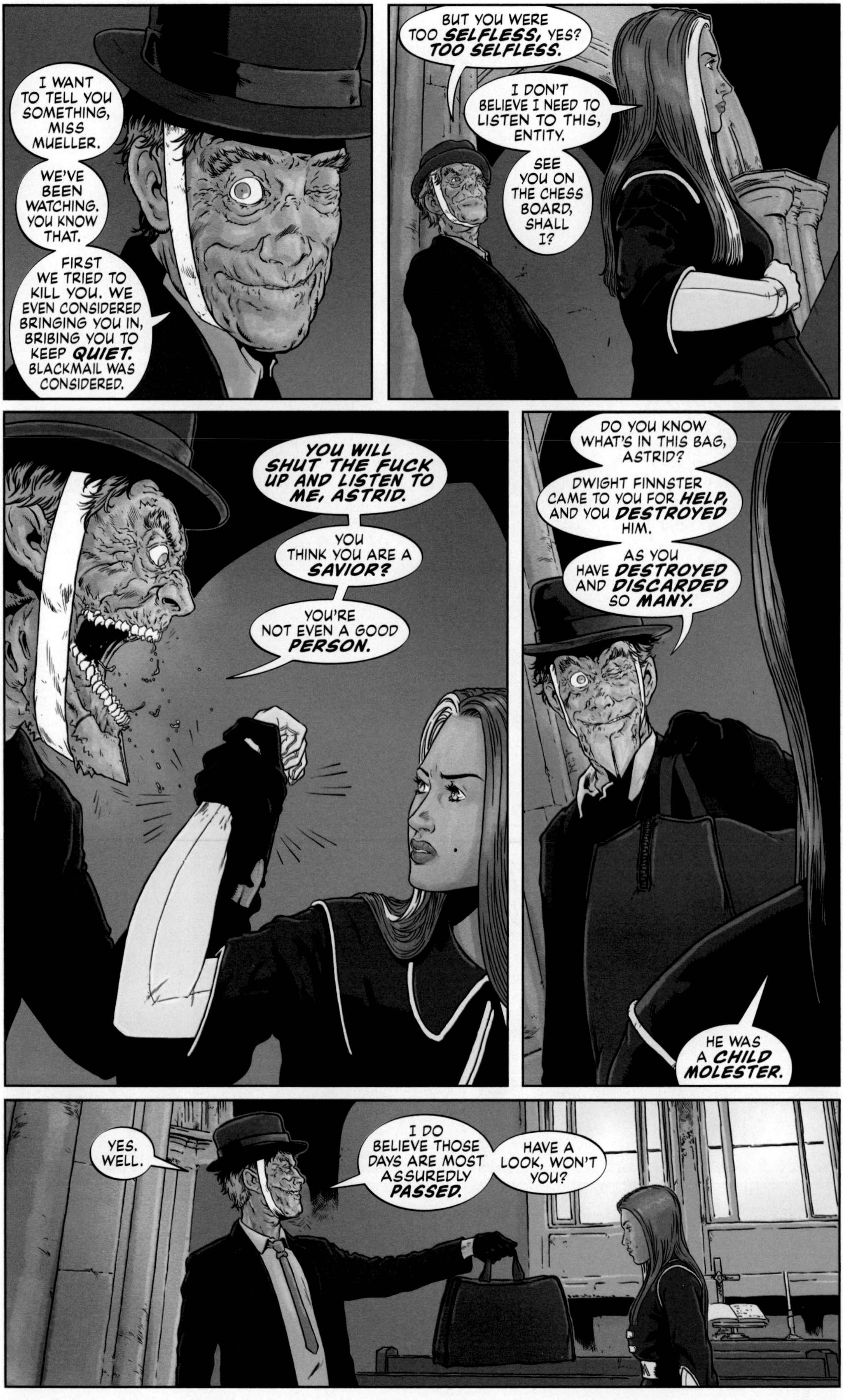
I WANT TO TELL YOU SOMETHING, MISS MUELLER.
WE'VE BEEN WATCHING. YOU KNOW THAT.
FIRST WE TRIED TO KILL YOU. WE EVEN CONSIDERED BRINGING YOU IN, BRIBING YOU TO KEEP QUIET. BLACKMAIL WAS CONSIDERED.
BUT YOU WERE TOO SELFLESS, YES? TOO SELFLESS.
I DON'T BELIEVE I NEED TO LISTEN TO THIS, ENTITY.
SEE YOU ON THE CHESS BOARD, SHALL I?
YOU WILL SHUT THE FUCK UP AND LISTEN TO ME, ASTRID.
YOU THINK YOU ARE A SAVIOR?
YOU'RE NOT EVEN A GOOD PERSON.
DO YOU KNOW WHAT'S IN THIS BAG, ASTRID?
DWIGHT FINNSTER CAME TO YOU FOR HELP, AND YOU DESTROYED HIM.
AS YOU HAVE DESTROYED AND DISCARDED SO MANY.
HE WAS A CHILD MOLESTER.
YES. WELL.
I DO BELIEVE THOSE DAYS ARE MOST ASSUREDLY PASSED.
HAVE A LOOK, WON'T YOU?

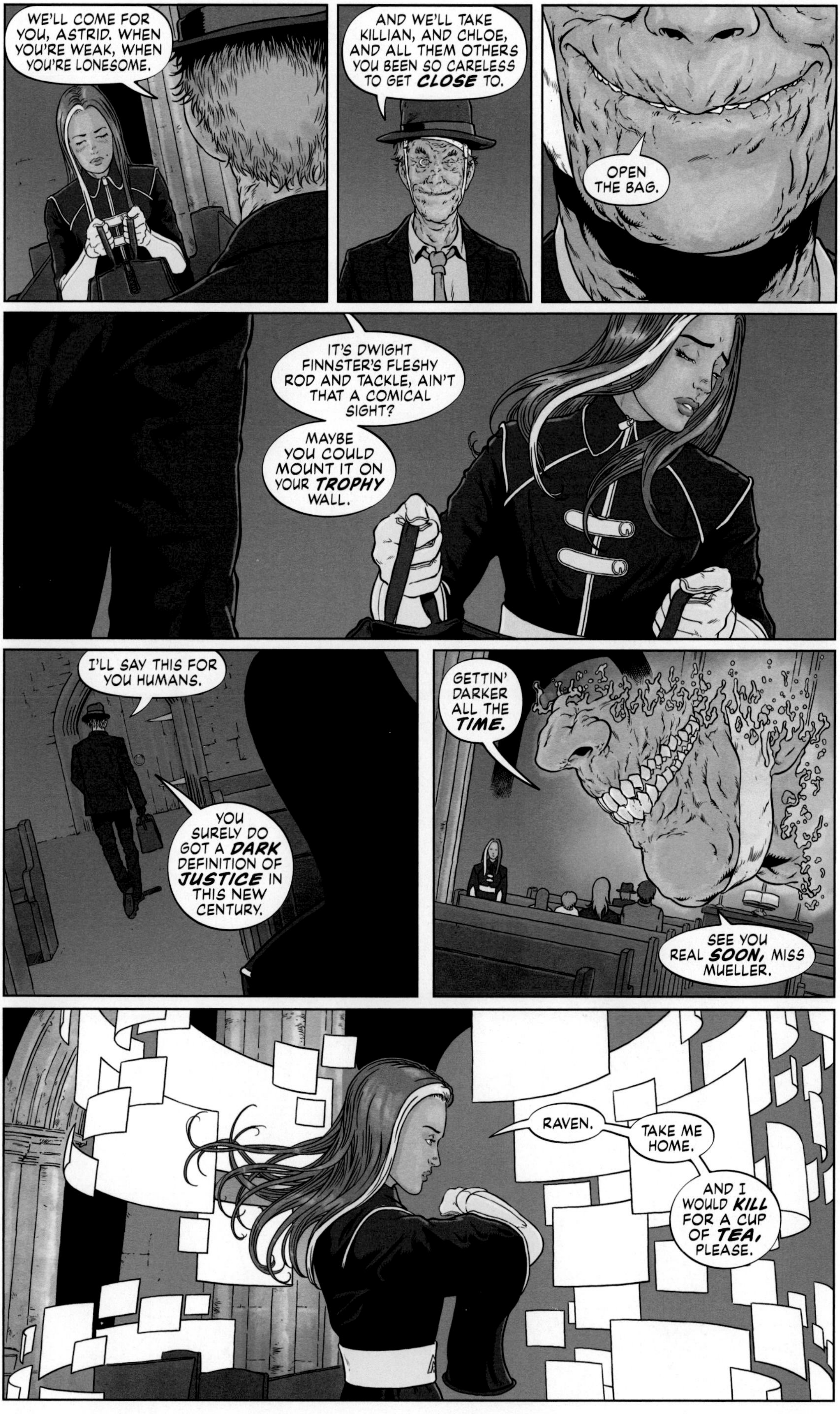
WE'LL COME FOR YOU, ASTRID. WHEN YOU'RE WEAK, WHEN YOU'RE LONESOME.
AND WE'LL TAKE KILLIAN, AND CHLOE, AND ALL THEM OTHERS YOU BEEN SO CARELESS TO GET CLOSE TO.
OPEN THE BAG.
IT'S DWIGHT FINNSTER'S FLESHY ROD AND TACKLE, AIN'T THAT A COMICAL SIGHT?
MAYBE YOU COULD MOUNT IT ON YOUR TROPHY WALL.
I'LL SAY THIS FOR YOU HUMANS.
YOU SURELY DO GOT A DARK DEFINITION OF JUSTICE IN THIS NEW CENTURY.
GETTIN' DARKER ALL THE TIME.
SEE YOU REAL SOON, MISS MUELLER.
RAVEN.
TAKE ME HOME.
AND I WOULD KILL FOR A CUP OF TEA, PLEASE.

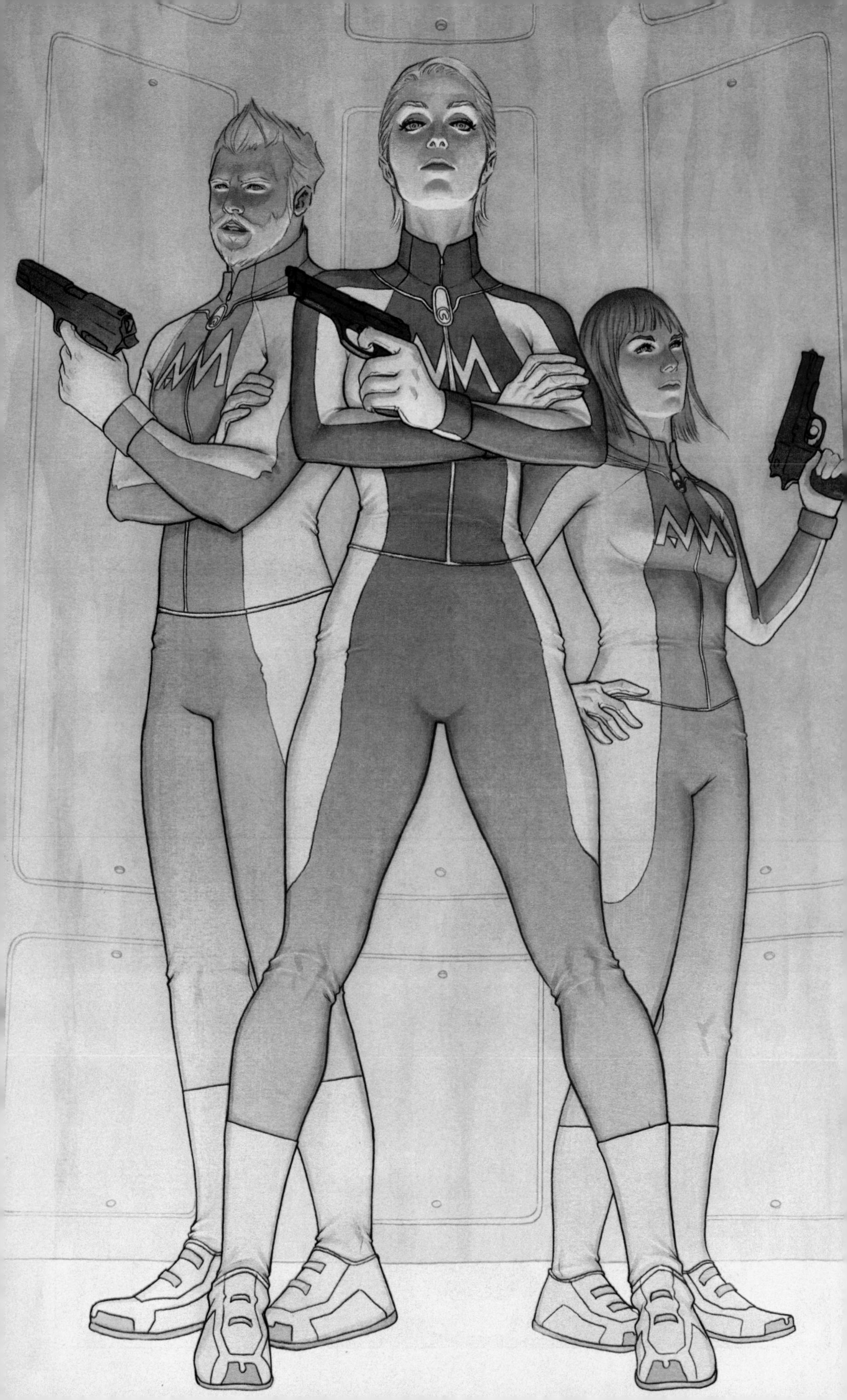

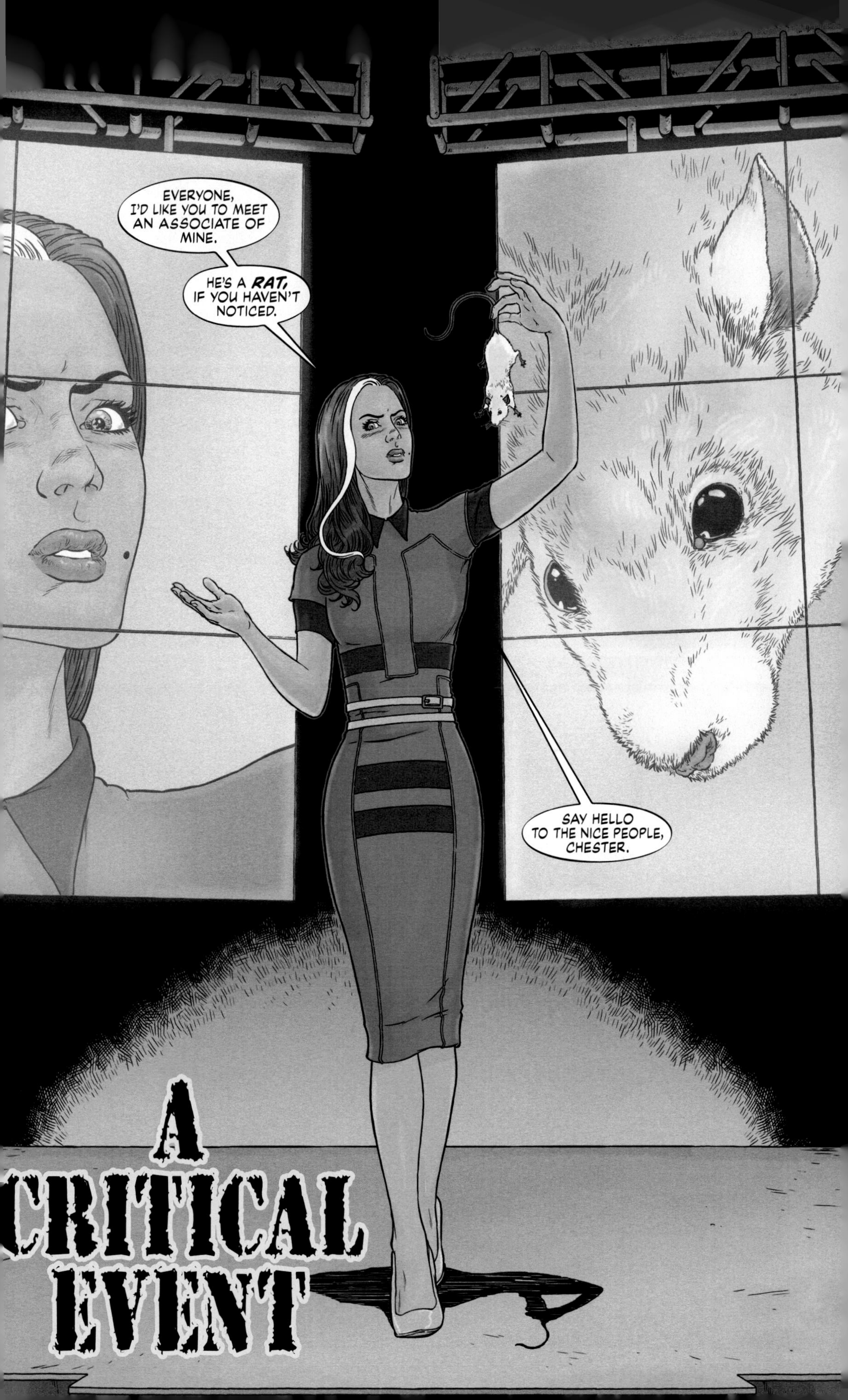
EVERYONE, I'D LIKE YOU TO MEET AN ASSOCIATE OF MINE.
HE'S A *RAT,* IF YOU HAVEN'T NOTICED.
SAY HELLO TO THE NICE PEOPLE, CHESTER.
A CRITICAL EVENT

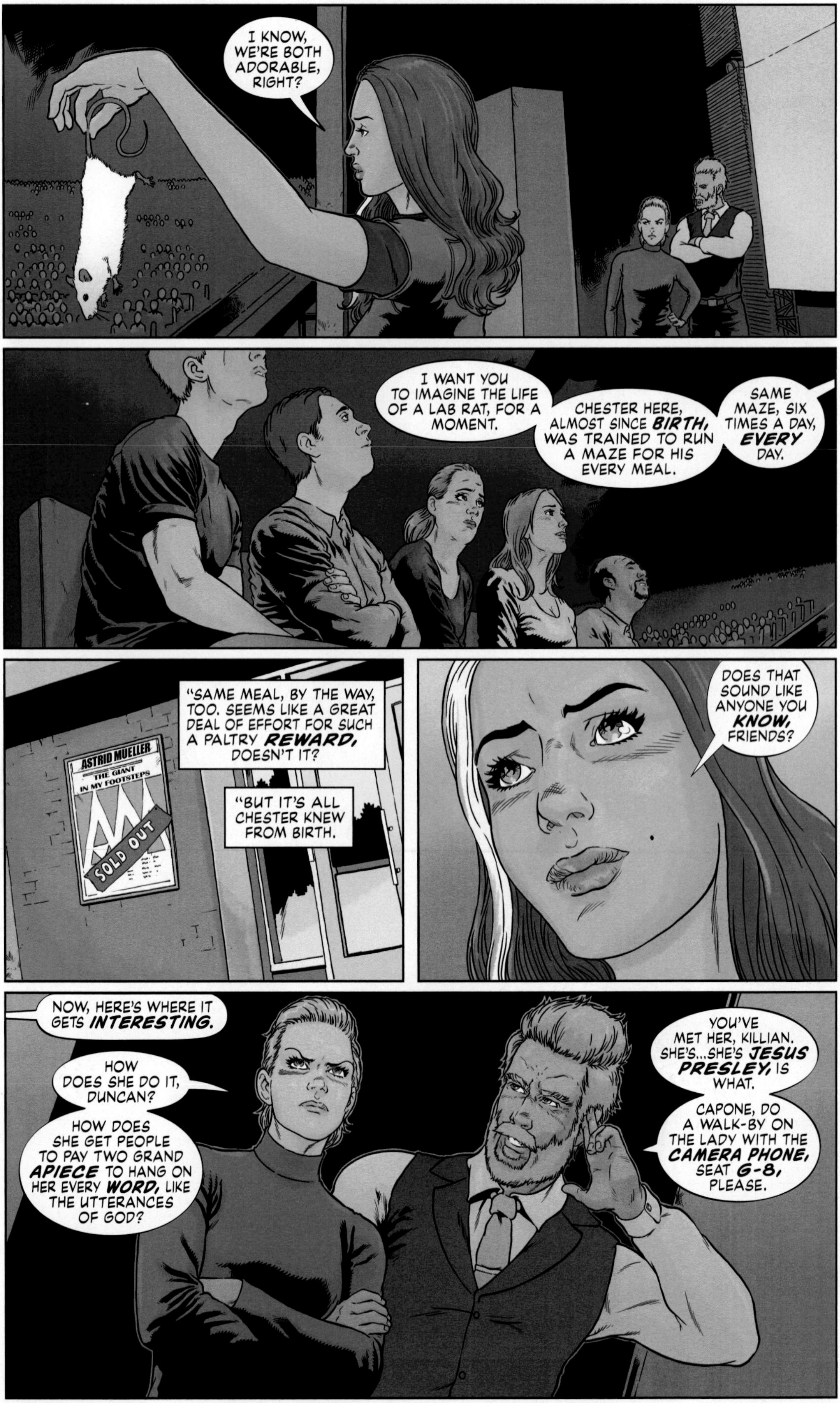
I KNOW, WE'RE BOTH ADORABLE, RIGHT?
I WANT YOU TO IMAGINE THE LIFE OF A LAB RAT, FOR A MOMENT.
CHESTER HERE, ALMOST SINCE BIRTH, WAS TRAINED TO RUN A MAZE FOR HIS EVERY MEAL.
SAME MAZE, SIX TIMES A DAY, EVERY DAY.
"SAME MEAL, BY THE WAY, TOO. SEEMS LIKE A GREAT DEAL OF EFFORT FOR SUCH A PALTRY REWARD, DOESN'T IT?
"BUT IT'S ALL CHESTER KNEW FROM BIRTH.
ASTRID MUELLER
THE GIANT IN MY FOOTSTEPS
SOLD OUT
DOES THAT SOUND LIKE ANYONE YOU KNOW, FRIENDS?
NOW, HERE'S WHERE IT GETS INTERESTING.
HOW DOES SHE DO IT, DUNCAN?
HOW DOES SHE GET PEOPLE TO PAY TWO GRAND APIECE TO HANG ON HER EVERY WORD, LIKE THE UTTERANCES OF GOD?
YOU'VE MET HER, KILLIAN. SHE'S...SHE'S JESUS PRESLEY, IS WHAT.
CAPONE, DO A WALK-BY ON THE LADY WITH THE CAMERA PHONE, SEAT G-8, PLEASE.

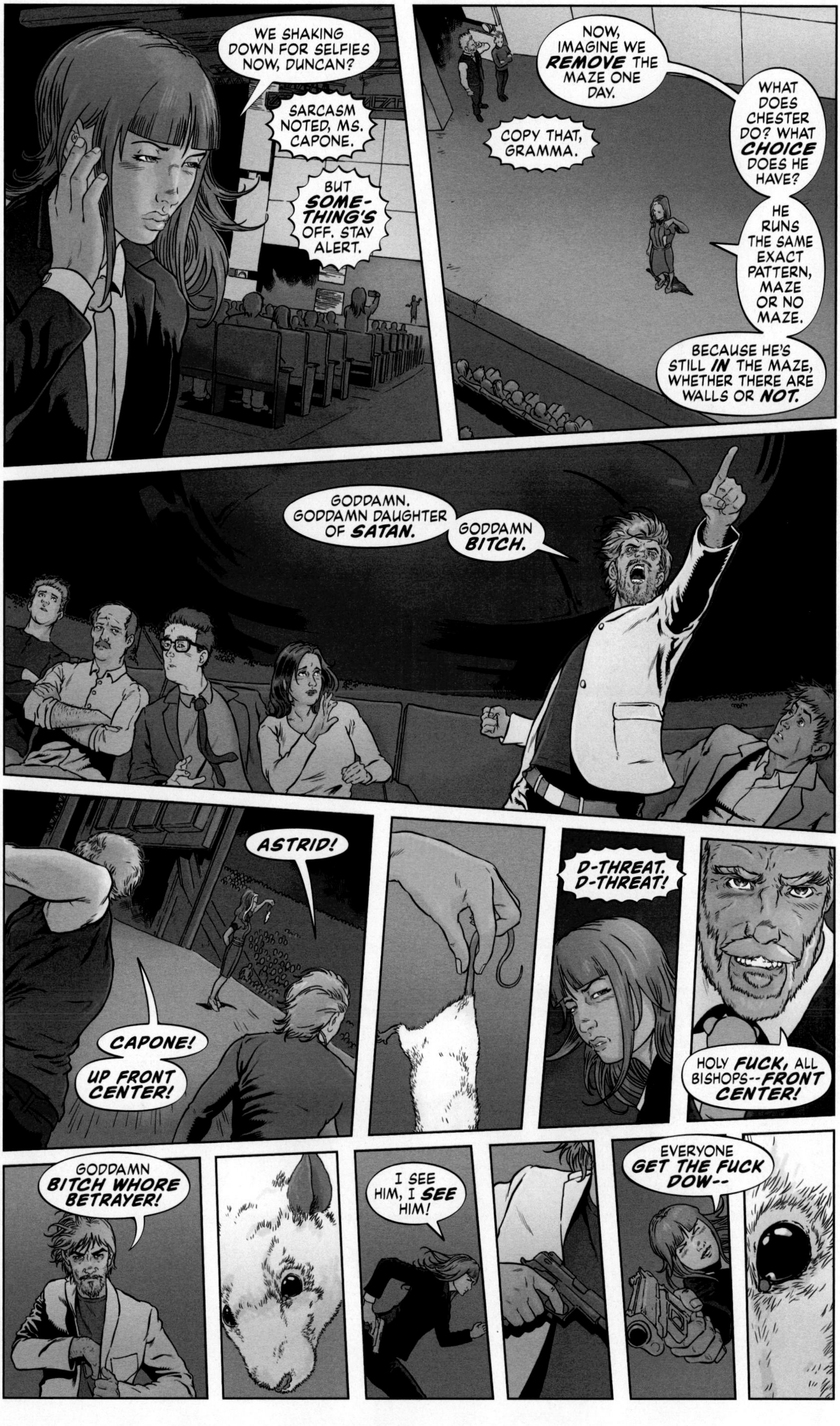
WE SHAKING DOWN FOR SELFIES NOW, DUNCAN?
SARCASM NOTED, MS. CAPONE.
BUT SOMETHING'S OFF. STAY ALERT.
NOW, IMAGINE WE REMOVE THE MAZE ONE DAY.
COPY THAT, GRAMMA.
WHAT DOES CHESTER DO? WHAT CHOICE DOES HE HAVE?
HE RUNS THE SAME EXACT PATTERN, MAZE OR NO MAZE.
BECAUSE HE'S STILL IN THE MAZE, WHETHER THERE ARE WALLS OR NOT.
GODDAMN. GODDAMN DAUGHTER OF SATAN.
GODDAMN BITCH.
ASTRID!
CAPONE!
UP FRONT CENTER!
D-THREAT. D-THREAT!
HOLY FUCK, ALL BISHOPS--FRONT CENTER!
GODDAMN BITCH WHORE BETRAYER!
I SEE HIM, I SEE HIM!
EVERYONE GET THE FUCK DOW--

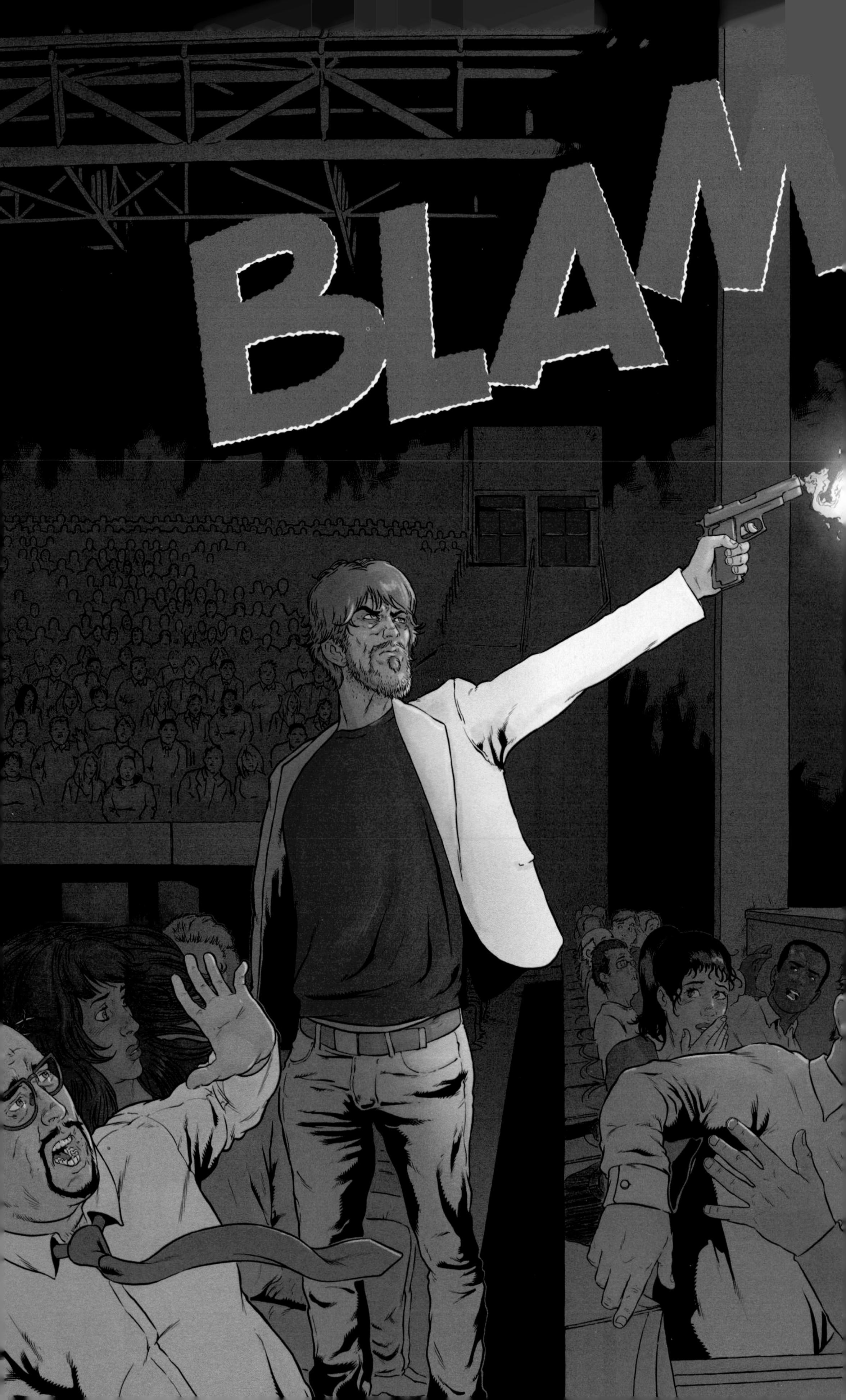
BLAM

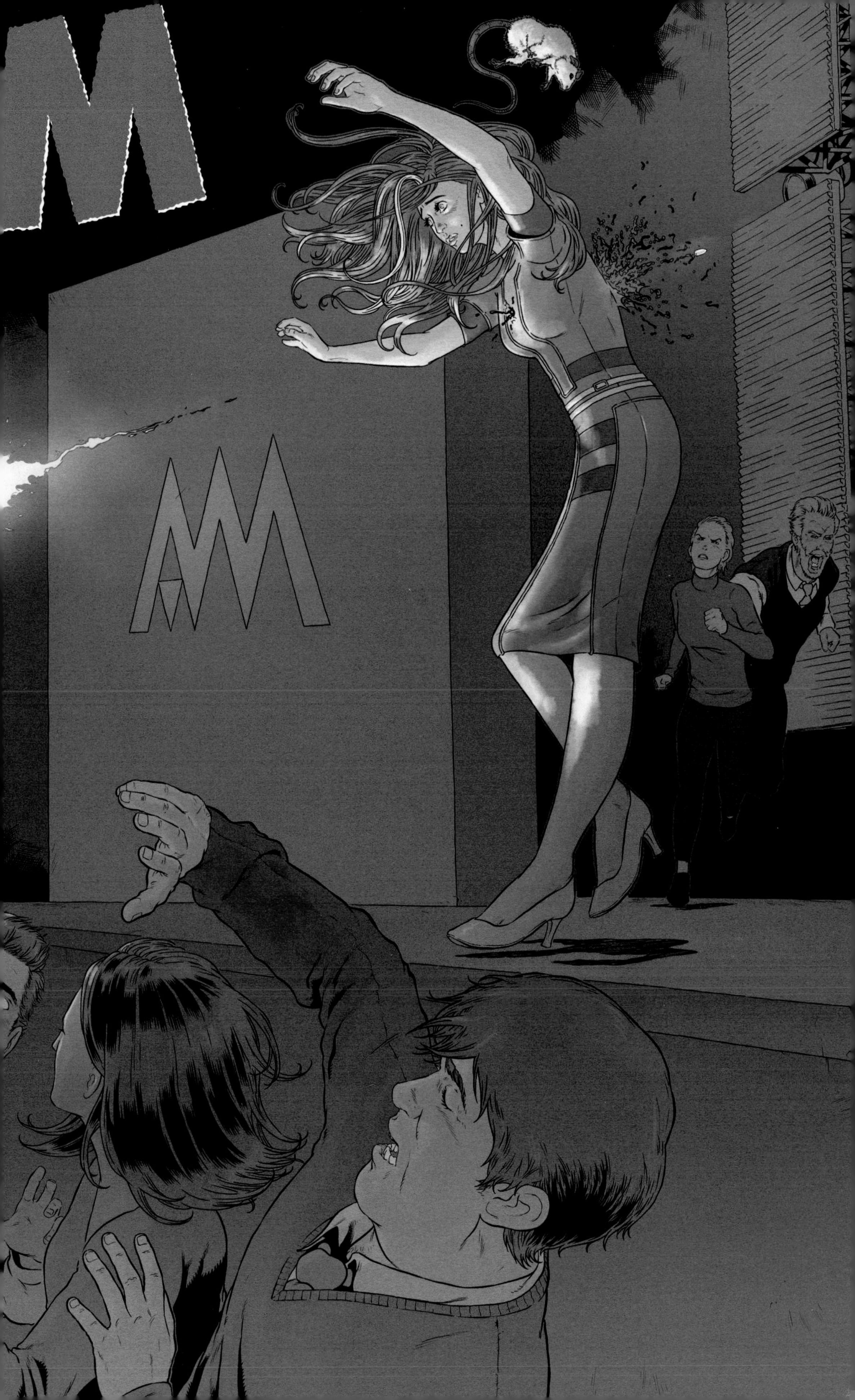

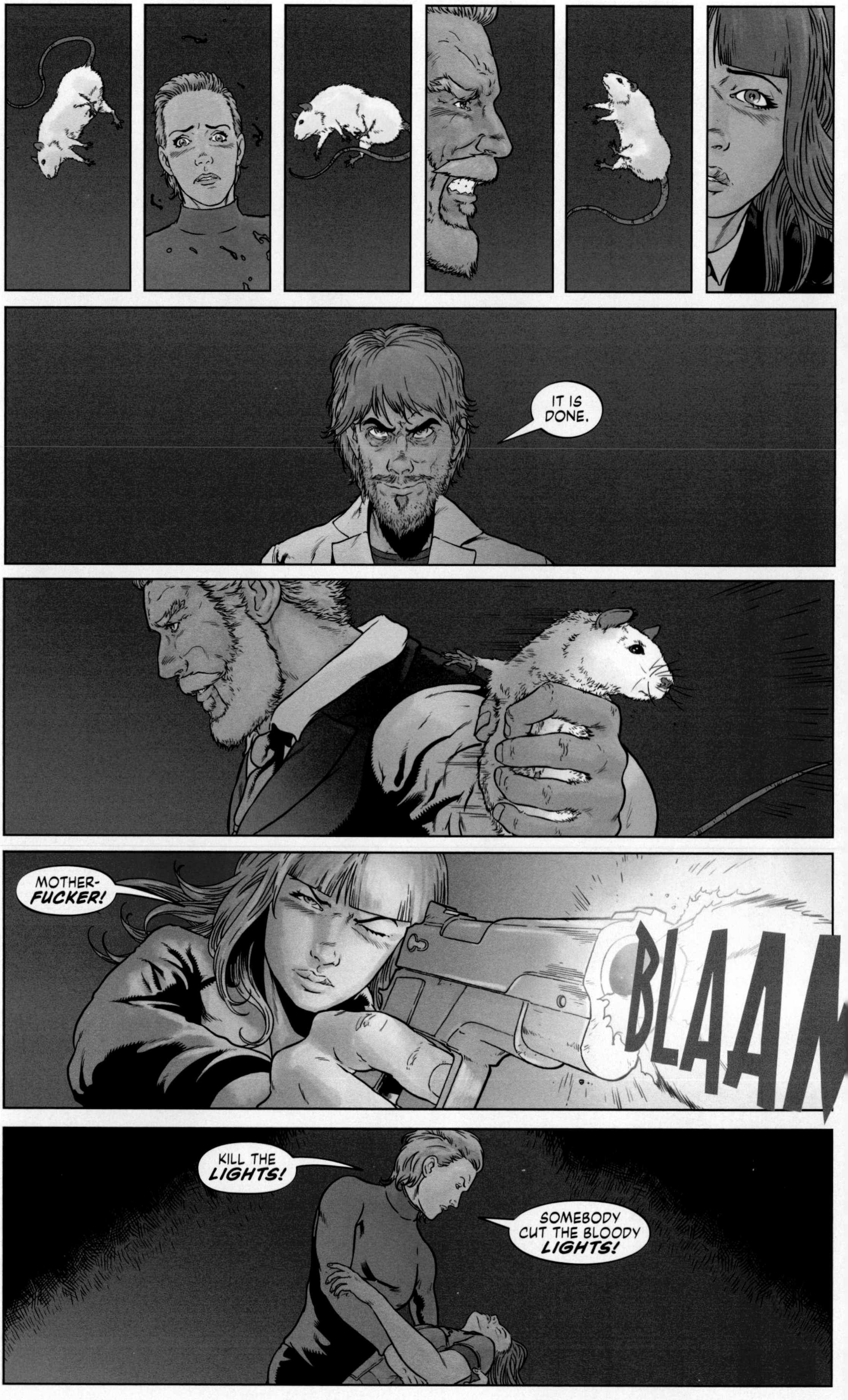
IT IS DONE.
MOTHER-FUCKER!
BLAAM
KILL THE LIGHTS!
SOMEBODY CUT THE BLOODY LIGHTS!

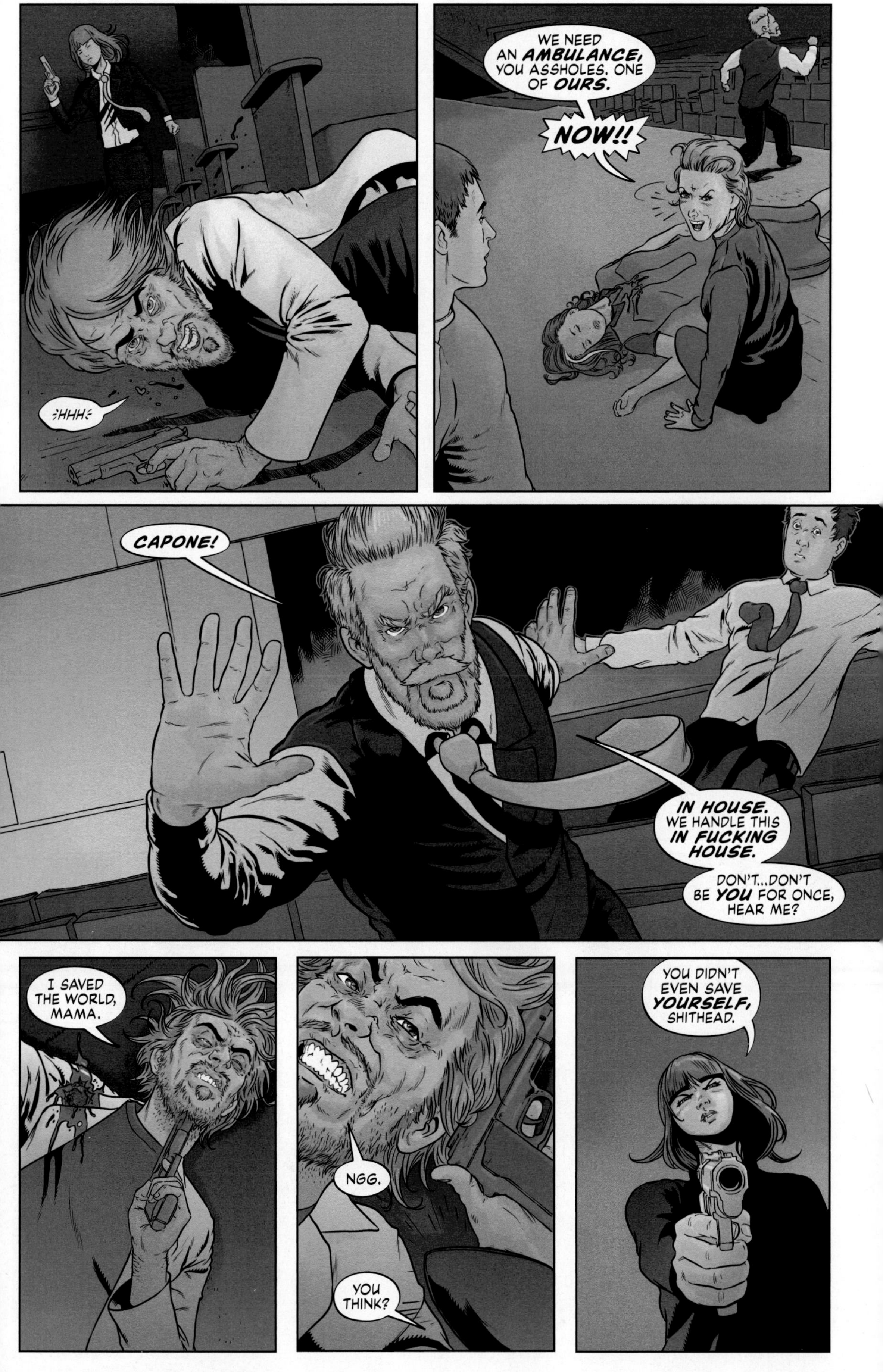

HHH
WE NEED AN AMBULANCE, YOU ASSHOLES. ONE OF OURS.
NOW!!
CAPONE!
IN HOUSE. WE HANDLE THIS IN FUCKING HOUSE.
DON'T...DON'T BE YOU FOR ONCE, HEAR ME?
I SAVED THE WORLD, MAMA.
NGG.
YOU THINK?
YOU DIDN'T EVEN SAVE YOURSELF, SHITHEAD.

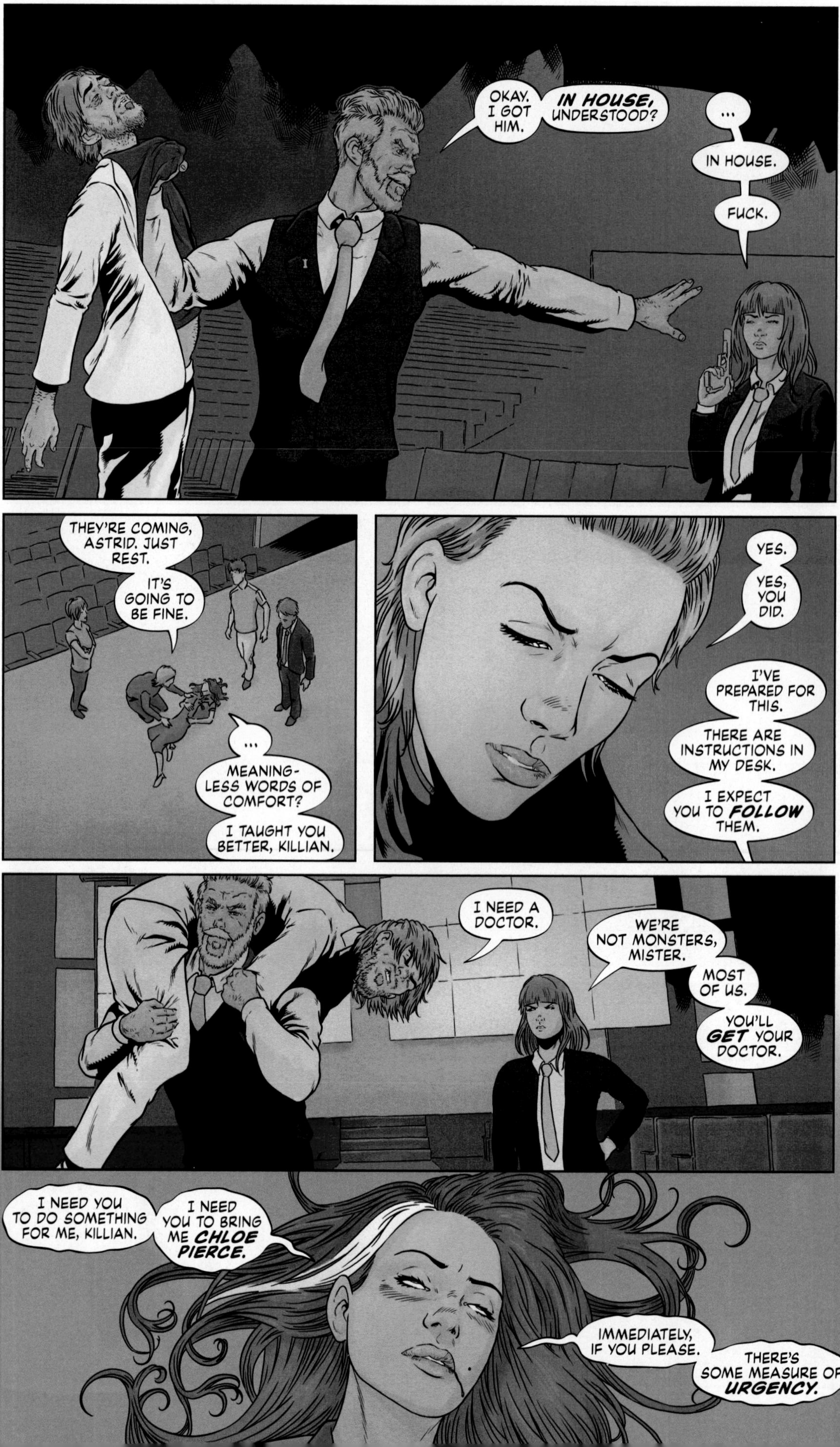
OKAY. I GOT HIM.
IN HOUSE, UNDERSTOOD?
...
IN HOUSE.
FUCK.
THEY'RE COMING, ASTRID. JUST REST.
IT'S GOING TO BE FINE.
...
MEANING-LESS WORDS OF COMFORT?
I TAUGHT YOU BETTER, KILLIAN.
YES.
YES, YOU DID.
I'VE PREPARED FOR THIS.
THERE ARE INSTRUCTIONS IN MY DESK.
I EXPECT YOU TO FOLLOW THEM.
I NEED A DOCTOR.
WE'RE NOT MONSTERS, MISTER.
MOST OF US.
YOU'LL GET YOUR DOCTOR.
I NEED YOU TO DO SOMETHING FOR ME, KILLIAN.
I NEED YOU TO BRING ME CHLOE PIERCE.
IMMEDIATELY, IF YOU PLEASE.
THERE'S SOME MEASURE OF URGENCY.

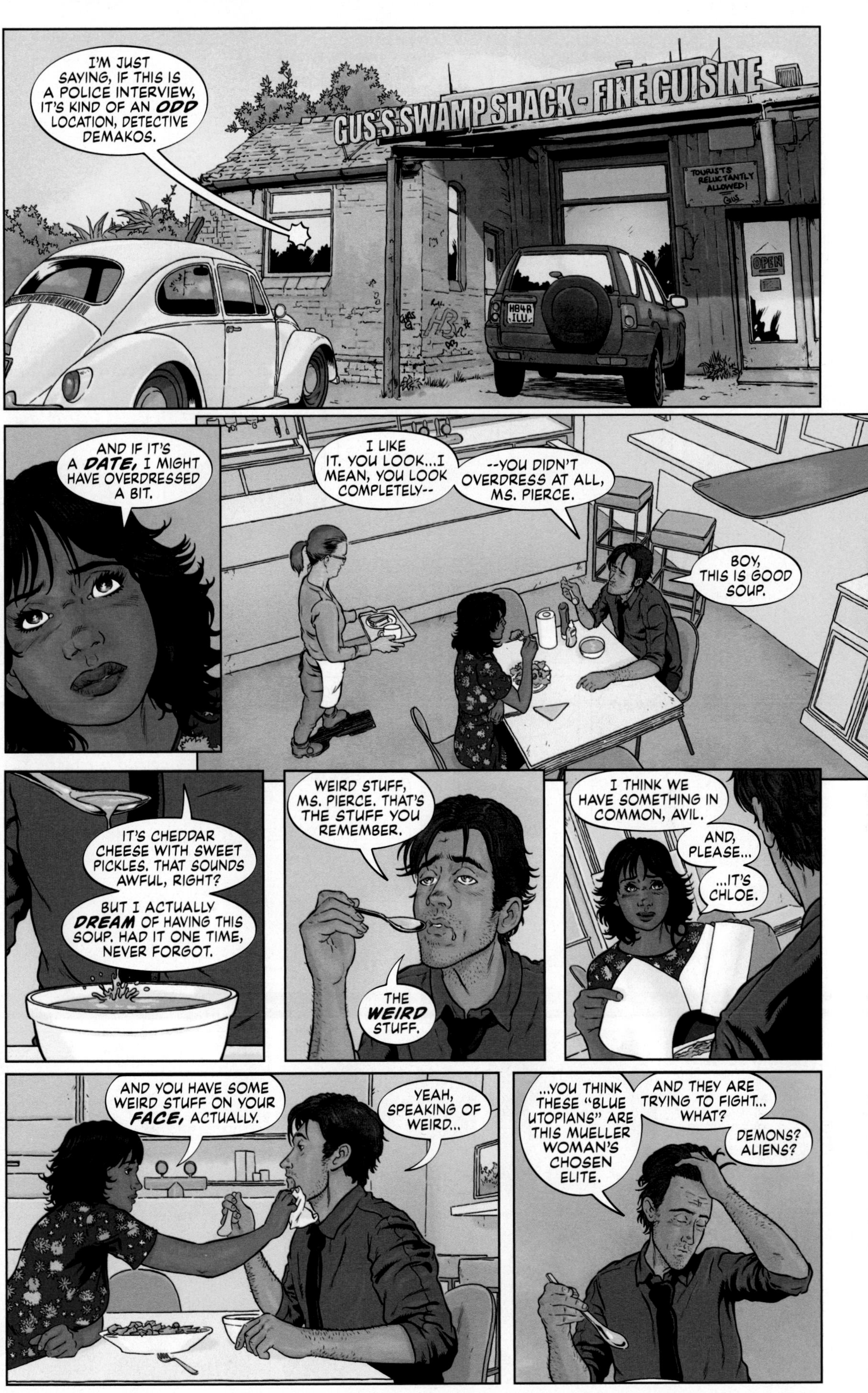
I'M JUST SAYING, IF THIS IS A POLICE INTERVIEW, IT'S KIND OF AN ODD LOCATION, DETECTIVE DEMAKOS.
GUS'S SWAMP SHACK - FINE CUISINE
TOURISTS RELUCTANTLY ALLOWED! GUS
OPEN
H84R ILU
AND IF IT'S A DATE, I MIGHT HAVE OVERDRESSED A BIT.
I LIKE IT. YOU LOOK...I MEAN, YOU LOOK COMPLETELY--
--YOU DIDN'T OVERDRESS AT ALL, MS. PIERCE.
BOY, THIS IS GOOD SOUP.
IT'S CHEDDAR CHEESE WITH SWEET PICKLES. THAT SOUNDS AWFUL, RIGHT?
BUT I ACTUALLY DREAM OF HAVING THIS SOUP. HAD IT ONE TIME, NEVER FORGOT.
WEIRD STUFF, MS. PIERCE. THAT'S THE STUFF YOU REMEMBER.
THE WEIRD STUFF.
I THINK WE HAVE SOMETHING IN COMMON, AVIL.
AND, PLEASE...
...IT'S CHLOE.
AND YOU HAVE SOME WEIRD STUFF ON YOUR FACE, ACTUALLY.
YEAH, SPEAKING OF WEIRD...
...YOU THINK THESE "BLUE UTOPIANS" ARE THIS MUELLER WOMAN'S CHOSEN ELITE.
AND THEY ARE TRYING TO FIGHT... WHAT?
DEMONS? ALIENS?

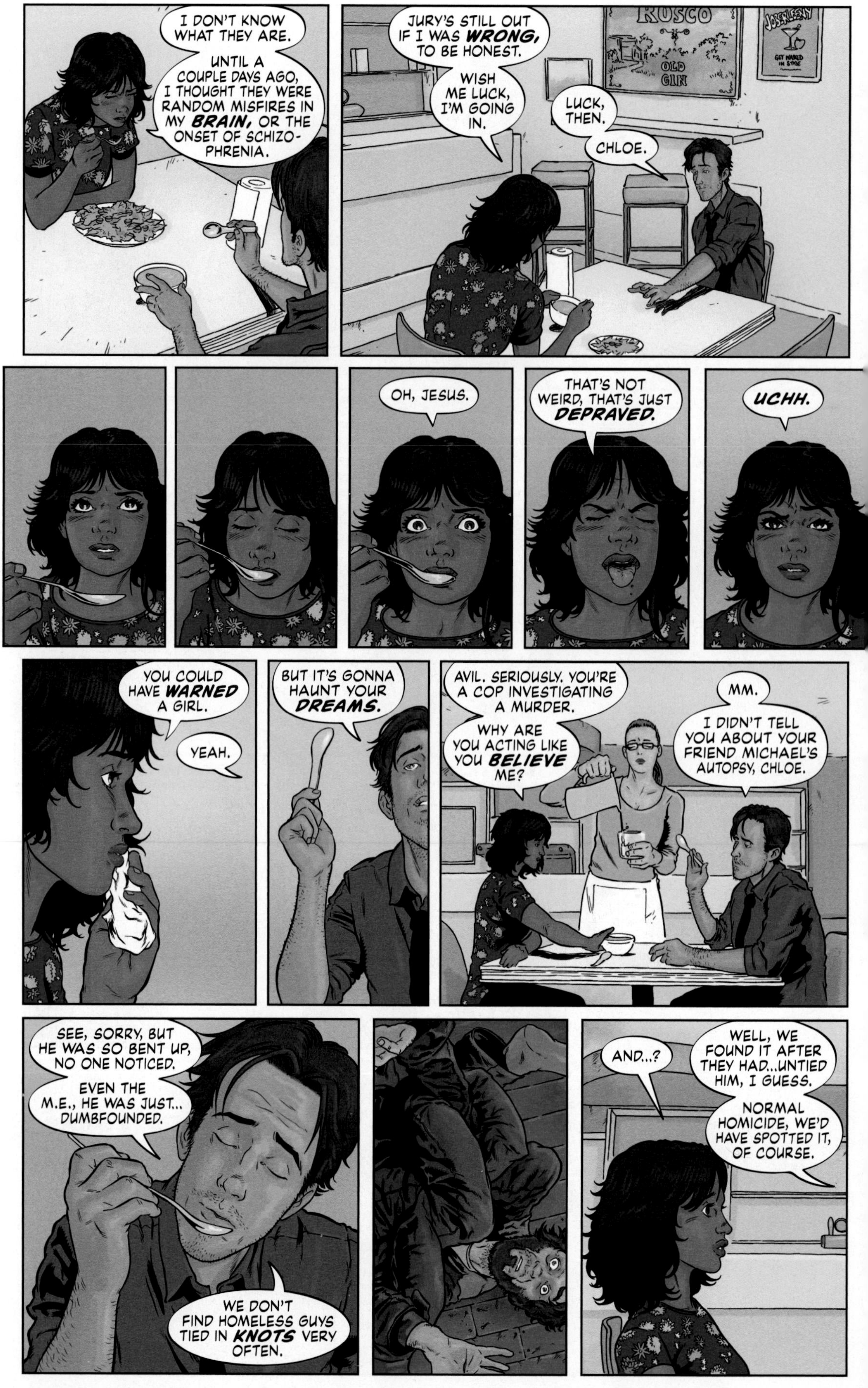
I DON'T KNOW WHAT THEY ARE.
UNTIL A COUPLE DAYS AGO, I THOUGHT THEY WERE RANDOM MISFIRES IN MY BRAIN, OR THE ONSET OF SCHIZO-PHRENIA.
JURY'S STILL OUT IF I WAS WRONG, TO BE HONEST.
WISH ME LUCK, I'M GOING IN.
ROSCO
OLD GIN
LUCK, THEN.
CHLOE.
OH, JESUS.
THAT'S NOT WEIRD, THAT'S JUST DEPRAVED.
UCHH.
YOU COULD HAVE WARNED A GIRL.
YEAH.
BUT IT'S GONNA HAUNT YOUR DREAMS.
AVIL. SERIOUSLY. YOU'RE A COP INVESTIGATING A MURDER.
WHY ARE YOU ACTING LIKE YOU BELIEVE ME?
MM.
I DIDN'T TELL YOU ABOUT YOUR FRIEND MICHAEL'S AUTOPSY, CHLOE.
SEE, SORRY, BUT HE WAS SO BENT UP, NO ONE NOTICED.
EVEN THE M.E., HE WAS JUST... DUMBFOUNDED.
WE DON'T FIND HOMELESS GUYS TIED IN KNOTS VERY OFTEN.
AND...?
WELL, WE FOUND IT AFTER THEY HAD...UNTIED HIM, I GUESS.
NORMAL HOMICIDE, WE'D HAVE SPOTTED IT, OF COURSE.

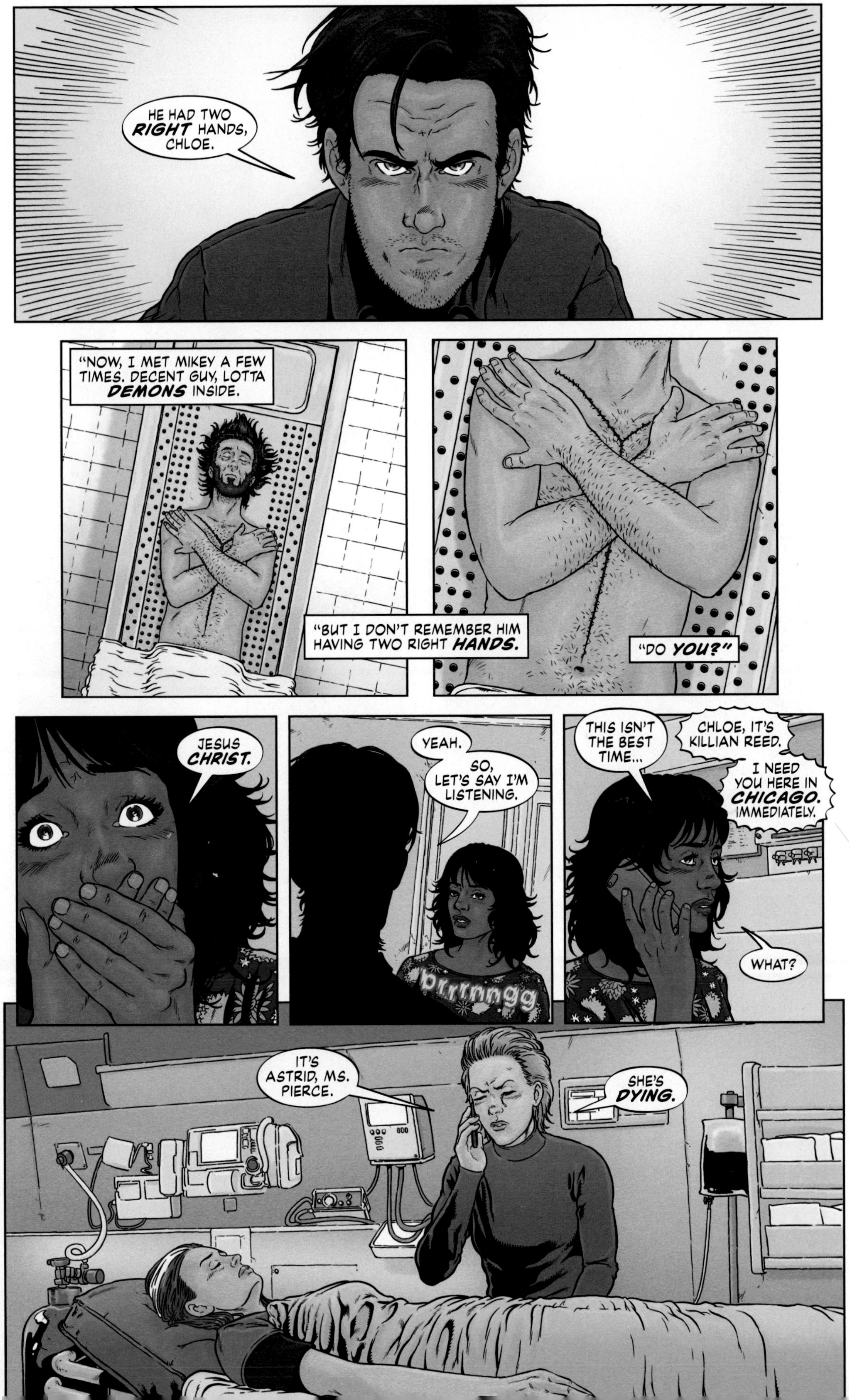
HE HAD TWO RIGHT HANDS, CHLOE.
"NOW, I MET MIKEY A FEW TIMES. DECENT GUY, LOTTA DEMONS INSIDE.
"BUT I DON'T REMEMBER HIM HAVING TWO RIGHT HANDS.
"DO YOU?"
JESUS CHRIST.
YEAH.
SO, LET'S SAY I'M LISTENING.
brrrrnngg
THIS ISN'T THE BEST TIME...
CHLOE, IT'S KILLIAN REED.
I NEED YOU HERE IN CHICAGO. IMMEDIATELY.
WHAT?
IT'S ASTRID, MS. PIERCE.
SHE'S DYING.

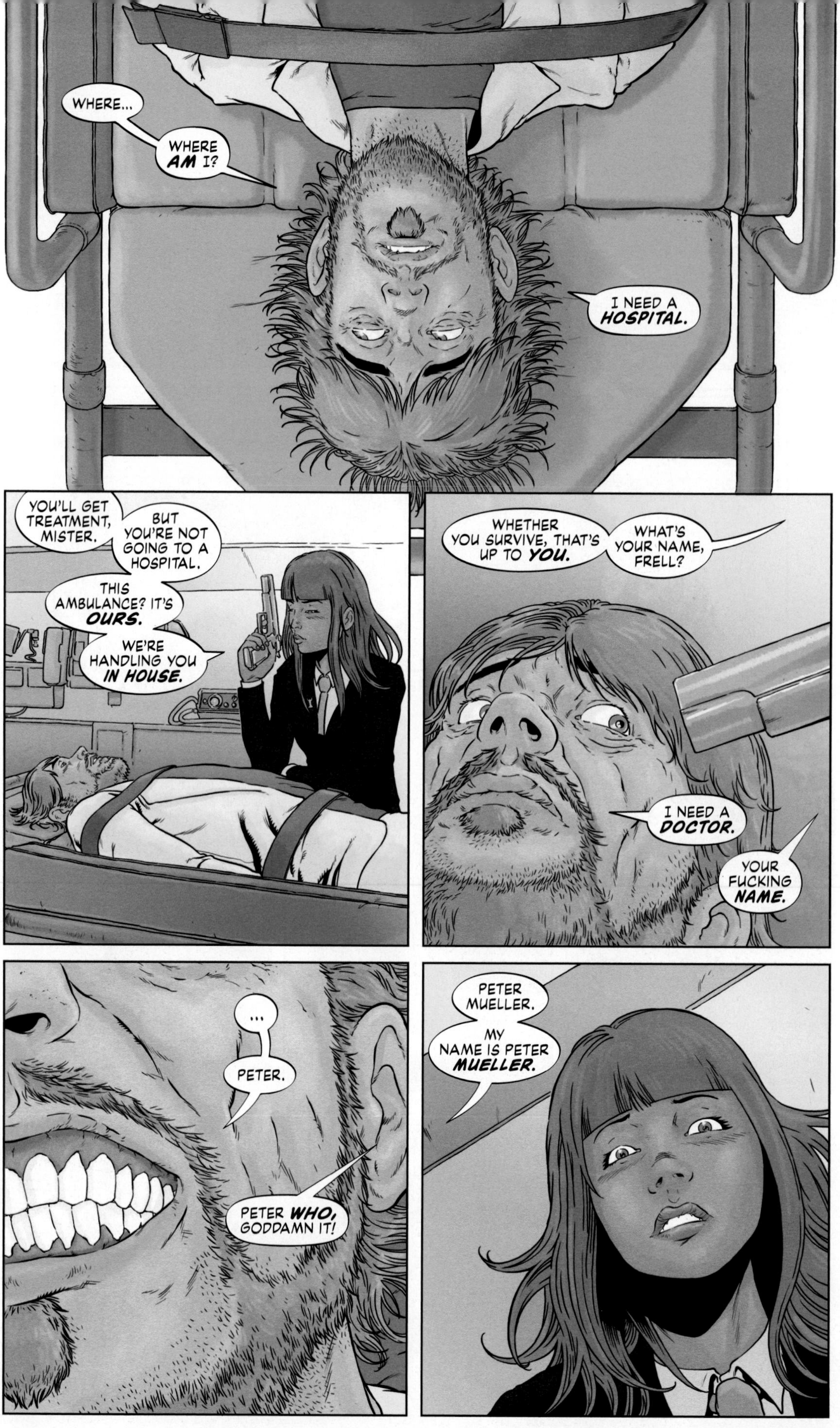
WHERE...
WHERE AM I?
I NEED A HOSPITAL.
YOU'LL GET TREATMENT, MISTER.
BUT YOU'RE NOT GOING TO A HOSPITAL.
THIS AMBULANCE? IT'S OURS.
WE'RE HANDLING YOU IN HOUSE.
WHETHER YOU SURVIVE, THAT'S UP TO YOU.
WHAT'S YOUR NAME, FRELL?
I NEED A DOCTOR.
YOUR FUCKING NAME.
...
PETER.
PETER WHO, GODDAMN IT!
PETER MUELLER.
MY NAME IS PETER MUELLER.

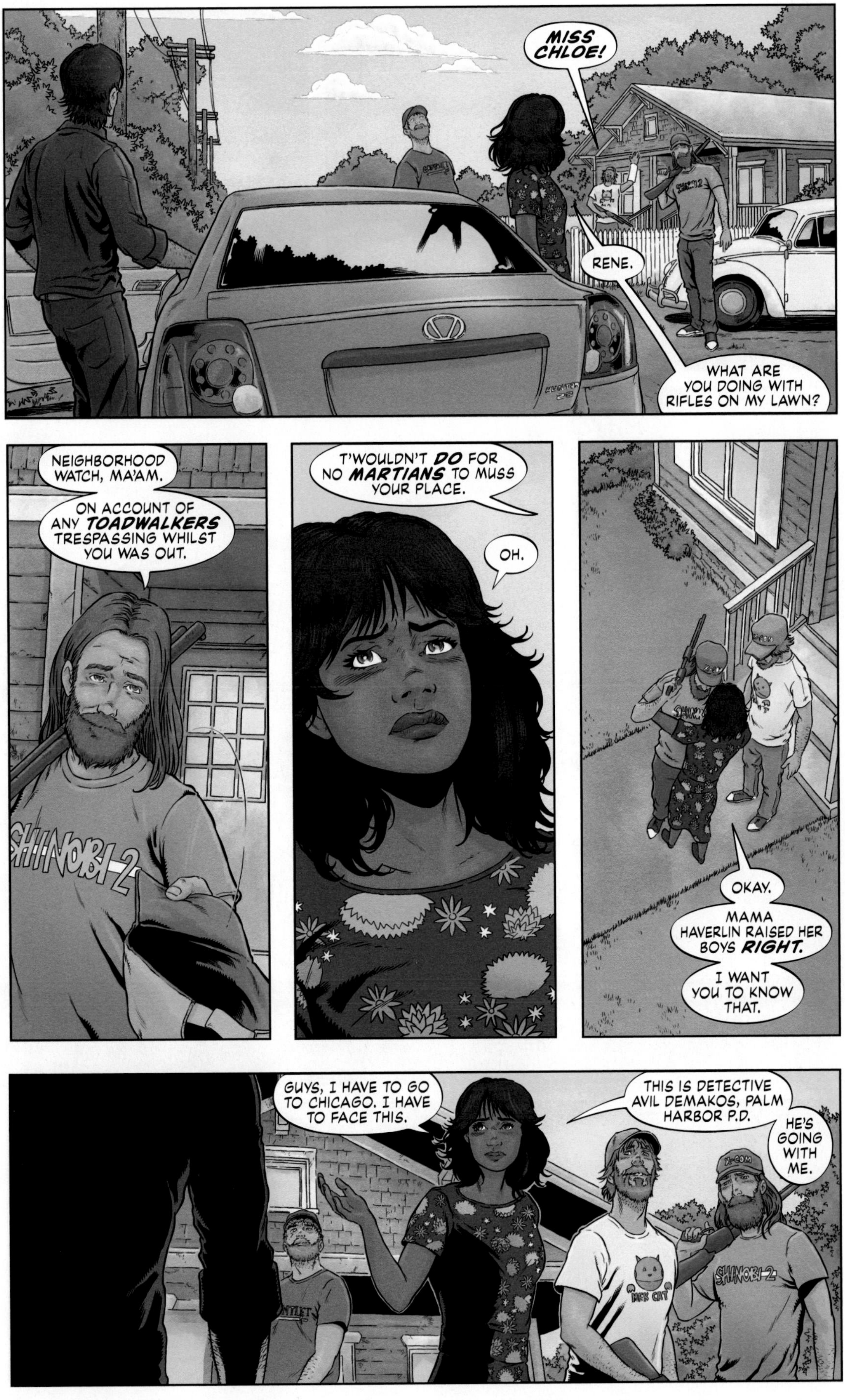
MISS CHLOE!
RENE.
WHAT ARE YOU DOING WITH RIFLES ON MY LAWN?
NEIGHBORHOOD WATCH, MA'AM.
ON ACCOUNT OF ANY TOADWALKERS TRESPASSING WHILST YOU WAS OUT.
T'WOULDN'T DO FOR NO MARTIANS TO MUSS YOUR PLACE.
OH.
OKAY.
MAMA HAVERLIN RAISED HER BOYS RIGHT.
I WANT YOU TO KNOW THAT.
GUYS, I HAVE TO GO TO CHICAGO. I HAVE TO FACE THIS.
THIS IS DETECTIVE AVIL DEMAKOS, PALM HARBOR P.D.
HE'S GOING WITH ME.

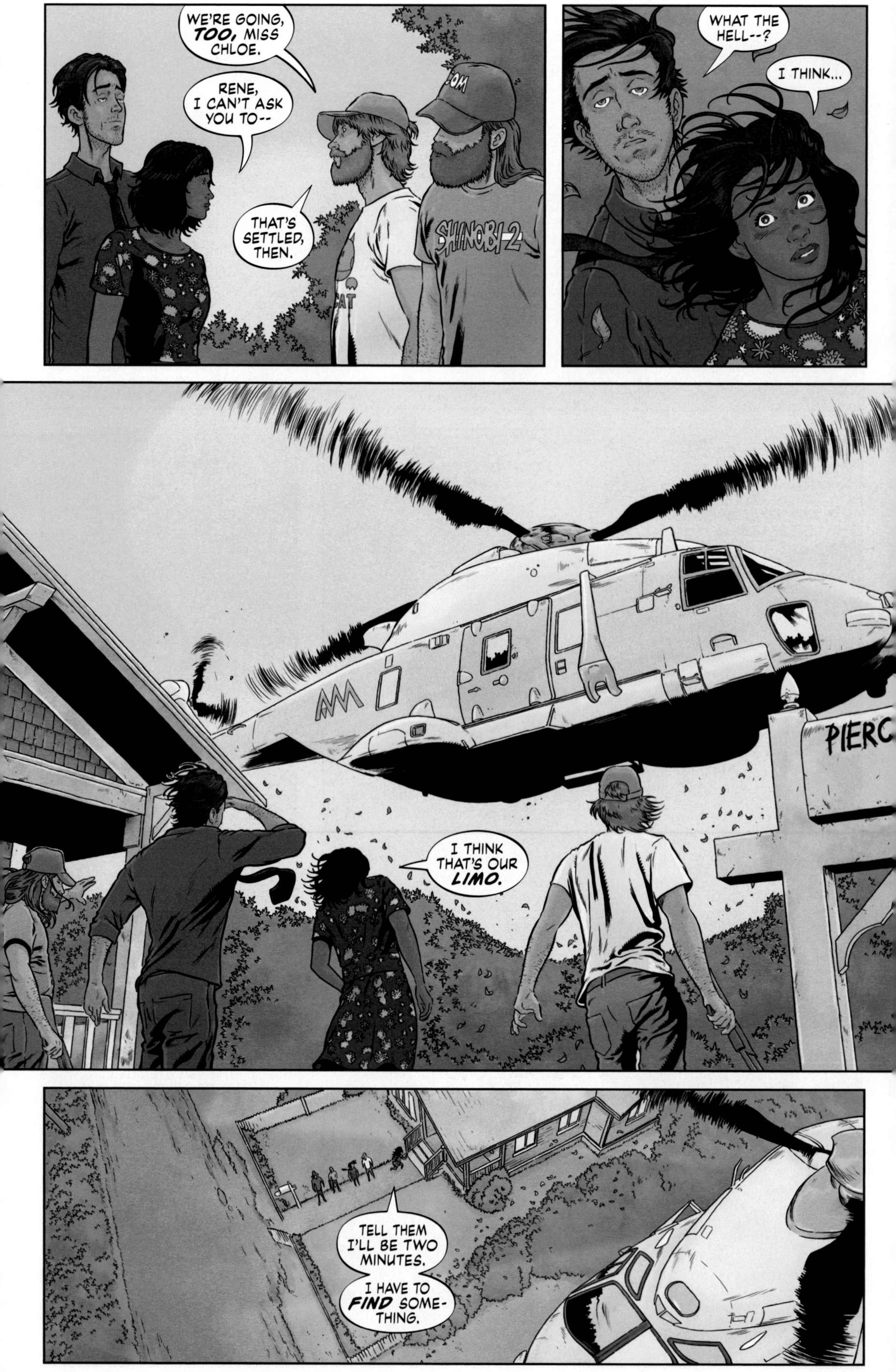
WE'RE GOING, **TOO,** MISS CHLOE.
RENE, I CAN'T ASK YOU TO--
THAT'S SETTLED, THEN.
SHINOBI-2
WHAT THE HELL--?
I THINK...
PIERC
I THINK THAT'S OUR **LIMO.**
TELL THEM I'LL BE TWO MINUTES.
I HAVE TO **FIND** SOME-THING.

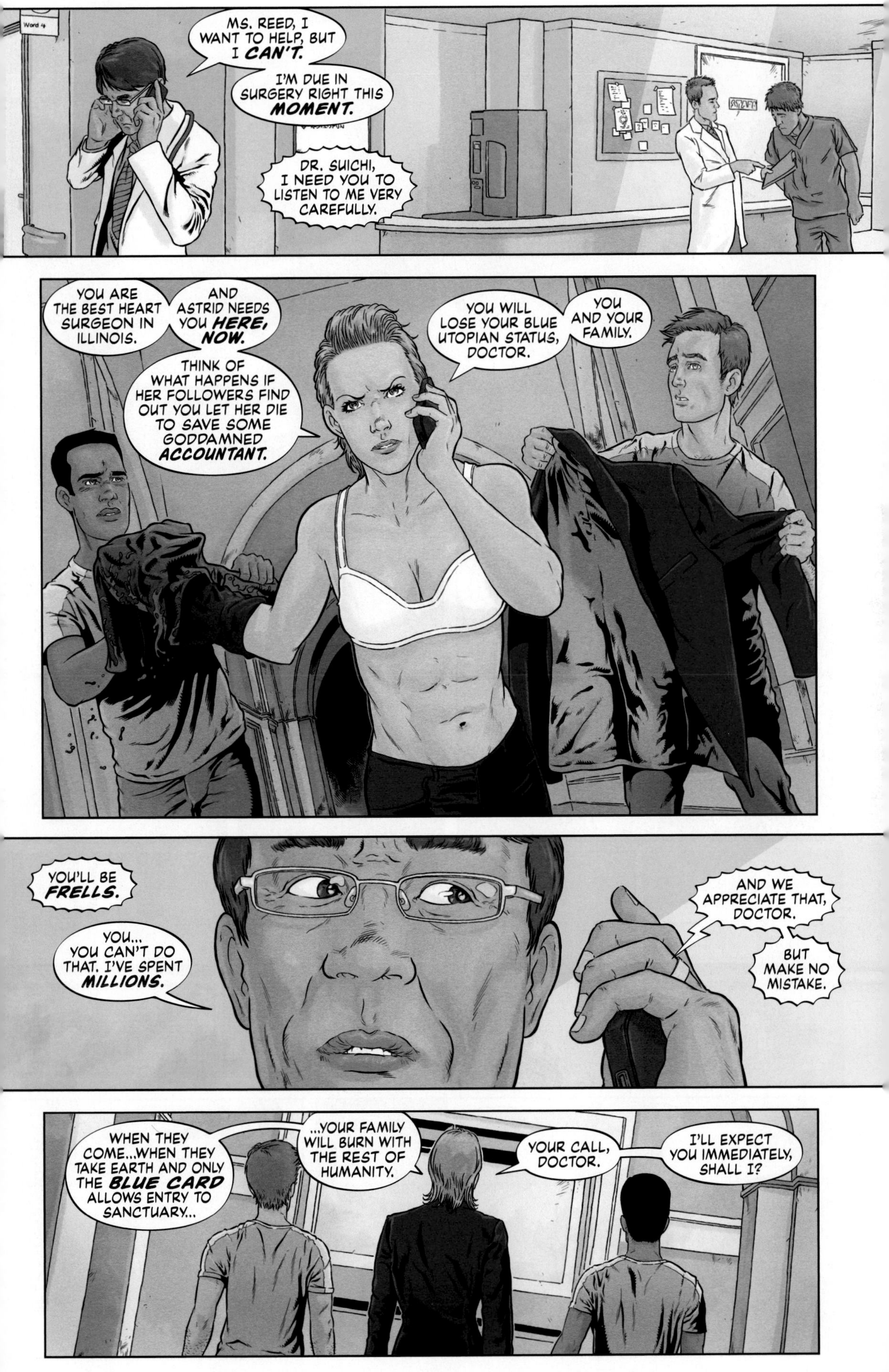
MS. REED, I WANT TO HELP, BUT I CAN'T.
I'M DUE IN SURGERY RIGHT THIS MOMENT.
DR. SUICHI, I NEED YOU TO LISTEN TO ME VERY CAREFULLY.
YOU ARE THE BEST HEART SURGEON IN ILLINOIS.
AND ASTRID NEEDS YOU HERE, NOW.
THINK OF WHAT HAPPENS IF HER FOLLOWERS FIND OUT YOU LET HER DIE TO SAVE SOME GODDAMNED ACCOUNTANT.
YOU WILL LOSE YOUR BLUE UTOPIAN STATUS, DOCTOR.
YOU AND YOUR FAMILY.
YOU'LL BE FRELLS.
YOU... YOU CAN'T DO THAT. I'VE SPENT MILLIONS.
AND WE APPRECIATE THAT, DOCTOR.
BUT MAKE NO MISTAKE.
WHEN THEY COME...WHEN THEY TAKE EARTH AND ONLY THE BLUE CARD ALLOWS ENTRY TO SANCTUARY...
...YOUR FAMILY WILL BURN WITH THE REST OF HUMANITY.
YOUR CALL, DOCTOR.
I'LL EXPECT YOU IMMEDIATELY, SHALL I?

SHE'S REQUESTED THAT THE SURGERY TAKE PLACE IN THE *CLEAN ROOM*. ALL NECESSARY EQUIPMENT IS BEING MOVED THERE.

I WANT FOUR BISHOP-LEVEL GUARDS OUTSIDE THE DOOR AT *ALL TIMES*.

NO ONE TALKS TO *ANYONE*, EXCEPT DUNCAN.

NOT POLICE, NOT MEDIA. UNDERSTOOD?

BUT MS. REED, DON'T YOU WANT TO BE WITH HER AT--

I MEAN, JUST IN CASE SHE--

I HAVE MY ORDERS, MR. VALIS.

SO DO *YOU*.

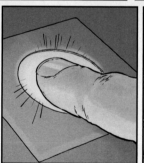

KILLIAN.

APPARENTLY, I AM EITHER DECEASED OR INCAPACITATED.

THIS VIDEO IS TO PREPARE YOU FOR WHAT YOU MUST DO TO CONTINUE OUR WORK.

THIS NEXT THING MIGHT BE A BIT OF A SHOCK.

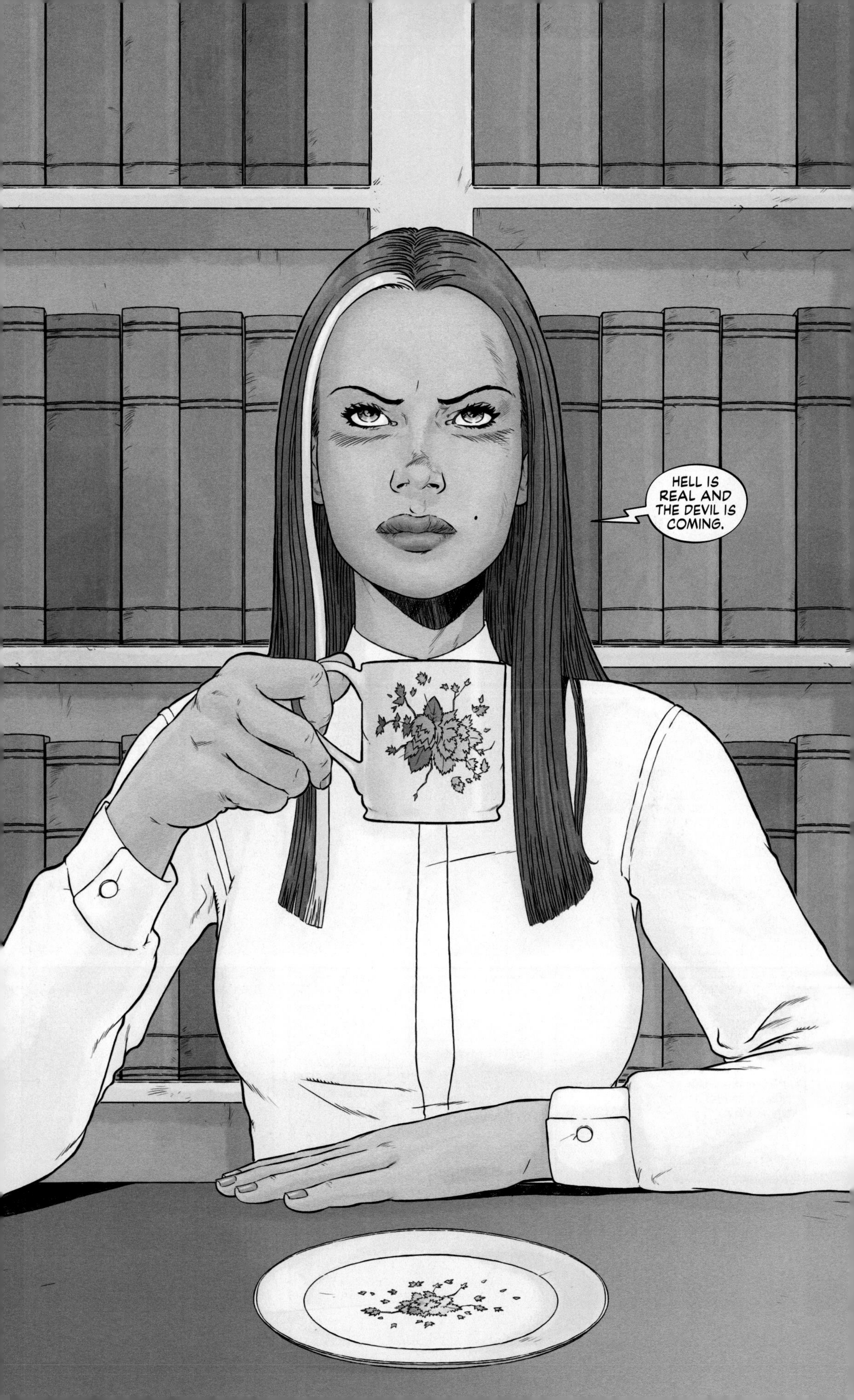
HELL IS REAL AND THE DEVIL IS COMING.

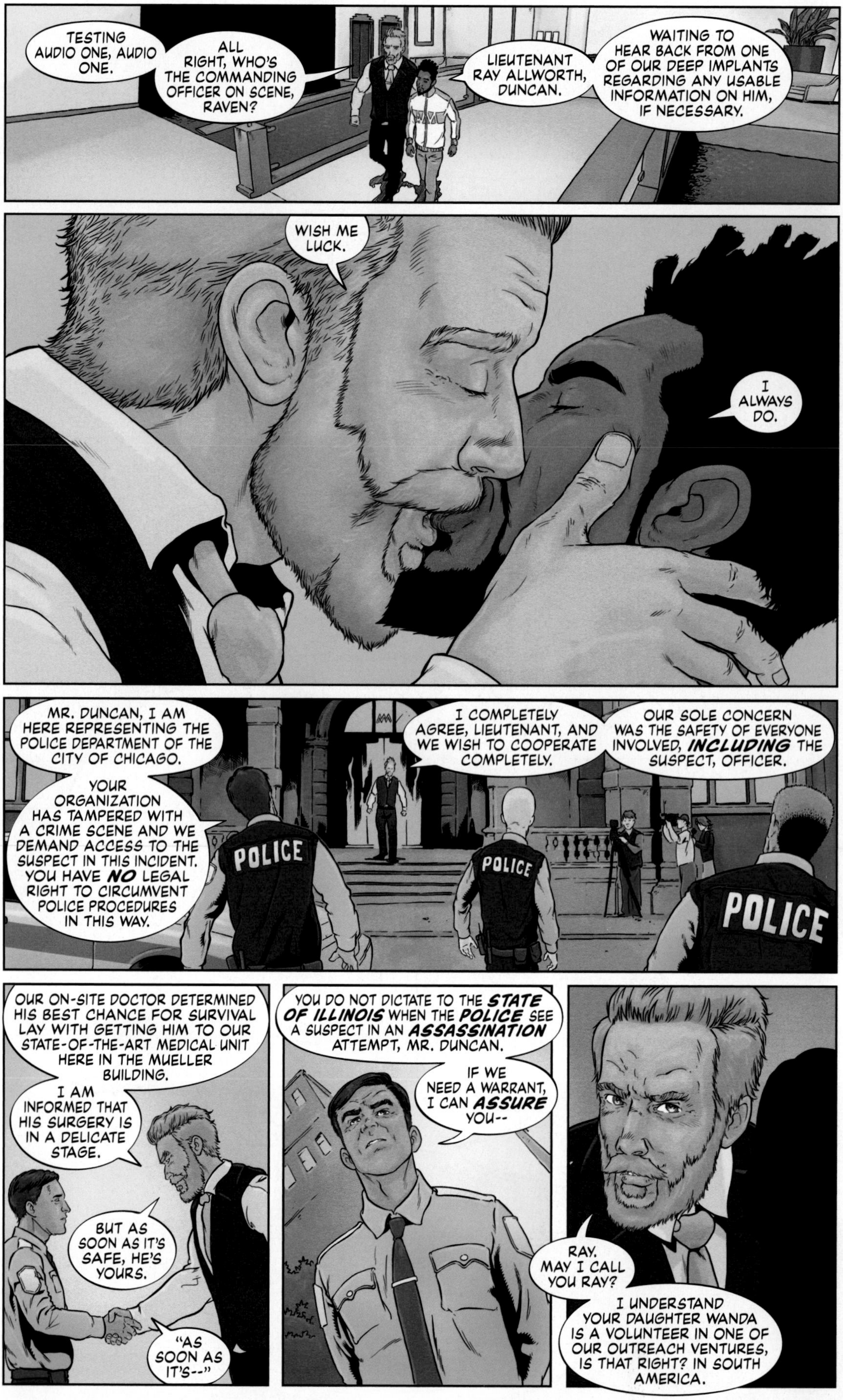

TESTING AUDIO ONE, AUDIO ONE.
ALL RIGHT, WHO'S THE COMMANDING OFFICER ON SCENE, RAVEN?
LIEUTENANT RAY ALLWORTH, DUNCAN.
WAITING TO HEAR BACK FROM ONE OF OUR DEEP IMPLANTS REGARDING ANY USABLE INFORMATION ON HIM, IF NECESSARY.
WISH ME LUCK.
I ALWAYS DO.
MR. DUNCAN, I AM HERE REPRESENTING THE POLICE DEPARTMENT OF THE CITY OF CHICAGO.
YOUR ORGANIZATION HAS TAMPERED WITH A CRIME SCENE AND WE DEMAND ACCESS TO THE SUSPECT IN THIS INCIDENT. YOU HAVE **NO** LEGAL RIGHT TO CIRCUMVENT POLICE PROCEDURES IN THIS WAY.
POLICE
POLICE
POLICE
I COMPLETELY AGREE, LIEUTENANT, AND WE WISH TO COOPERATE COMPLETELY.
OUR SOLE CONCERN WAS THE SAFETY OF EVERYONE INVOLVED, ***INCLUDING*** THE SUSPECT, OFFICER.
OUR ON-SITE DOCTOR DETERMINED HIS BEST CHANCE FOR SURVIVAL LAY WITH GETTING HIM TO OUR STATE-OF-THE-ART MEDICAL UNIT HERE IN THE MUELLER BUILDING.
I AM INFORMED THAT HIS SURGERY IS IN A DELICATE STAGE.
BUT AS SOON AS IT'S SAFE, HE'S YOURS.
"AS SOON AS IT'S--"
YOU DO NOT DICTATE TO THE ***STATE OF ILLINOIS*** WHEN THE ***POLICE*** SEE A SUSPECT IN AN ***ASSASSINATION*** ATTEMPT, MR. DUNCAN.
IF WE NEED A WARRANT, I CAN ***ASSURE*** YOU--
RAY. MAY I CALL YOU RAY?
I UNDERSTAND YOUR DAUGHTER WANDA IS A VOLUNTEER IN ONE OF OUR OUTREACH VENTURES, IS THAT RIGHT? IN SOUTH AMERICA.

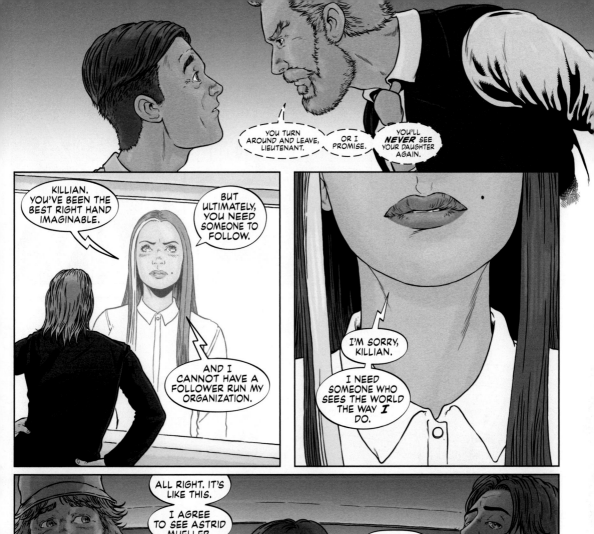

YOU TURN AROUND AND LEAVE, LIEUTENANT.

OR I PROMISE.

YOU'LL *NEVER* SEE YOUR DAUGHTER AGAIN.

KILLIAN. YOU'VE BEEN THE BEST RIGHT HAND IMAGINABLE.

BUT ULTIMATELY, YOU NEED SOMEONE TO FOLLOW.

AND I CANNOT HAVE A FOLLOWER RUN MY ORGANIZATION.

I'M SORRY, KILLIAN.

I NEED SOMEONE WHO SEES THE WORLD THE WAY *I* DO.

ALL RIGHT. IT'S LIKE THIS.

I AGREE TO SEE ASTRID MUELLER.

UNDER ONE CONDITION.

I WON'T GO BACK INTO THAT ROOM ALONE.

I'M TAKING MY NEIGHBOR AS A *WITNESS.*

MS. PIERCE, SURELY YOU UNDERSTAND... WE CAN'T *ALLOW*...

IT'S SIMPLY NOT *POSSIBLE*...

FINE. GIVE HER WHATEVER SHE WANTS. IT DOESN'T MATTER NOW.

WE DID THE FULL DEEP EVAL ON HER NEIGHBORS DAYS AGO. THEY'RE NOTHING AND **NO ONE,** SIMPLE IGNORANT REDNECKS.

JUST **GET** HER HERE.

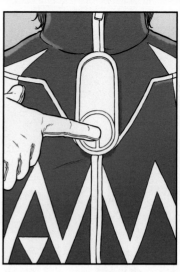

MS. REED. IT'S **BAD,** I'M AFRAID.

SHE HAS BULLET FRAGMENTS LODGED IN HER HEART, AND SHE'S GOT A HEMOTHRAX.

I CAN KEEP HER ALIVE. FOR A WHILE.

I'M SORRY. I'M SO, **SO** SORRY.

...A SECOND TRAGEDY IN AS MANY WEEKS FOR THE SELF-HELP GURU, WHO RECENTLY SUFFERED SEVERE PUBLIC-RELATIONS DAMAGE REGARDING THE SUICIDE OF CELEBRITY ADHERENT **RAND TANNER.**

BUT TONIGHT, IT'S MUELLER **HERSELF** WHO FIGHTS FOR HER LIFE, ACCORDING TO CHICAGO POLICE.

THE MUELLER ORGANIZATION HAS BEEN FULLY COOPERATING WITH US AT EVERY JUNCTURE, AND ANY SUGGESTION OF INFLUENCE OR IMPROPRIETY IS COMPLETELY UNFOUNDED AND, MAY I SAY, **INHUMANE** AT THIS TIME.

THANK YOU.

HAPPENING NOW
LT. RAY ALLWORTH, CHICAGO P.D.

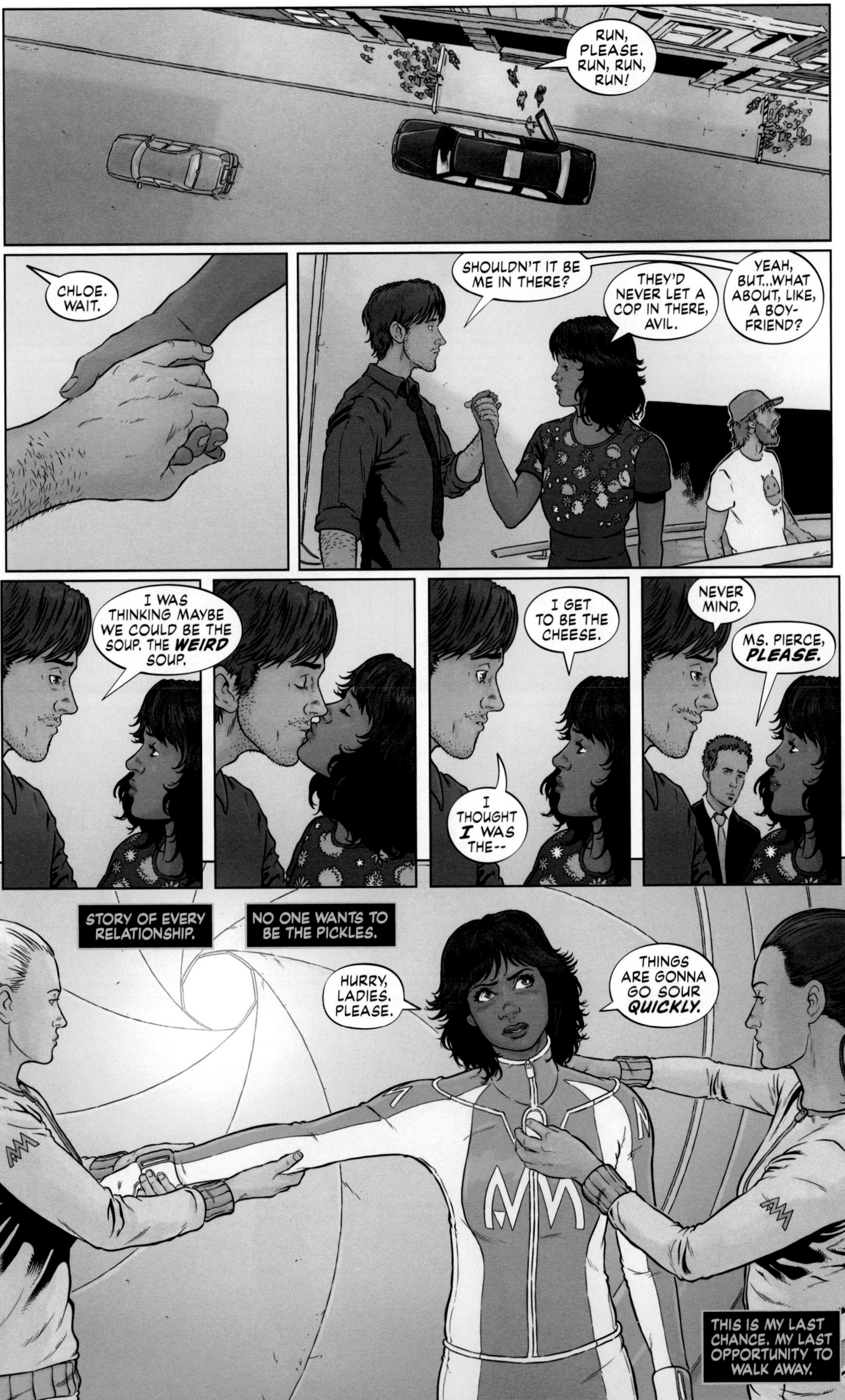
RUN, PLEASE. RUN, RUN, RUN!
CHLOE. WAIT.
SHOULDN'T IT BE ME IN THERE?
THEY'D NEVER LET A COP IN THERE, AVIL.
YEAH, BUT...WHAT ABOUT, LIKE, A BOY-FRIEND?
I WAS THINKING MAYBE WE COULD BE THE SOUP. THE WEIRD SOUP.
I GET TO BE THE CHEESE.
I THOUGHT I WAS THE--
NEVER MIND.
MS. PIERCE, PLEASE.
STORY OF EVERY RELATIONSHIP.
NO ONE WANTS TO BE THE PICKLES.
HURRY, LADIES. PLEASE.
THINGS ARE GONNA GO SOUR QUICKLY.
THIS IS MY LAST CHANCE. MY LAST OPPORTUNITY TO WALK AWAY.

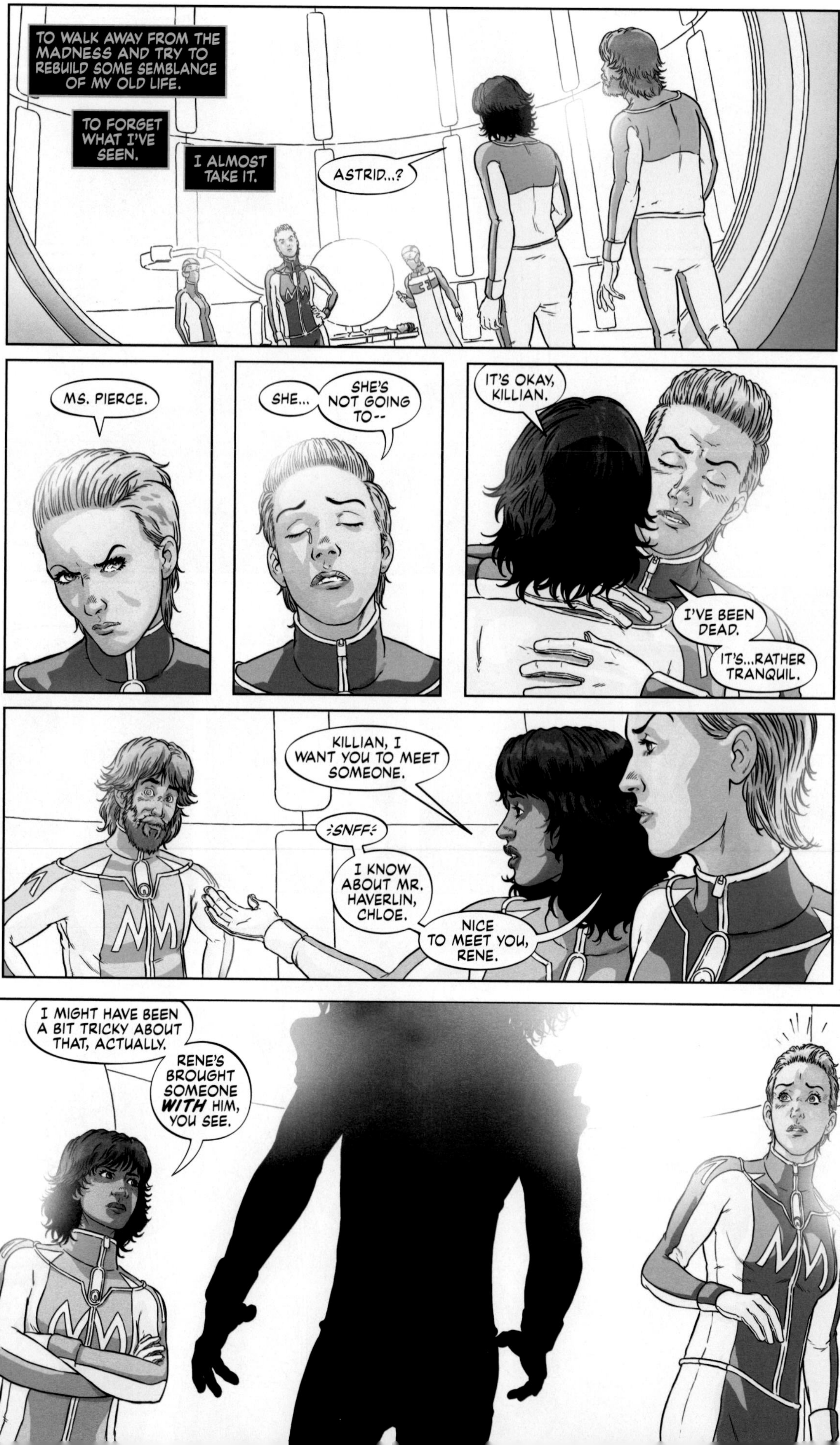
TO WALK AWAY FROM THE MADNESS AND TRY TO REBUILD SOME SEMBLANCE OF MY OLD LIFE.
TO FORGET WHAT I'VE SEEN.
I ALMOST TAKE IT.
ASTRID...?
MS. PIERCE.
SHE...
SHE'S NOT GOING TO--
IT'S OKAY, KILLIAN.
I'VE BEEN DEAD.
IT'S...RATHER TRANQUIL.
KILLIAN, I WANT YOU TO MEET SOMEONE.
SNFF
I KNOW ABOUT MR. HAVERLIN, CHLOE.
NICE TO MEET YOU, RENE.
I MIGHT HAVE BEEN A BIT TRICKY ABOUT THAT, ACTUALLY.
RENE'S BROUGHT SOMEONE WITH HIM, YOU SEE.

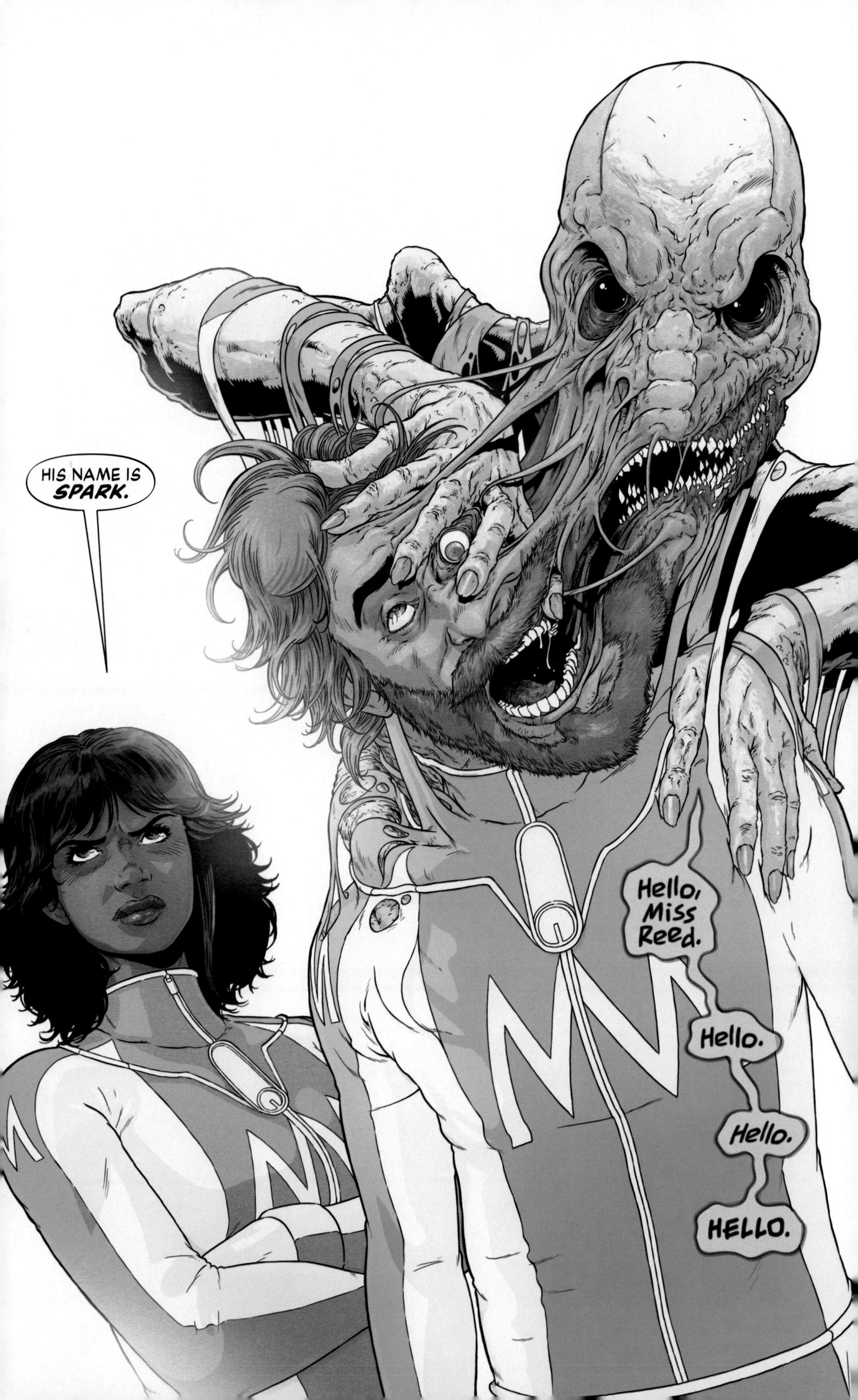
HIS NAME IS *SPARK.*
Hello, Miss Reed.
Hello.
Hello.
HELLO.

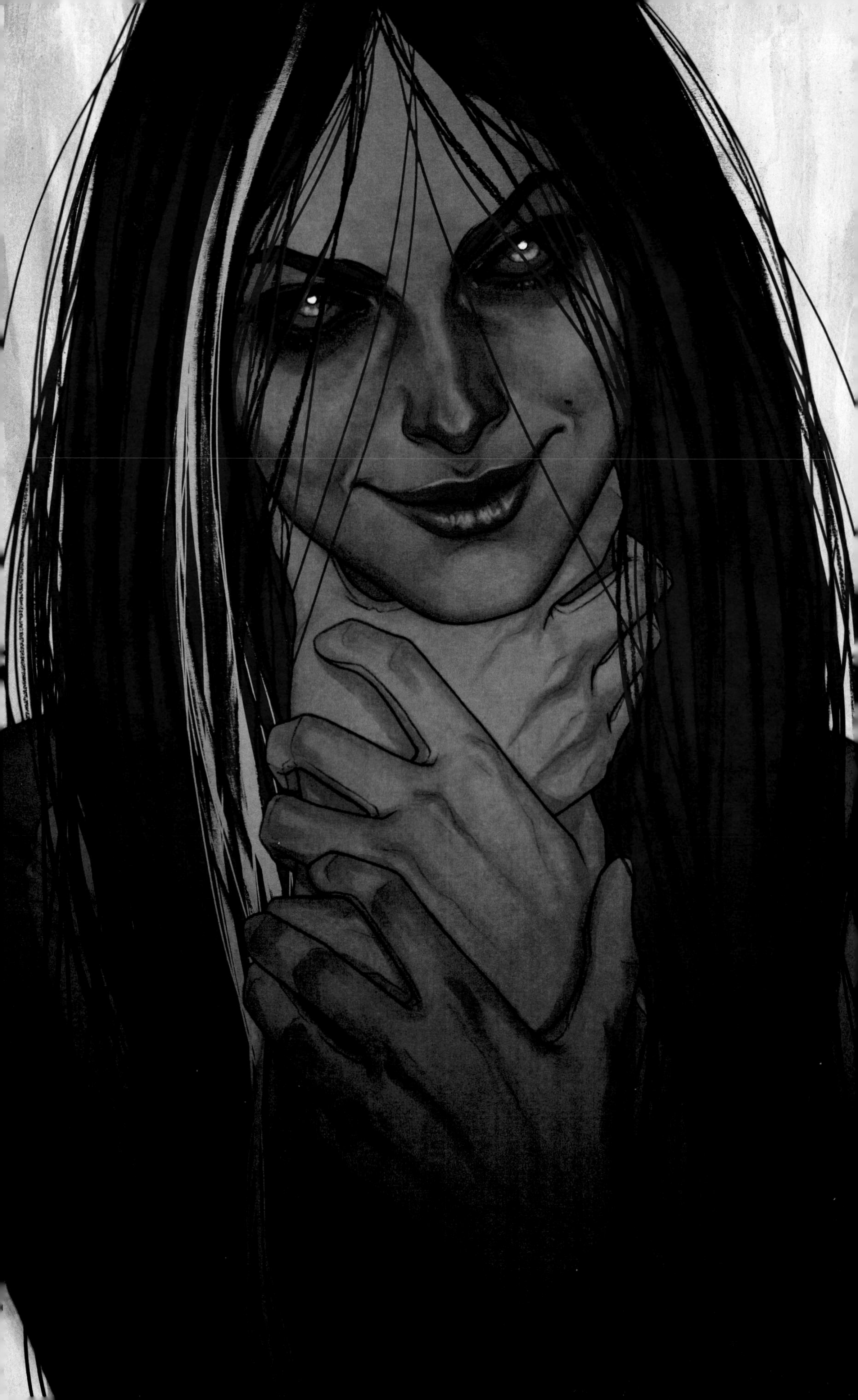

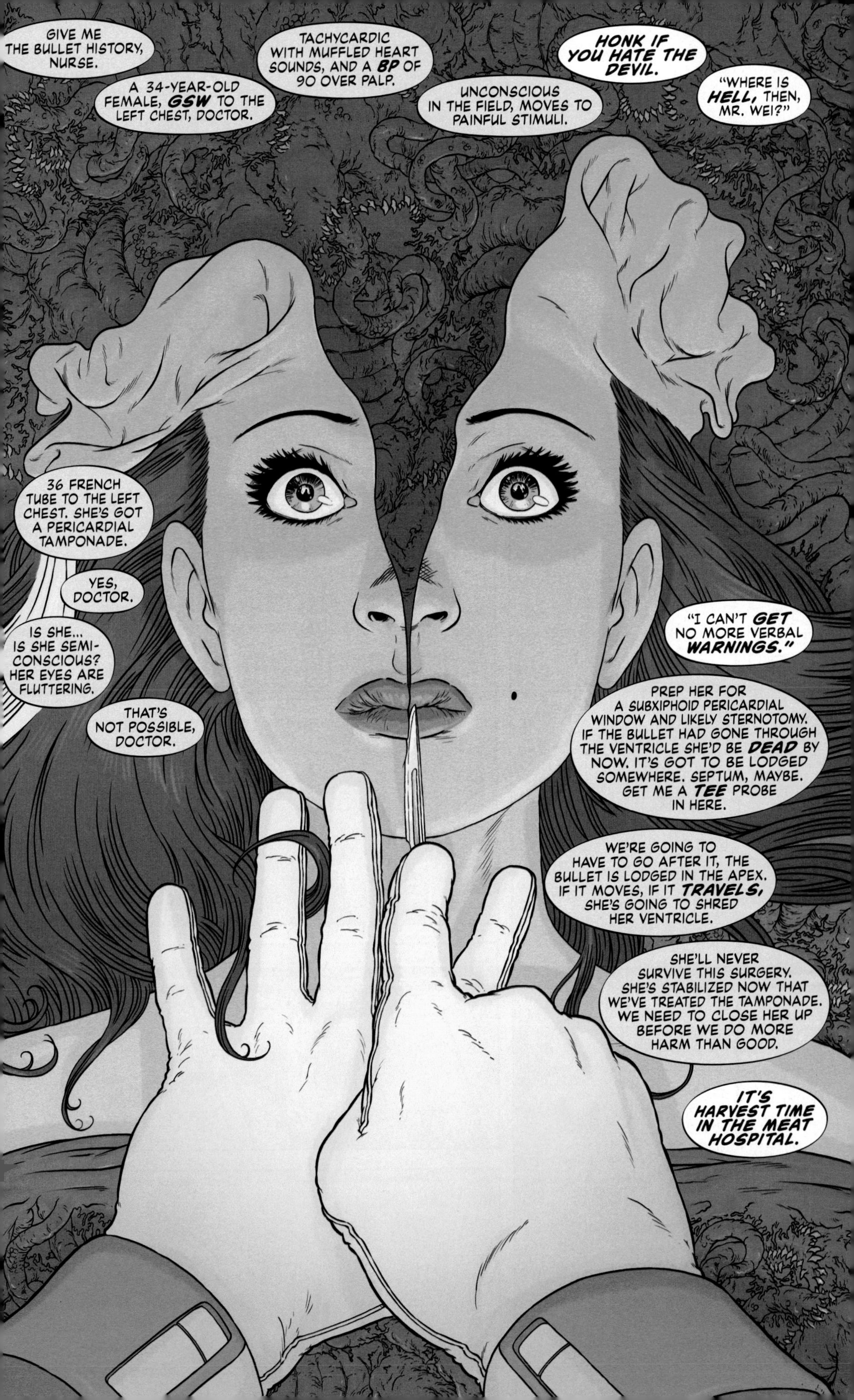
GIVE ME THE BULLET HISTORY, NURSE.
A 34-YEAR-OLD FEMALE, GSW TO THE LEFT CHEST, DOCTOR.
TACHYCARDIC WITH MUFFLED HEART SOUNDS, AND A BP OF 90 OVER PALP.
UNCONSCIOUS IN THE FIELD, MOVES TO PAINFUL STIMULI.
HONK IF YOU HATE THE DEVIL.
"WHERE IS HELL, THEN, MR. WEI?"
36 FRENCH TUBE TO THE LEFT CHEST. SHE'S GOT A PERICARDIAL TAMPONADE.
YES, DOCTOR.
IS SHE... IS SHE SEMI-CONSCIOUS? HER EYES ARE FLUTTERING.
THAT'S NOT POSSIBLE, DOCTOR.
"I CAN'T GET NO MORE VERBAL WARNINGS."
PREP HER FOR A SUBXIPHOID PERICARDIAL WINDOW AND LIKELY STERNOTOMY. IF THE BULLET HAD GONE THROUGH THE VENTRICLE SHE'D BE DEAD BY NOW. IT'S GOT TO BE LODGED SOMEWHERE. SEPTUM, MAYBE. GET ME A TEE PROBE IN HERE.
WE'RE GOING TO HAVE TO GO AFTER IT, THE BULLET IS LODGED IN THE APEX. IF IT MOVES, IF IT TRAVELS, SHE'S GOING TO SHRED HER VENTRICLE.
SHE'LL NEVER SURVIVE THIS SURGERY. SHE'S STABILIZED NOW THAT WE'VE TREATED THE TAMPONADE. WE NEED TO CLOSE HER UP BEFORE WE DO MORE HARM THAN GOOD.
IT'S HARVEST TIME IN THE MEAT HOSPITAL.

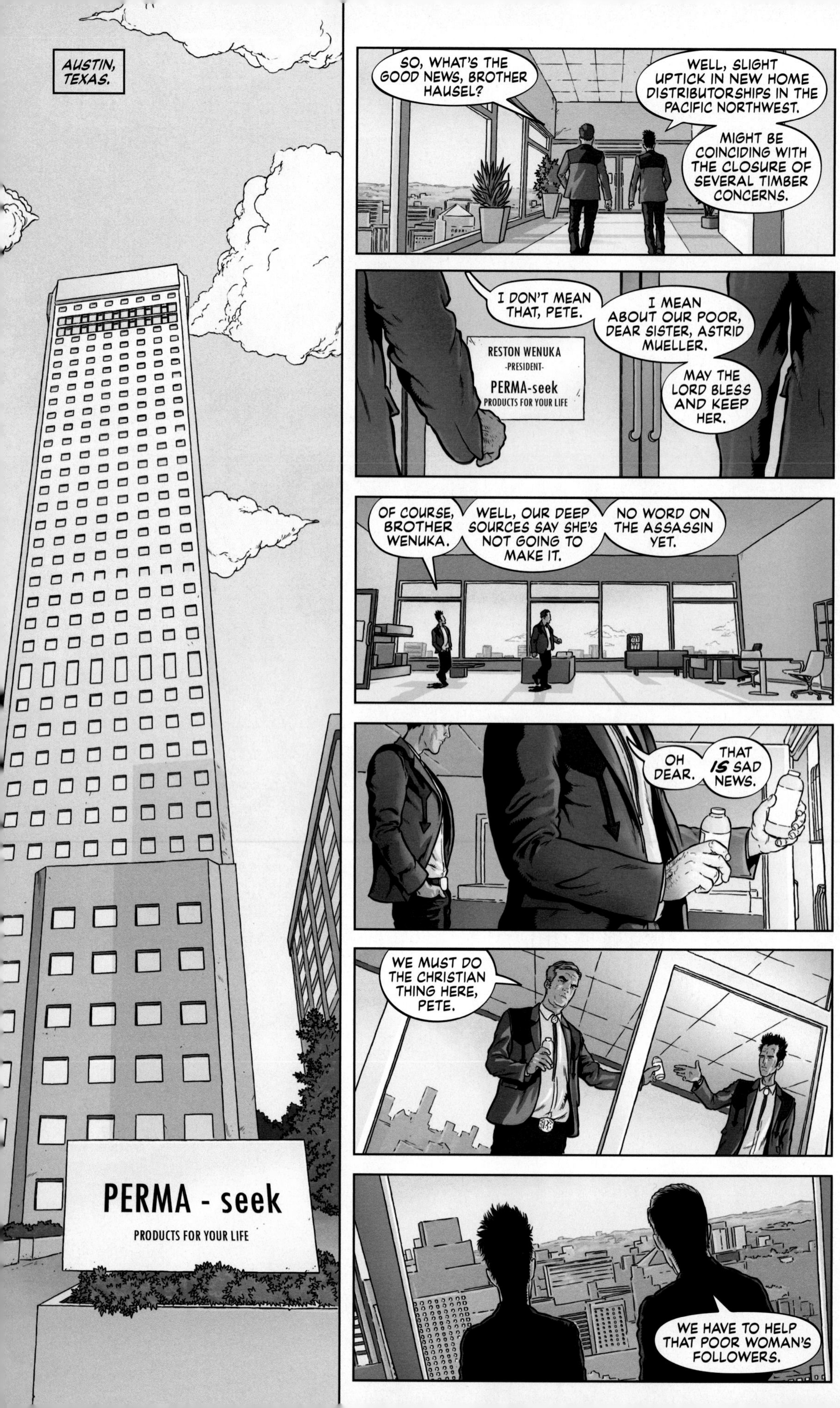
AUSTIN, TEXAS.
PERMA - seek
PRODUCTS FOR YOUR LIFE
SO, WHAT'S THE GOOD NEWS, BROTHER HAUSEL?
WELL, SLIGHT UPTICK IN NEW HOME DISTRIBUTORSHIPS IN THE PACIFIC NORTHWEST.
MIGHT BE COINCIDING WITH THE CLOSURE OF SEVERAL TIMBER CONCERNS.
I DON'T MEAN THAT, PETE.
RESTON WENUKA
-PRESIDENT-
PERMA-seek
PRODUCTS FOR YOUR LIFE
I MEAN ABOUT OUR POOR, DEAR SISTER, ASTRID MUELLER.
MAY THE LORD BLESS AND KEEP HER.
OF COURSE, BROTHER WENUKA.
WELL, OUR DEEP SOURCES SAY SHE'S NOT GOING TO MAKE IT.
NO WORD ON THE ASSASSIN YET.
OH DEAR.
THAT *IS* SAD NEWS.
WE MUST DO THE CHRISTIAN THING HERE, PETE.
WE HAVE TO HELP THAT POOR WOMAN'S FOLLOWERS.

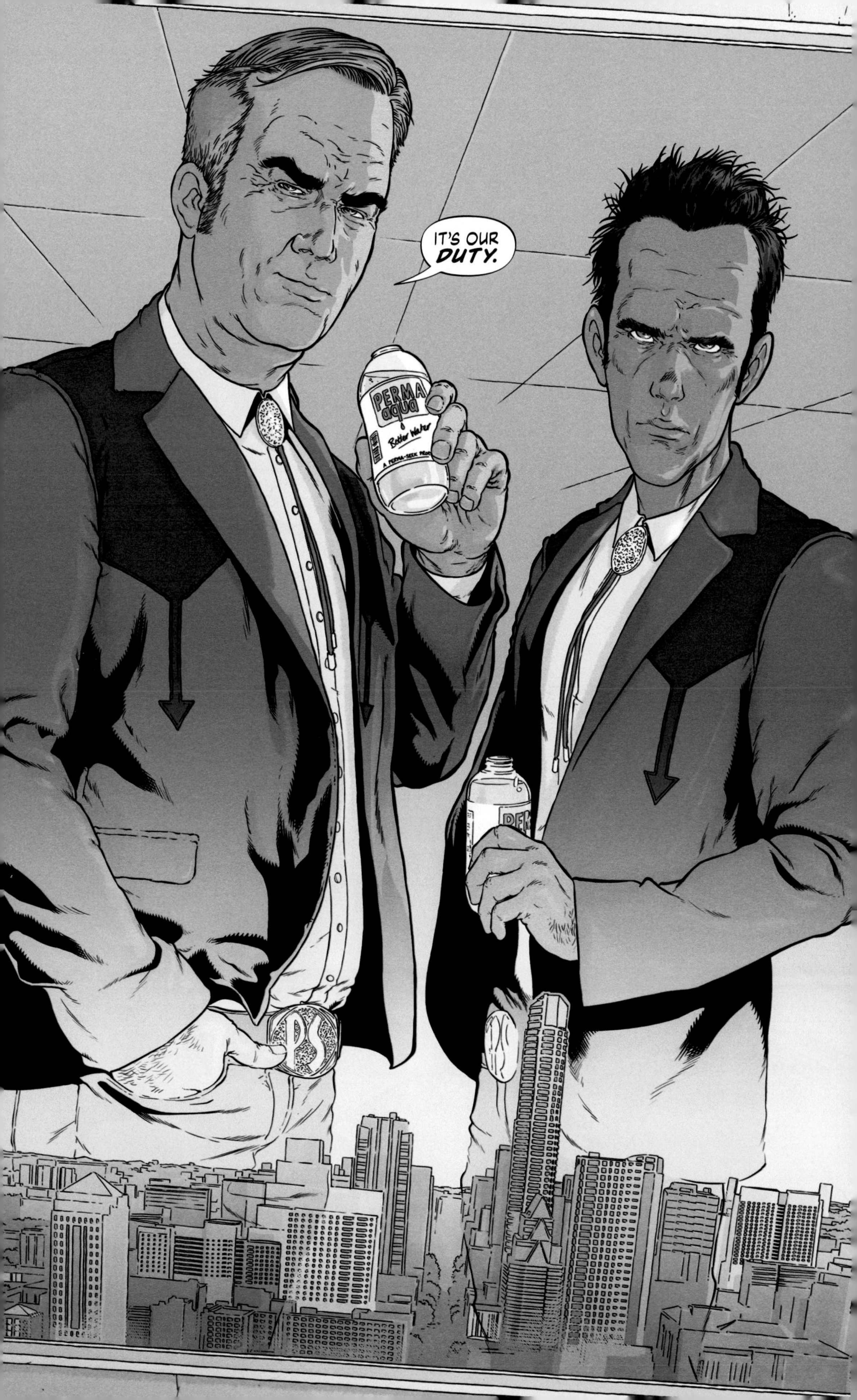
IT'S OUR DUTY.
PERMA aqua
Better Water

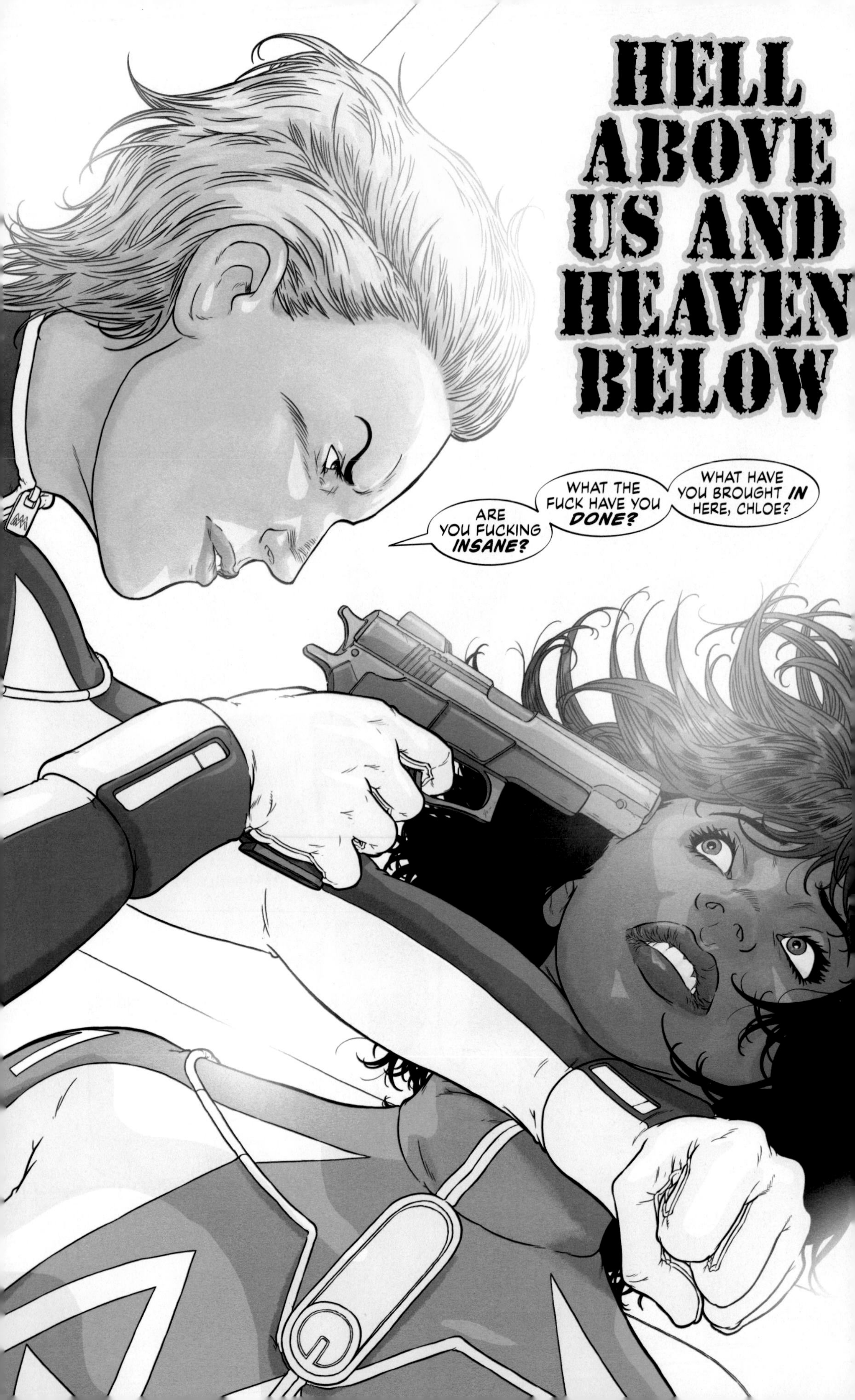
HELL ABOVE US AND HEAVEN BELOW
WHAT HAVE YOU BROUGHT IN HERE, CHLOE?
WHAT THE FUCK HAVE YOU DONE?
ARE YOU FUCKING INSANE?

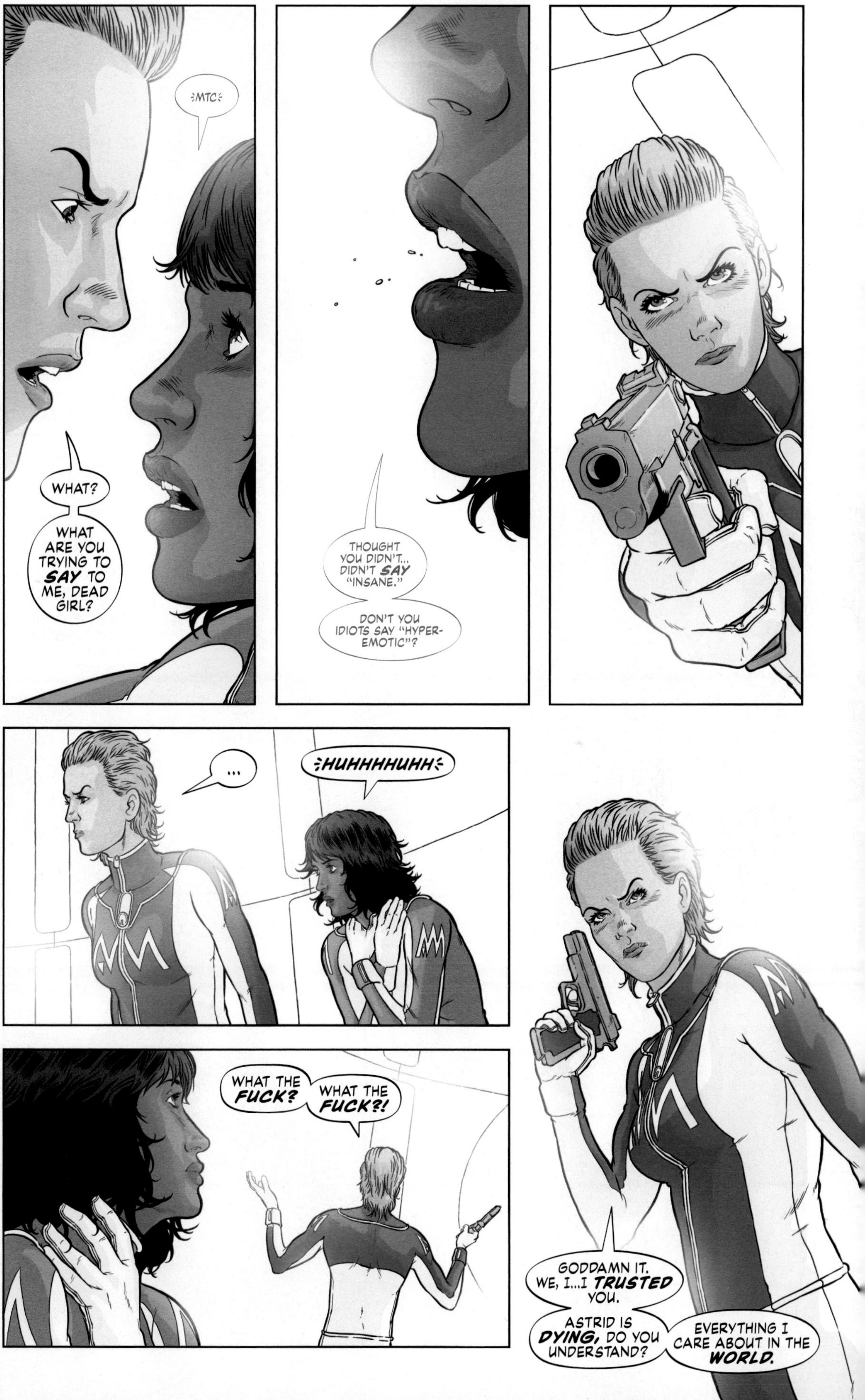
MTC
WHAT?
WHAT ARE YOU TRYING TO SAY TO ME, DEAD GIRL?
THOUGHT YOU DIDN'T... DIDN'T SAY "INSANE."
DON'T YOU IDIOTS SAY "HYPER-EMOTIC"?
...
HUHHHHUHH
WHAT THE FUCK?
WHAT THE FUCK?!
GODDAMN IT. WE, I...I TRUSTED YOU.
ASTRID IS DYING, DO YOU UNDERSTAND?
EVERYTHING I CARE ABOUT IN THE WORLD.

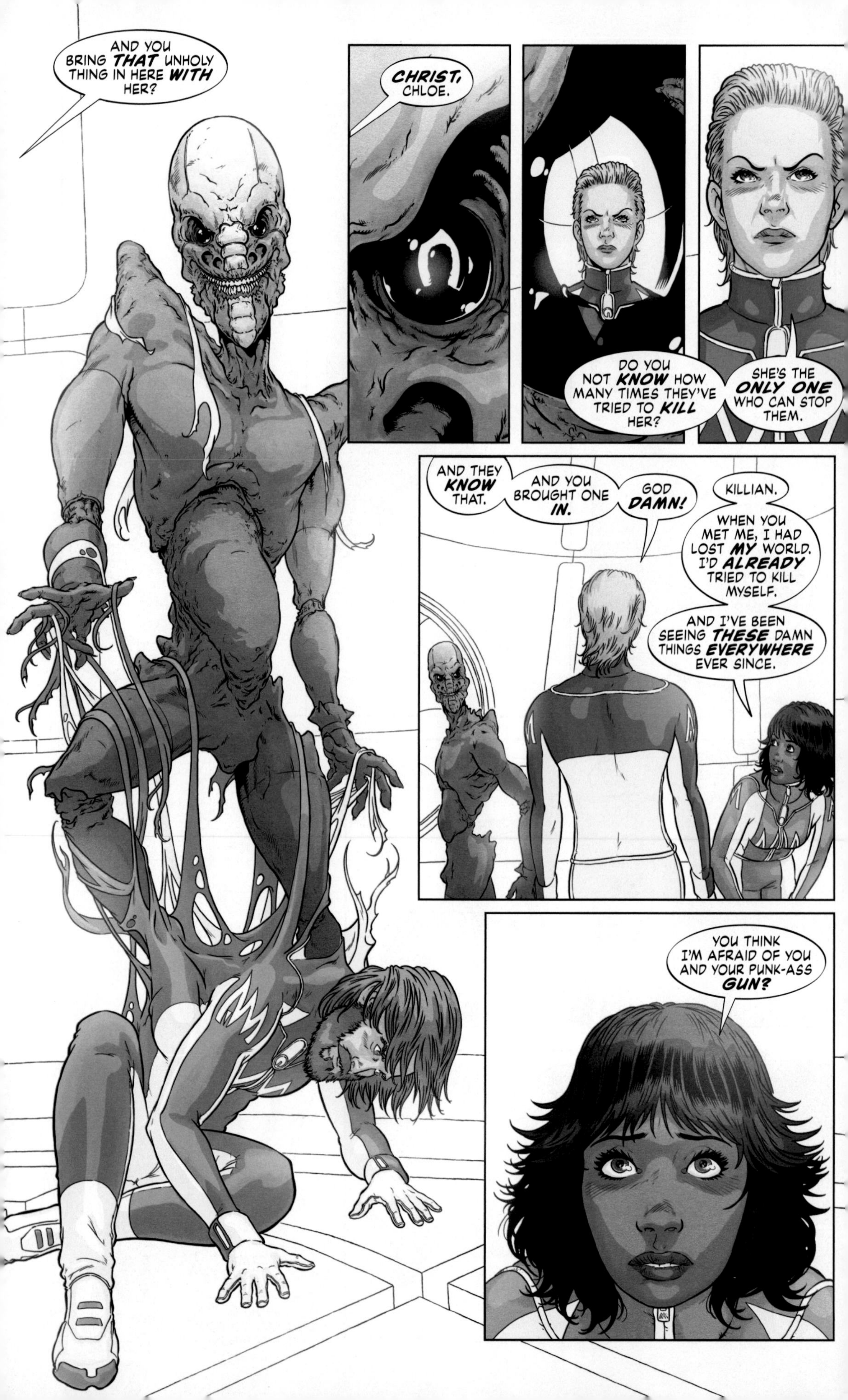
AND YOU BRING **THAT** UNHOLY THING IN HERE **WITH** HER?
CHRIST, CHLOE.
DO YOU NOT **KNOW** HOW MANY TIMES THEY'VE TRIED TO **KILL** HER?
SHE'S THE **ONLY ONE** WHO CAN STOP THEM.
AND THEY **KNOW** THAT.
AND YOU BROUGHT ONE **IN.**
GOD **DAMN!**
KILLIAN.
WHEN YOU MET ME, I HAD LOST **MY** WORLD. I'D **ALREADY** TRIED TO KILL MYSELF.
AND I'VE BEEN SEEING **THESE** DAMN THINGS **EVERYWHERE** EVER SINCE.
YOU THINK I'M AFRAID OF YOU AND YOUR PUNK-ASS **GUN?**

MAYBE NOT.

SO MAYBE I NEED A BIGGER GUN.

RAVEN.

YES, MS. REED?

DO YOU HAVE THE TARGET ON VISUAL?

YES, MS. REED.

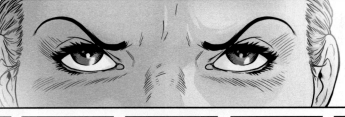

BURN THE FUCKING ABOMINATION TO *ASH* THEN, IF YOU WOULD BE SO KIND.

YES, MS. REED.

NO.

KILLIAN. *LISTEN* TO ME.

YOU CAN'T *DO* THIS!

XZRXX!

GODDAMN IT, *LISTEN* TO ME!

KILLIAN. CHLOE.

PLEASE. STOP QUARRELING.

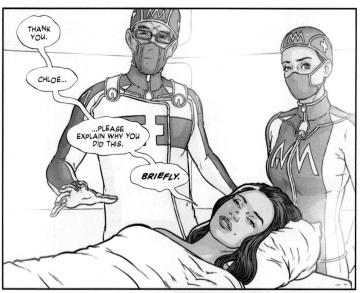

THANK YOU.

CHLOE...

...PLEASE EXPLAIN WHY YOU DID THIS.

BRIEFLY.

THIS...THIS IS *NOT* POSSIBLE. SHE SHOULD BE UNDER.

HUSH, DR. SUICHI, PLEASE.

CHLOE.

ALL RIGHT.

WHATEVER THESE...*THINGS* ARE, THESE *ENTITIES*...

"...PEOPLE HAVE BEEN MISTAKING THEM FOR DEMONS FOR *HUNDREDS* OF *YEARS*.

"SCARING CHILDREN. PERFORMING *EXORCISMS*.

"THEY CAN BE LIKE PARASITES. 'RIDING PEOPLE,' THEY CALL IT.

"AND SOMETIMES, THE PRIESTS WOULD BE CALLED UPON TO GET THEM *OUT* OF A HOST BODY."

AND SOMETIMES IT WORKED.

HOW FASCINATING.

THIS IS *SPARK*.

HE WAS BLESSED BY THE CHURCH RIGHT THE FUCK *OUT* OF A YOUNG SPANISH GIRL, GOD KNOWS WHEN.

AND HE'S HERE NOW. FOR ME.

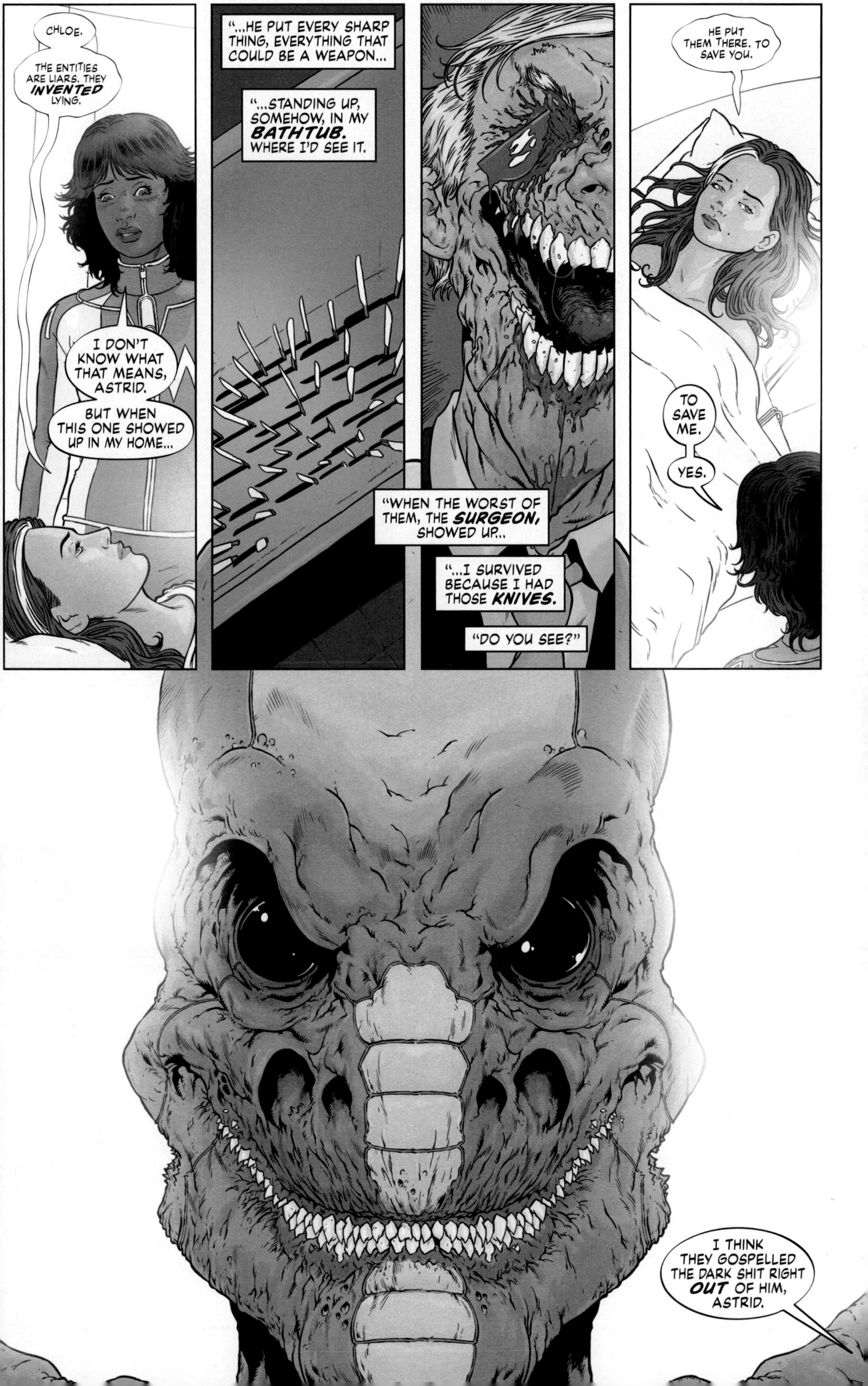
CHLOE.
THE ENTITIES ARE LIARS. THEY INVENTED LYING.
I DON'T KNOW WHAT THAT MEANS, ASTRID.
BUT WHEN THIS ONE SHOWED UP IN MY HOME...
"...HE PUT EVERY SHARP THING, EVERYTHING THAT COULD BE A WEAPON...
"...STANDING UP, SOMEHOW, IN MY BATHTUB. WHERE I'D SEE IT.
"WHEN THE WORST OF THEM, THE SURGEON, SHOWED UP...
"...I SURVIVED BECAUSE I HAD THOSE KNIVES.
"DO YOU SEE?"
HE PUT THEM THERE. TO SAVE YOU.
TO SAVE ME.
YES.
I THINK THEY GOSPELLED THE DARK SHIT RIGHT OUT OF HIM, ASTRID.

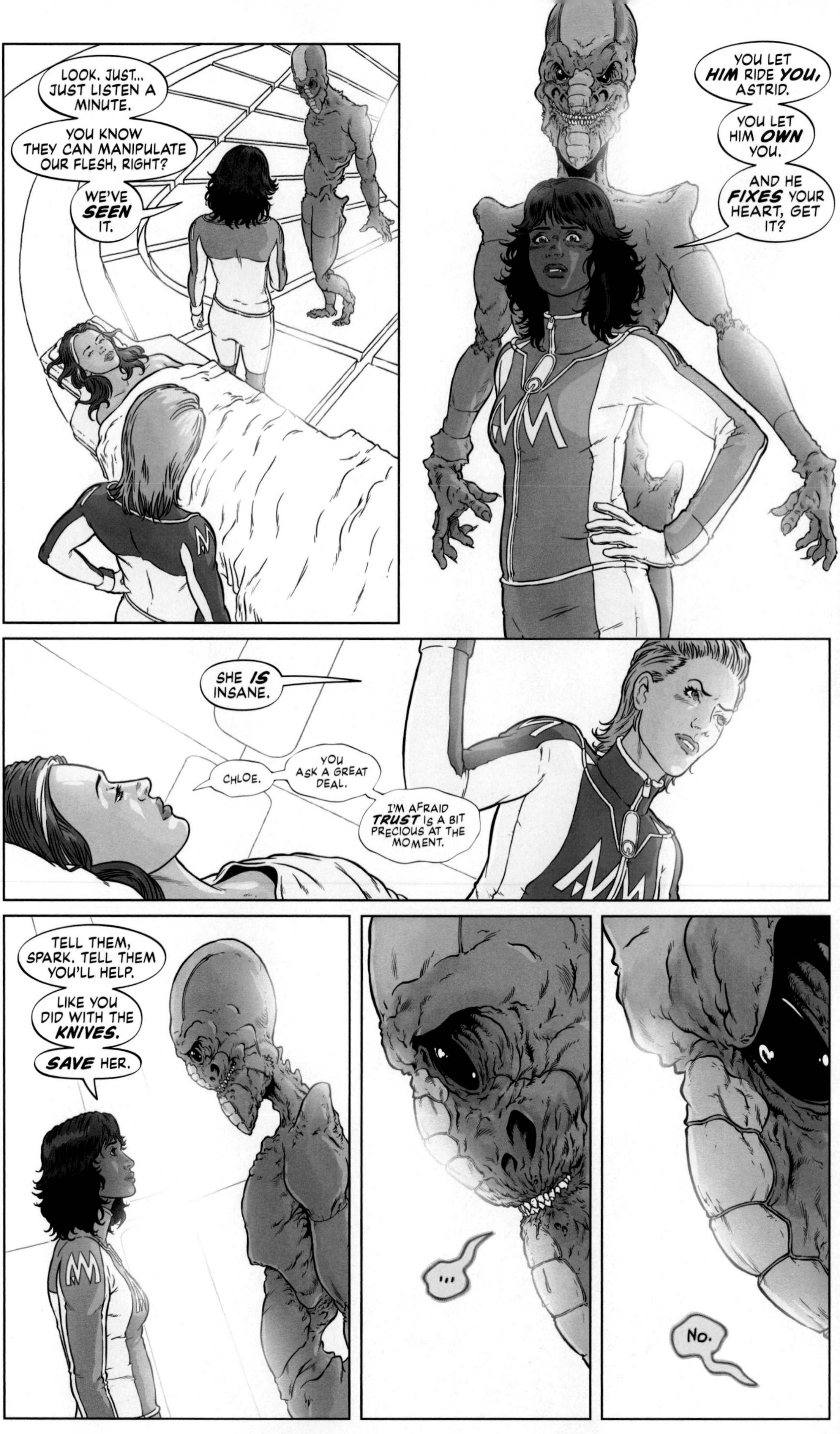
LOOK. JUST... JUST LISTEN A MINUTE.
YOU KNOW THEY CAN MANIPULATE OUR FLESH, RIGHT?
WE'VE SEEN IT.
YOU LET HIM RIDE YOU, ASTRID.
YOU LET HIM OWN YOU.
AND HE FIXES YOUR HEART, GET IT?
SHE IS INSANE.
CHLOE.
YOU ASK A GREAT DEAL.
I'M AFRAID TRUST IS A BIT PRECIOUS AT THE MOMENT.
TELL THEM, SPARK. TELL THEM YOU'LL HELP.
LIKE YOU DID WITH THE KNIVES.
SAVE HER.
...
NO.

EEEEEEEEEEEEEEEEE

OH DEAR GOD.

SHE'S IN *VF18*.

CHARGING TO 200, EVERYBODY *CLEAR*.

WE'RE *LOSING HER*.

NO.

PLEASE.

SPARK! WHAT ARE YOU DOING? WE *NEED* YOU!

Don't *LIKE* it here.

Don't *LIKE IT HERE*, Chloe Clim Clam.

Don't like it *HERE* and I don't like *HER*.

ASYSTOLE!

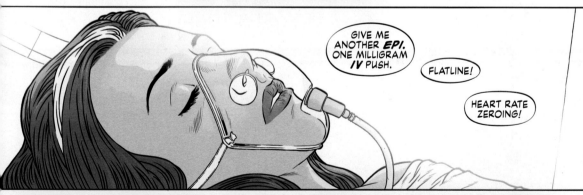

GIVE ME ANOTHER *EPI*. ONE MILLIGRAM *IV* PUSH.

FLATLINE!

HEART RATE ZEROING!

ASTRID?

PLEASE.

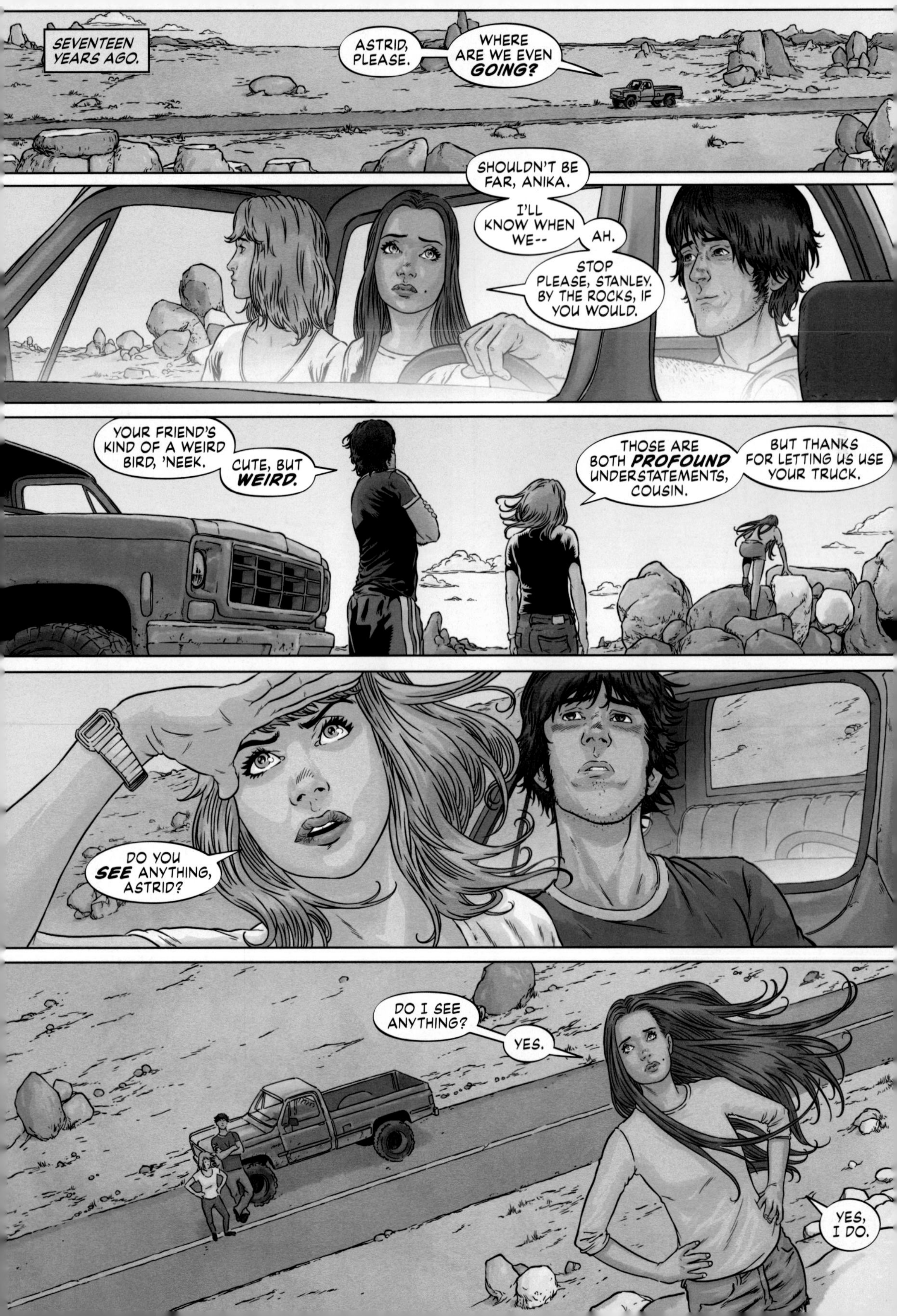
SEVENTEEN YEARS AGO.
ASTRID, PLEASE.
WHERE ARE WE EVEN GOING?
SHOULDN'T BE FAR, ANIKA.
I'LL KNOW WHEN WE--
AH.
STOP PLEASE, STANLEY. BY THE ROCKS, IF YOU WOULD.
YOUR FRIEND'S KIND OF A WEIRD BIRD, 'NEEK.
CUTE, BUT WEIRD.
THOSE ARE BOTH PROFOUND UNDERSTATEMENTS, COUSIN.
BUT THANKS FOR LETTING US USE YOUR TRUCK.
DO YOU SEE ANYTHING, ASTRID?
DO I SEE ANYTHING?
YES.
YES, I DO.

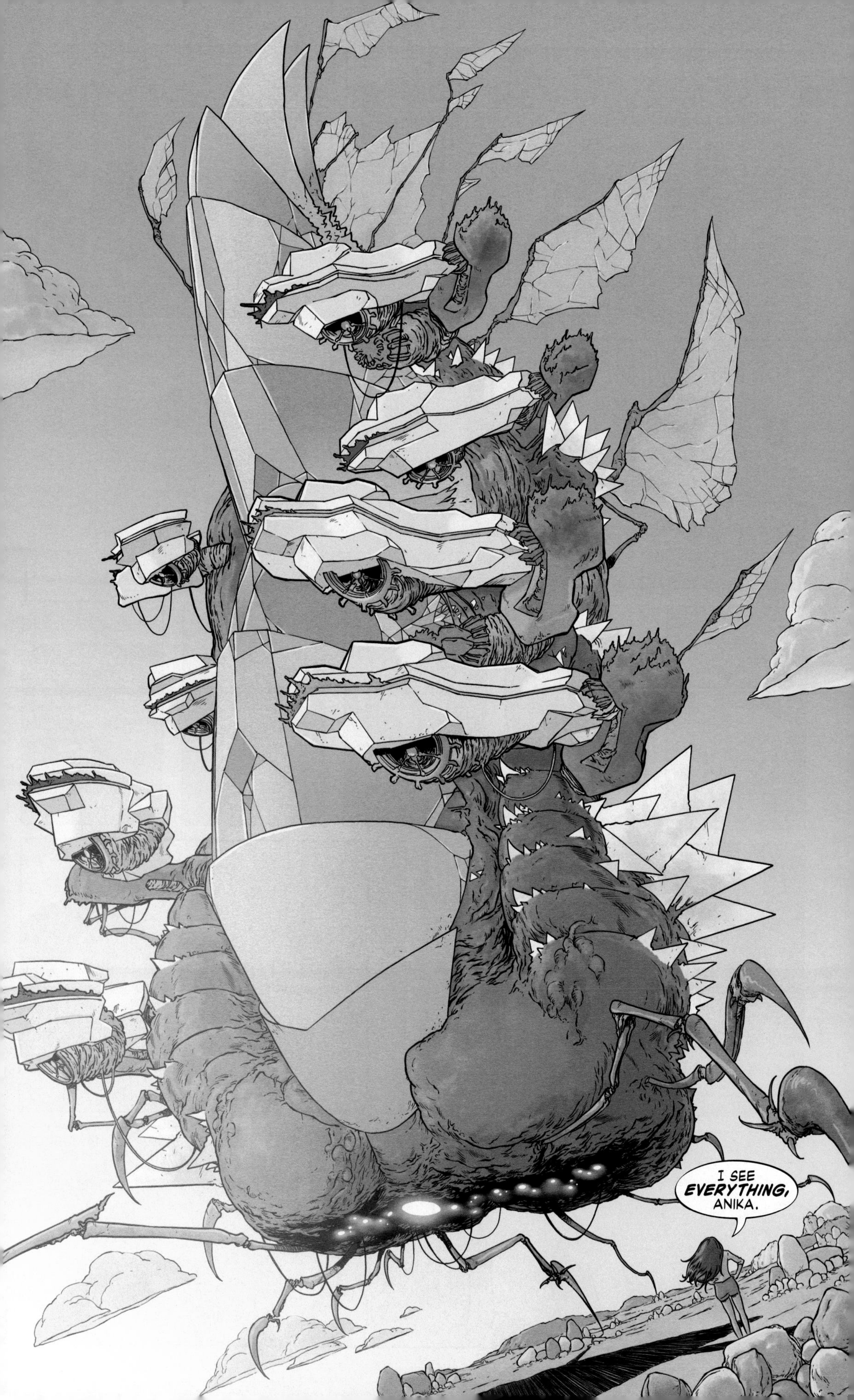
I SEE *EVERYTHING,* ANIKA.

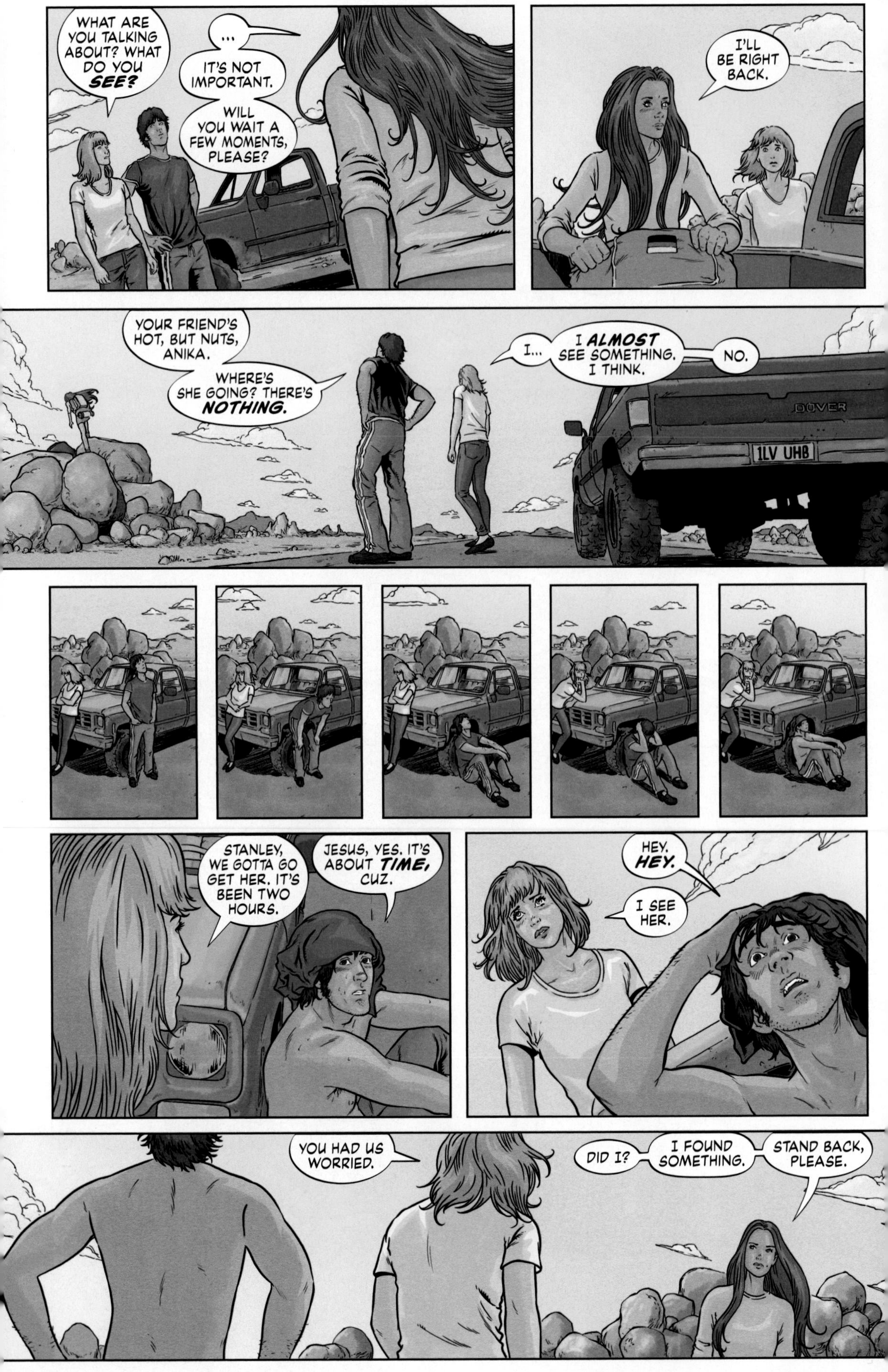
WHAT ARE YOU TALKING ABOUT? WHAT DO YOU **SEE?**
...
IT'S NOT IMPORTANT.
WILL YOU WAIT A FEW MOMENTS, PLEASE?
I'LL BE RIGHT BACK.
YOUR FRIEND'S HOT, BUT NUTS, ANIKA.
WHERE'S SHE GOING? THERE'S **NOTHING.**
I...
I **ALMOST** SEE SOMETHING. I THINK.
NO.
DOVER
1LV UHB
STANLEY, WE GOTTA GO GET HER. IT'S BEEN TWO HOURS.
JESUS, YES. IT'S ABOUT **TIME,** CUZ.
HEY. **HEY.**
I SEE HER.
YOU HAD US WORRIED.
DID I?
I FOUND SOMETHING.
STAND BACK, PLEASE.

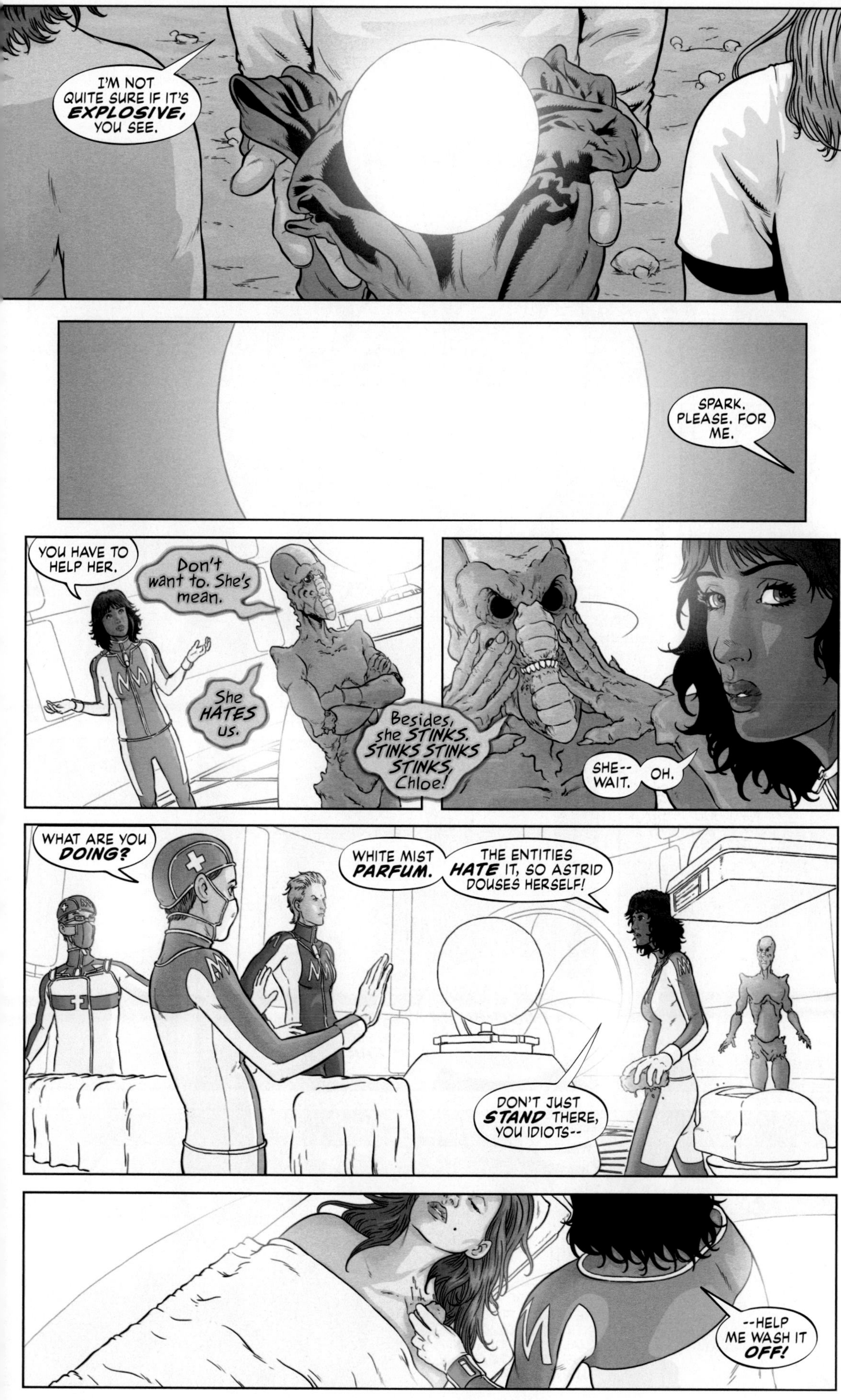

I'M NOT QUITE SURE IF IT'S *EXPLOSIVE,* YOU SEE.
SPARK. PLEASE. FOR ME.
YOU HAVE TO HELP HER.
Don't want to. She's mean.
She *HATES* us.
Besides, she *STINKS. STINKS STINKS STINKS,* Chloe!
SHE-- WAIT.
OH.
WHAT ARE YOU *DOING?*
WHITE MIST *PARFUM.*
THE ENTITIES *HATE* IT, SO ASTRID DOUSES HERSELF!
DON'T JUST *STAND* THERE, YOU IDIOTS--
--HELP ME WASH IT *OFF!*

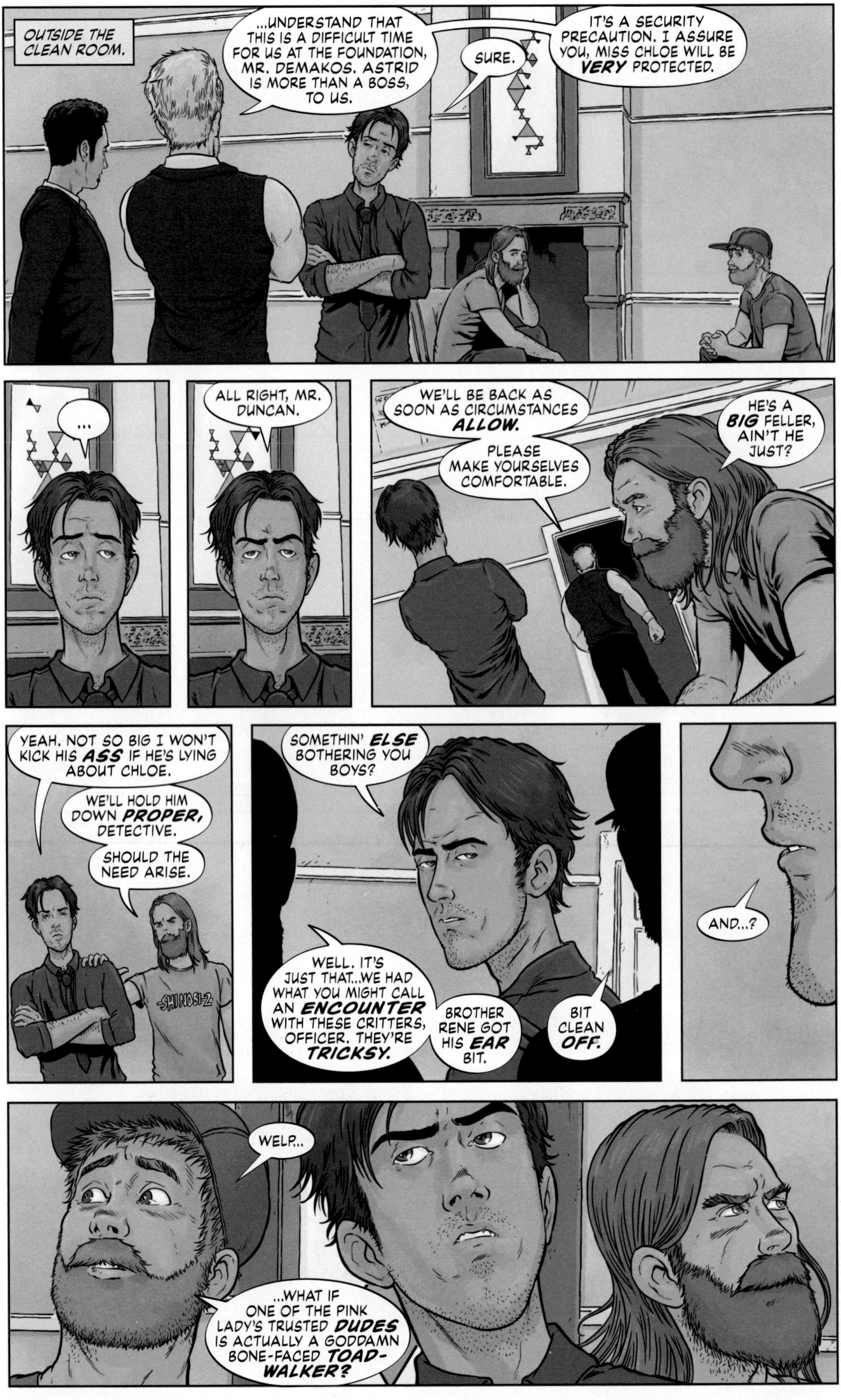
OUTSIDE THE CLEAN ROOM.
...UNDERSTAND THAT THIS IS A DIFFICULT TIME FOR US AT THE FOUNDATION, MR. DEMAKOS. ASTRID IS MORE THAN A BOSS, TO US.
SURE.
IT'S A SECURITY PRECAUTION. I ASSURE YOU, MISS CHLOE WILL BE VERY PROTECTED.
...
ALL RIGHT, MR. DUNCAN.
WE'LL BE BACK AS SOON AS CIRCUMSTANCES ALLOW.
PLEASE MAKE YOURSELVES COMFORTABLE.
HE'S A BIG FELLER, AIN'T HE JUST?
YEAH. NOT SO BIG I WON'T KICK HIS ASS IF HE'S LYING ABOUT CHLOE.
WE'LL HOLD HIM DOWN PROPER, DETECTIVE.
SHOULD THE NEED ARISE.
SHINOBI-2
SOMETHIN' ELSE BOTHERING YOU BOYS?
WELL. IT'S JUST THAT...WE HAD WHAT YOU MIGHT CALL AN ENCOUNTER WITH THESE CRITTERS, OFFICER. THEY'RE TRICKSY.
BROTHER RENE GOT HIS EAR BIT.
BIT CLEAN OFF.
AND...?
WELP...
...WHAT IF ONE OF THE PINK LADY'S TRUSTED DUDES IS ACTUALLY A GODDAMN BONE-FACED TOAD-WALKER?

SPARK. PLEASE.

YOU'VE BEEN EXORCISED. YOU DON'T HAVE ANY EVIL LEFT IN YOU.

HELP HER. THERE'S NO TIME LEFT.

HELP HER.

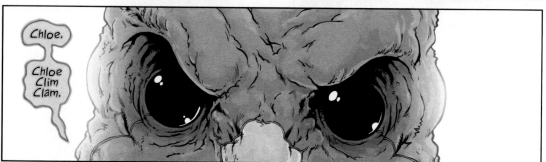

Chloe.

Chloe Clim Clam.

She'll hurt me. She'll burn me and poke me.

SHE WILL *NOT*.

I WON'T *LET* HER.

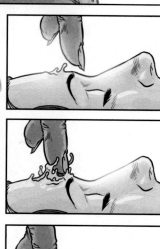

You'll feel a little prick.

A little prickity prick.

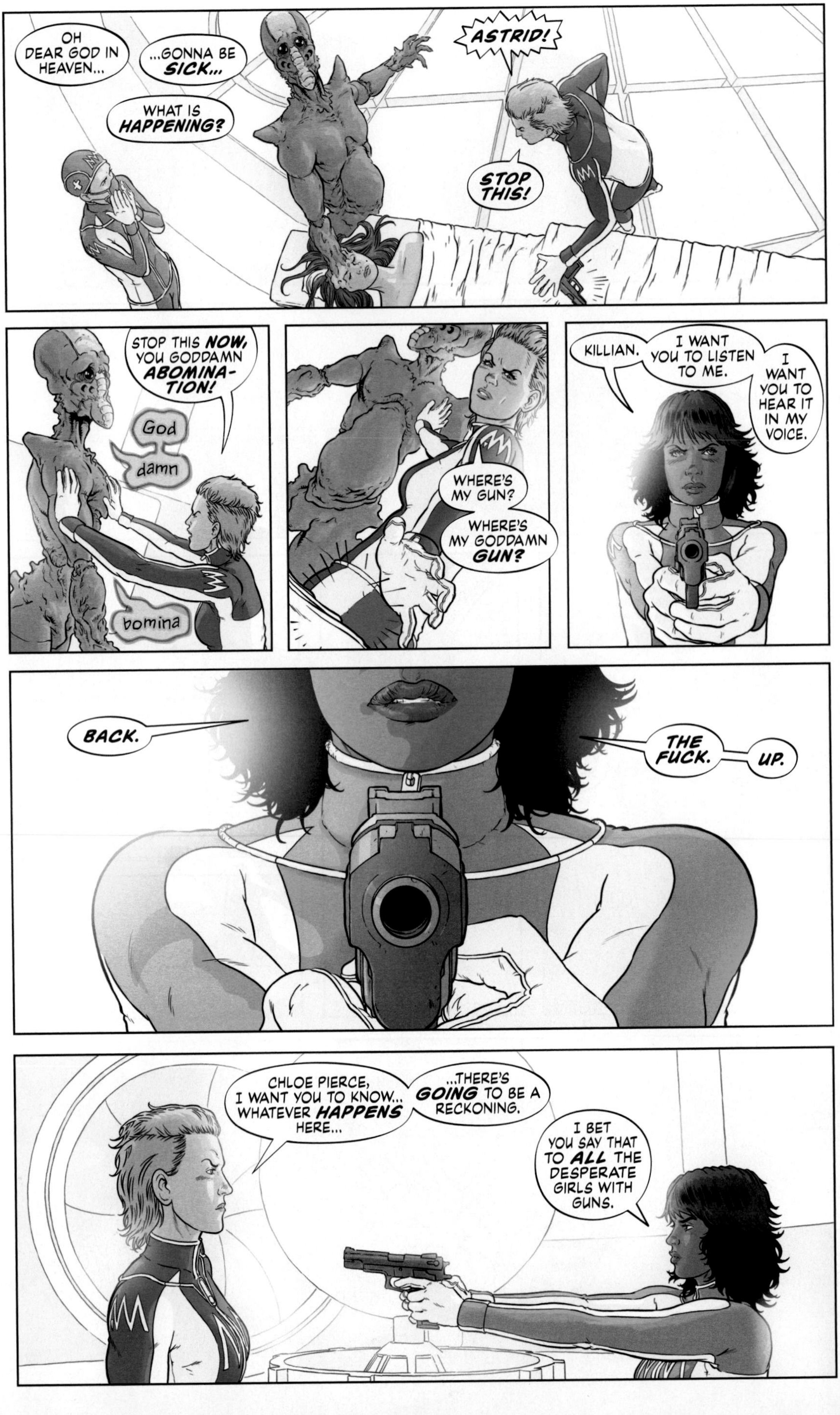
OH DEAR GOD IN HEAVEN...
...GONNA BE SICK...
WHAT IS HAPPENING?
ASTRID!
STOP THIS!
STOP THIS NOW, YOU GODDAMN ABOMINA-TION!
God
damn
bomina
WHERE'S MY GUN?
WHERE'S MY GODDAMN GUN?
KILLIAN.
I WANT YOU TO LISTEN TO ME.
I WANT YOU TO HEAR IT IN MY VOICE.
BACK.
THE FUCK.
UP.
CHLOE PIERCE, I WANT YOU TO KNOW... WHATEVER HAPPENS HERE...
...THERE'S GOING TO BE A RECKONING.
I BET YOU SAY THAT TO ALL THE DESPERATE GIRLS WITH GUNS.

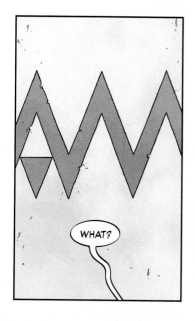

WHAT?

WHAT'S...

HELLO, SLEEPY-HEAD.

WE'VE RESTRAINED YOU FOR YOUR OWN SAFETY, MR. MUELLER.

I ALSO CONVINCED THE SURGEON IN ATTENDANCE THAT IT WOULD BE BEST NOT TO RISK ANY PAINKILLERS AT THIS JUNCTURE.

THAT BULLET WOUND'S BOUND TO *STING* A BIT, I IMAGINE.

;GGHH;

PETER, YOU CLAIM TO BE ASTRID MUELLER'S BROTHER.

SO THEN WHY, OH *WHY* DID YOU TRY TO ASSASSINATE HER?

I'M SIMPLY *EVER* SO CURIOUS.

BECAUSE... *GHHH!*

BECAUSE SHE'S A LITTLE GOD-CURSED *WHORE*. LIKE *YOU*.

AND BECAUSE...AND BECAUSE...

...BECAUSE SHE MURDERED OUR *FATHER*.

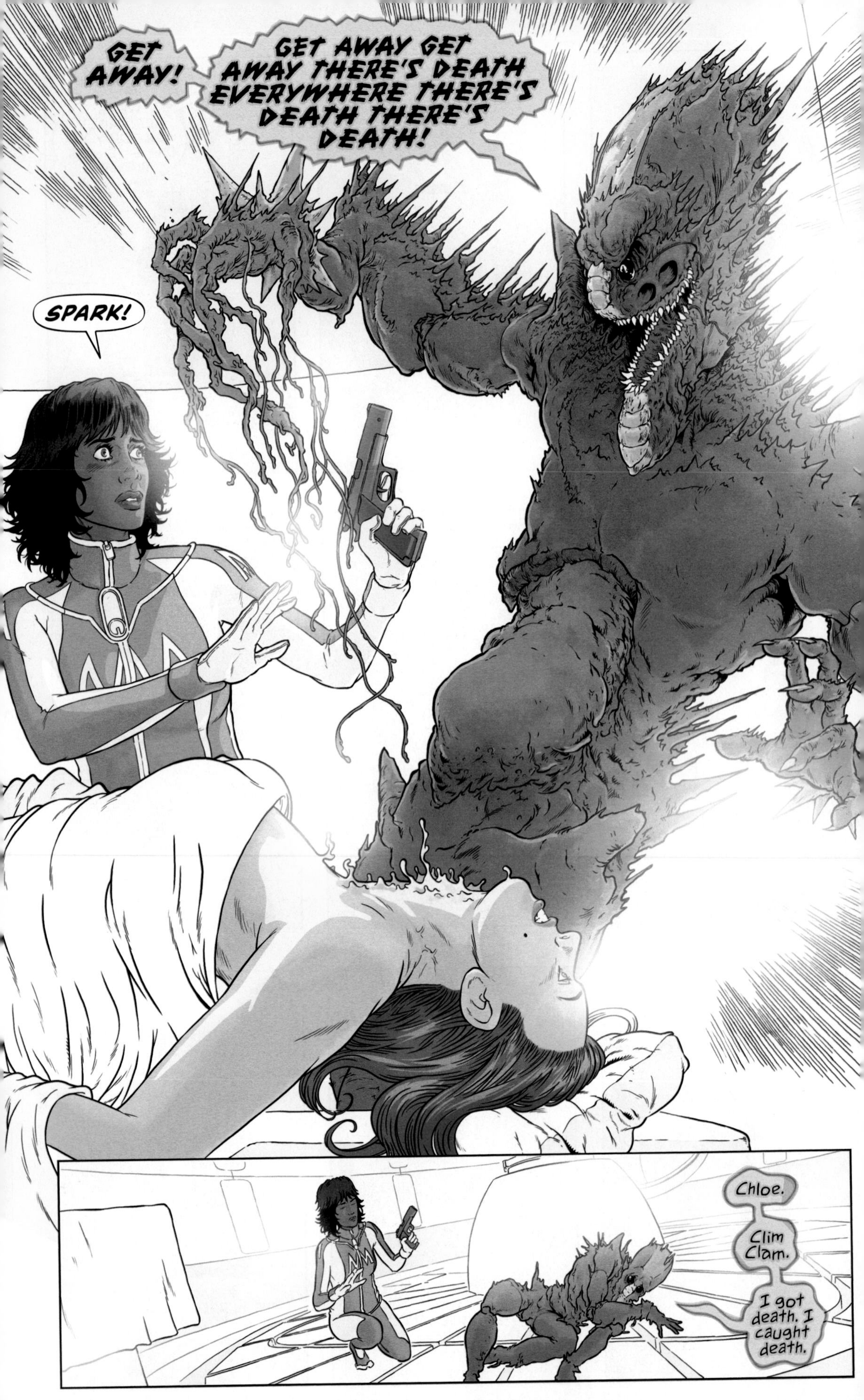
GET AWAY!
GET AWAY GET AWAY THERE'S DEATH EVERYWHERE THERE'S DEATH THERE'S DEATH!
SPARK!
Chloe.
Clim Clam.
I got death. I caught death.

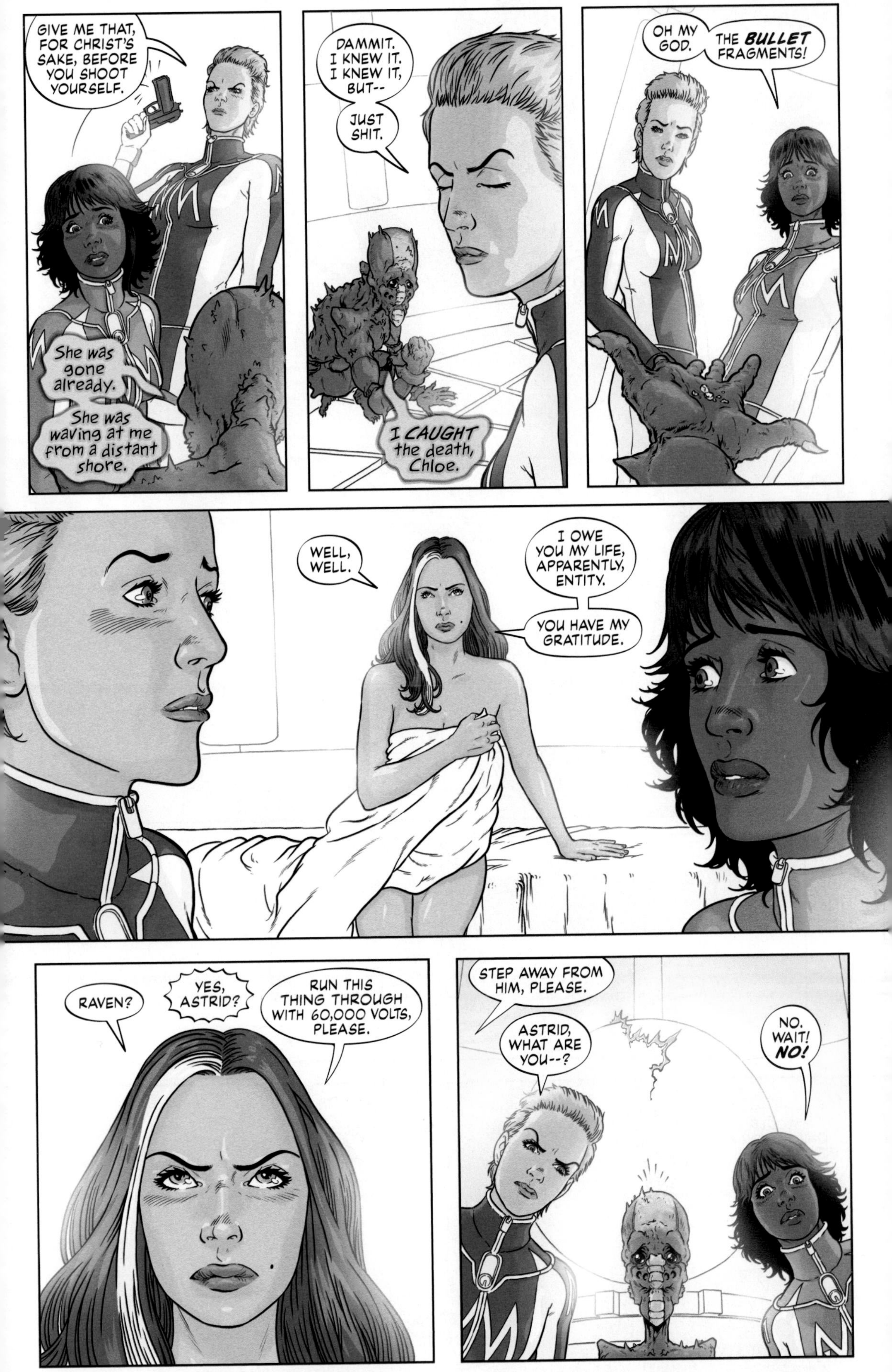
GIVE ME THAT, FOR CHRIST'S SAKE, BEFORE YOU SHOOT YOURSELF.
She was gone already.
She was waving at me from a distant shore.
DAMMIT. I KNEW IT. I KNEW IT, BUT--
JUST SHIT.
I CAUGHT the death, Chloe.
OH MY GOD.
THE BULLET FRAGMENTS!
WELL, WELL.
I OWE YOU MY LIFE, APPARENTLY, ENTITY.
YOU HAVE MY GRATITUDE.
RAVEN?
YES, ASTRID?
RUN THIS THING THROUGH WITH 60,000 VOLTS, PLEASE.
STEP AWAY FROM HIM, PLEASE.
ASTRID, WHAT ARE YOU--?
NO. WAIT! NO!

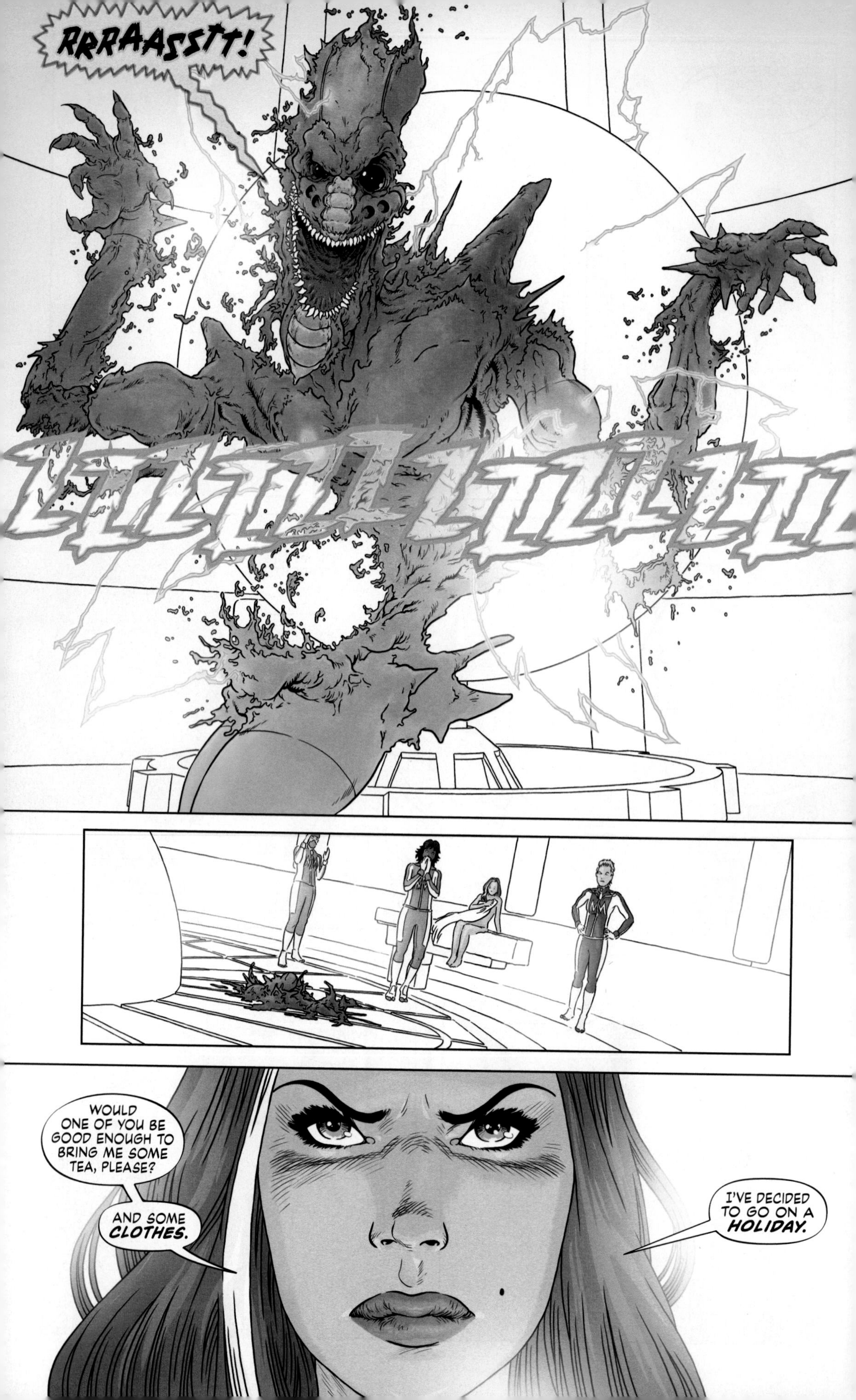
RRRAASSTT!
ZZZZZZZZZZZ
WOULD ONE OF YOU BE GOOD ENOUGH TO BRING ME SOME TEA, PLEASE?
AND SOME CLOTHES.
I'VE DECIDED TO GO ON A HOLIDAY.

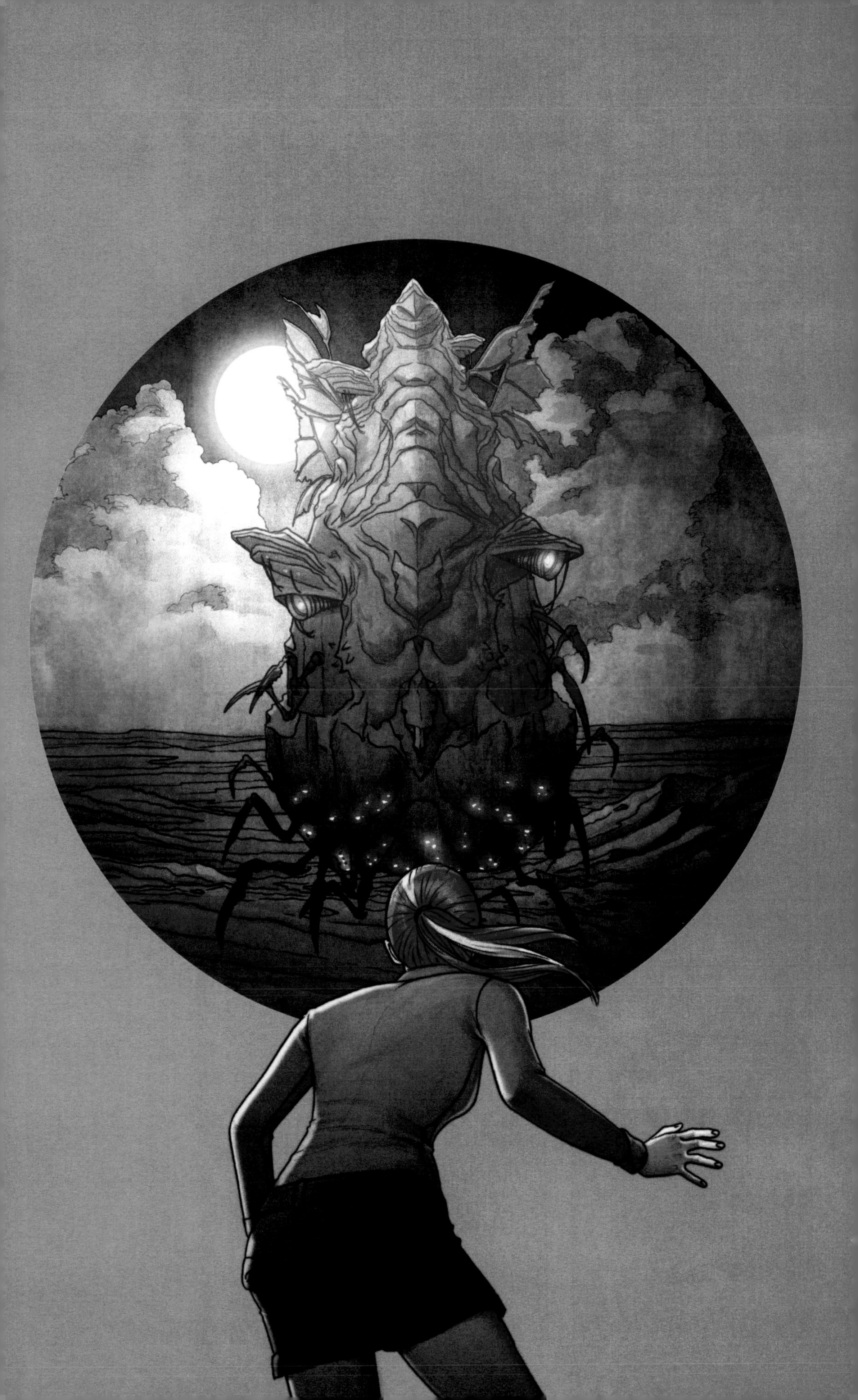

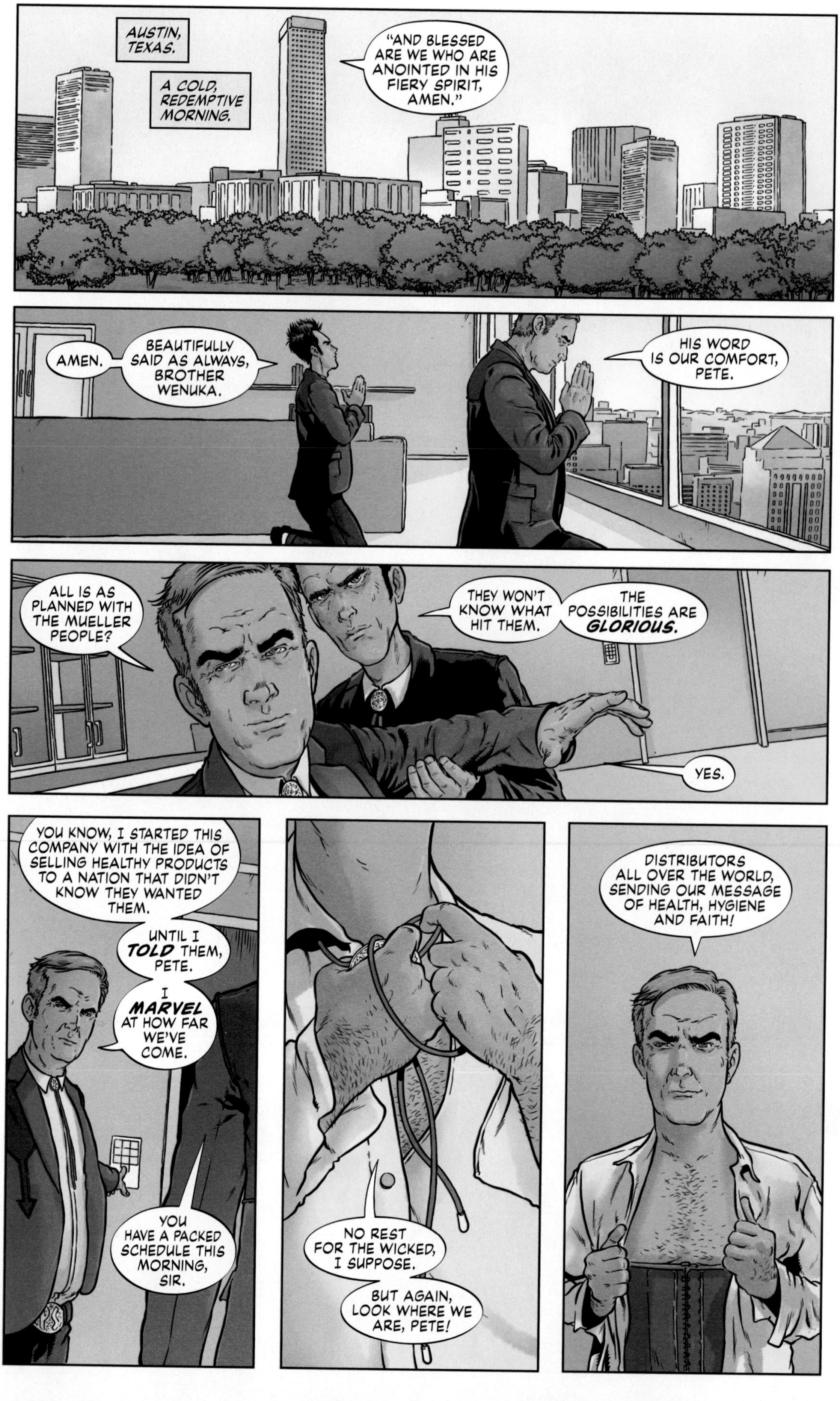
AUSTIN, TEXAS.
A COLD, REDEMPTIVE MORNING.
"AND BLESSED ARE WE WHO ARE ANOINTED IN HIS FIERY SPIRIT, AMEN."
AMEN.
BEAUTIFULLY SAID AS ALWAYS, BROTHER WENUKA.
HIS WORD IS OUR COMFORT, PETE.
ALL IS AS PLANNED WITH THE MUELLER PEOPLE?
THEY WON'T KNOW WHAT HIT THEM.
THE POSSIBILITIES ARE GLORIOUS.
YES.
YOU KNOW, I STARTED THIS COMPANY WITH THE IDEA OF SELLING HEALTHY PRODUCTS TO A NATION THAT DIDN'T KNOW THEY WANTED THEM.
UNTIL I TOLD THEM, PETE.
I MARVEL AT HOW FAR WE'VE COME.
YOU HAVE A PACKED SCHEDULE THIS MORNING, SIR.
NO REST FOR THE WICKED, I SUPPOSE.
BUT AGAIN, LOOK WHERE WE ARE, PETE!
DISTRIBUTORS ALL OVER THE WORLD, SENDING OUR MESSAGE OF HEALTH, HYGIENE AND FAITH!

NORMAL, DECENT FOLKS, JUST LIKE YOU AND ME.

WE HAVE A REAL OPPORTUNITY HERE, BROTHER RUSSEL.

A CHANCE TO NOT JUST EXPAND OUR USER AND DISTRIBUTION BASES BY 300 PERCENT...

...BUT TO *ALSO* STEER THE HEARTS AND MINDS OF THAT WOMAN'S POOR FOLLOWERS TOWARDS A HIGHER PATH.

PRAISE JESUS.

SO, WHO ARE WE MINISTERING TO THIS FINE MORNING, PETE?

IT'S A SAD ONE, I'M NOT GONNA LIE TO YOU.

LOVELY COUPLE, TRIPLE JAGUAR-LEVEL SALES UNTIL THIS YEAR.

BEEN MISSING SALES QUOTAS SOMETHING *FIERCE*.

GAVE ME SOME UNRIGHTEOUS NONSENSE THAT THE WIFE'S BEEN SUFFERING *DEPRESSION*.

HER *MOTHER* DIED, IS THE BIG CALAMITY. YOU BELIEVE THAT?

WAS ALL I COULD DO NOT TO SPIT IN THEIR GODDAMN *FACES*.

A LITTLE *COMPASSION*, PLEASE, PETE.

SOMETIMES PEOPLE FORGET OUR SIMPLE TEACHINGS, AND JUST NEED TO BE REMINDED.

OF COURSE, SIR.

THEIR NAMES ARE TODD AND SANDY GALLAGHER, GREATER TULSA REGION.

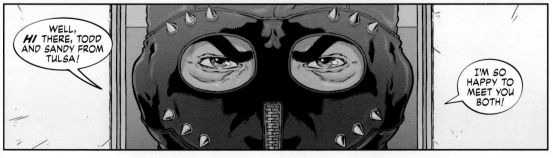

WELL, *HI* THERE, TODD AND SANDY FROM TULSA!

I'M SO HAPPY TO MEET YOU BOTH!

THE LAST BREATH OF AN EXILE

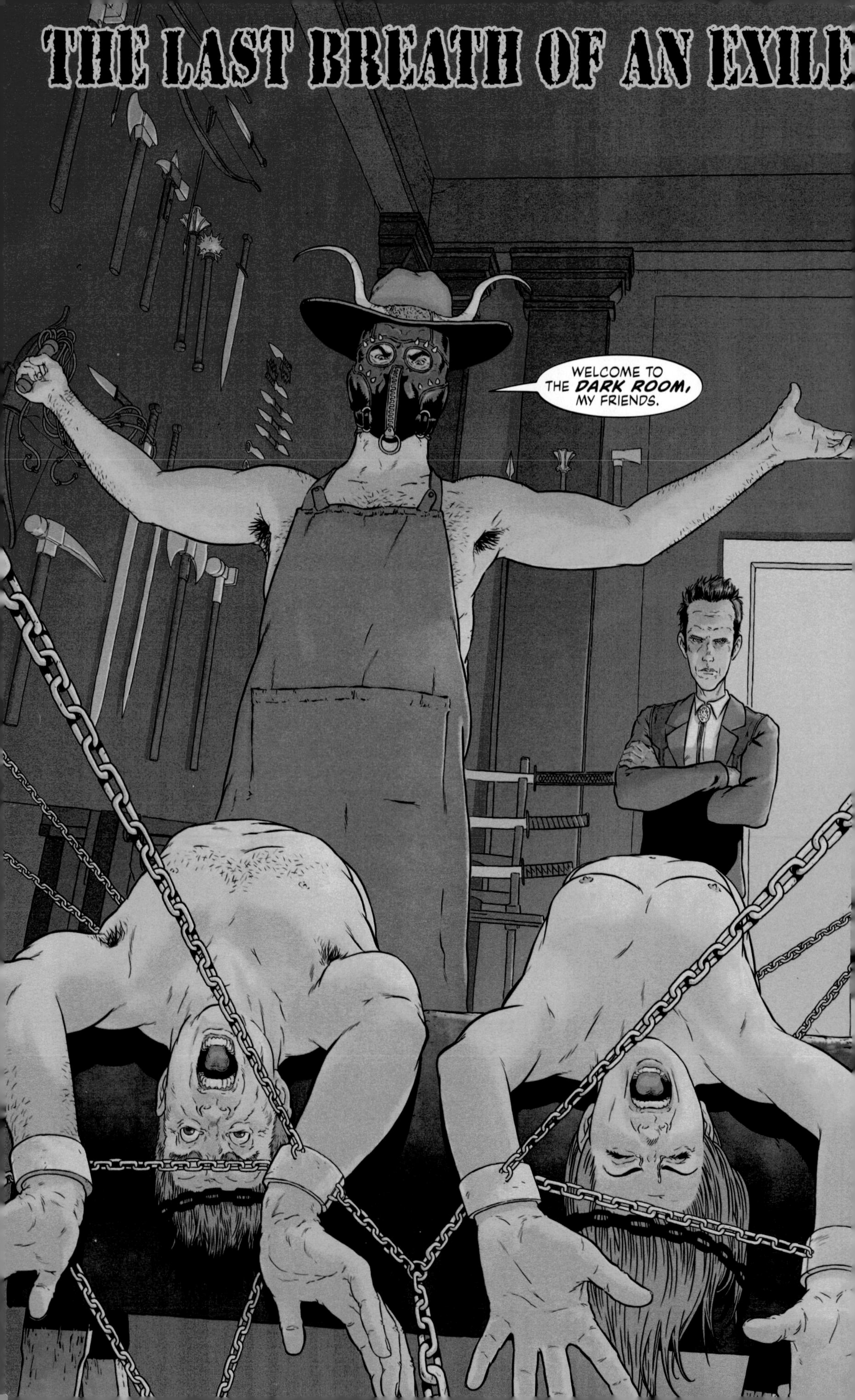
WELCOME TO THE DARK ROOM, MY FRIENDS.

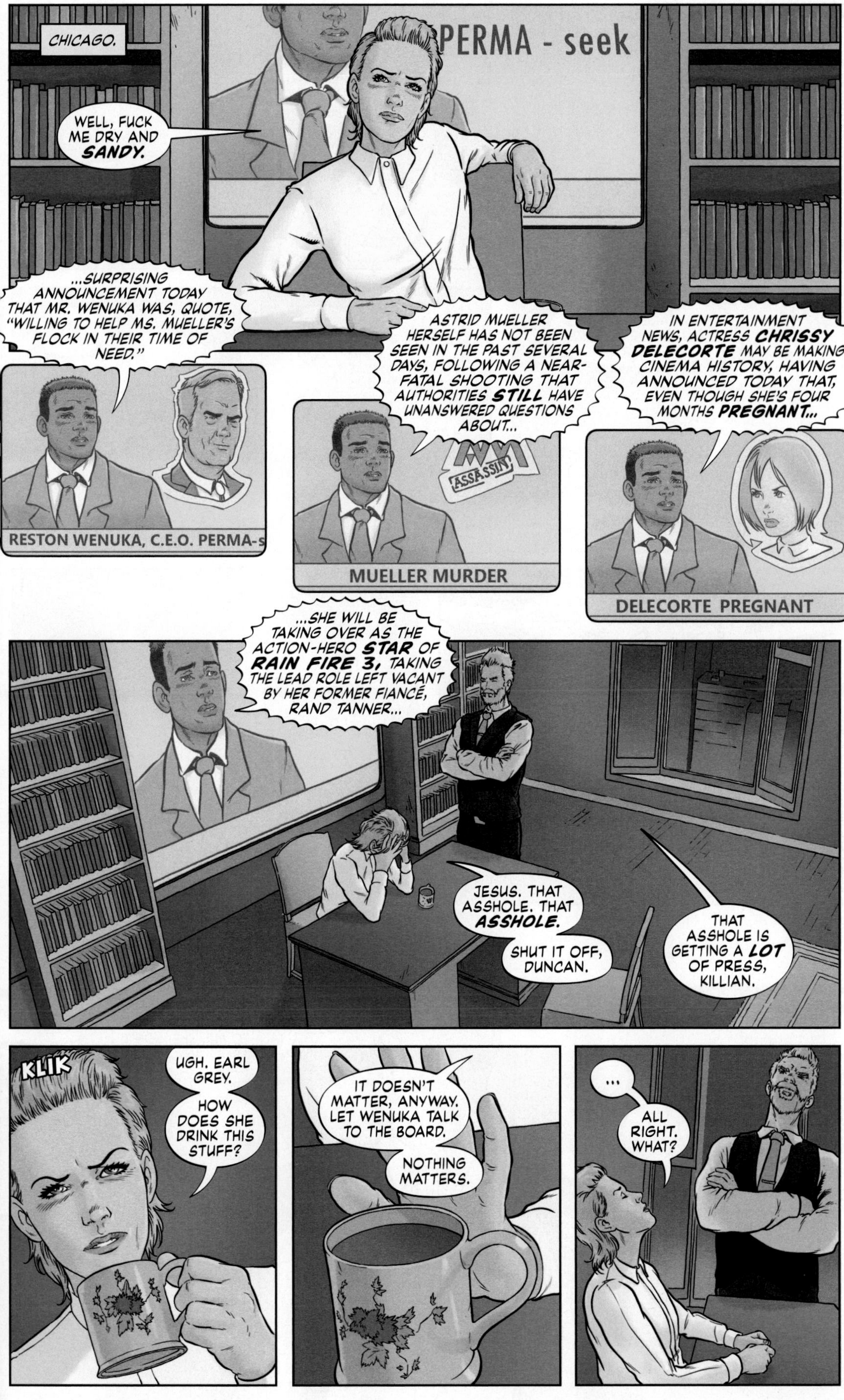

CHICAGO.
WELL, FUCK ME DRY AND SANDY.
PERMA - seek
...SURPRISING ANNOUNCEMENT TODAY THAT MR. WENUKA WAS, QUOTE, "WILLING TO HELP MS. MUELLER'S FLOCK IN THEIR TIME OF NEED."
RESTON WENUKA, C.E.O. PERMA-s
ASTRID MUELLER HERSELF HAS NOT BEEN SEEN IN THE PAST SEVERAL DAYS, FOLLOWING A NEAR-FATAL SHOOTING THAT AUTHORITIES STILL HAVE UNANSWERED QUESTIONS ABOUT...
ASSASSIN
MUELLER MURDER
IN ENTERTAINMENT NEWS, ACTRESS CHRISSY DELECORTE MAY BE MAKING CINEMA HISTORY, HAVING ANNOUNCED TODAY THAT, EVEN THOUGH SHE'S FOUR MONTHS PREGNANT...
DELECORTE PREGNANT
...SHE WILL BE TAKING OVER AS THE ACTION-HERO STAR OF RAIN FIRE 3, TAKING THE LEAD ROLE LEFT VACANT BY HER FORMER FIANCÉ, RAND TANNER...
JESUS. THAT ASSHOLE. THAT ASSHOLE.
SHUT IT OFF, DUNCAN.
THAT ASSHOLE IS GETTING A LOT OF PRESS, KILLIAN.
KLIK
UGH. EARL GREY.
HOW DOES SHE DRINK THIS STUFF?
IT DOESN'T MATTER, ANYWAY. LET WENUKA TALK TO THE BOARD.
NOTHING MATTERS.
...
ALL RIGHT. WHAT?

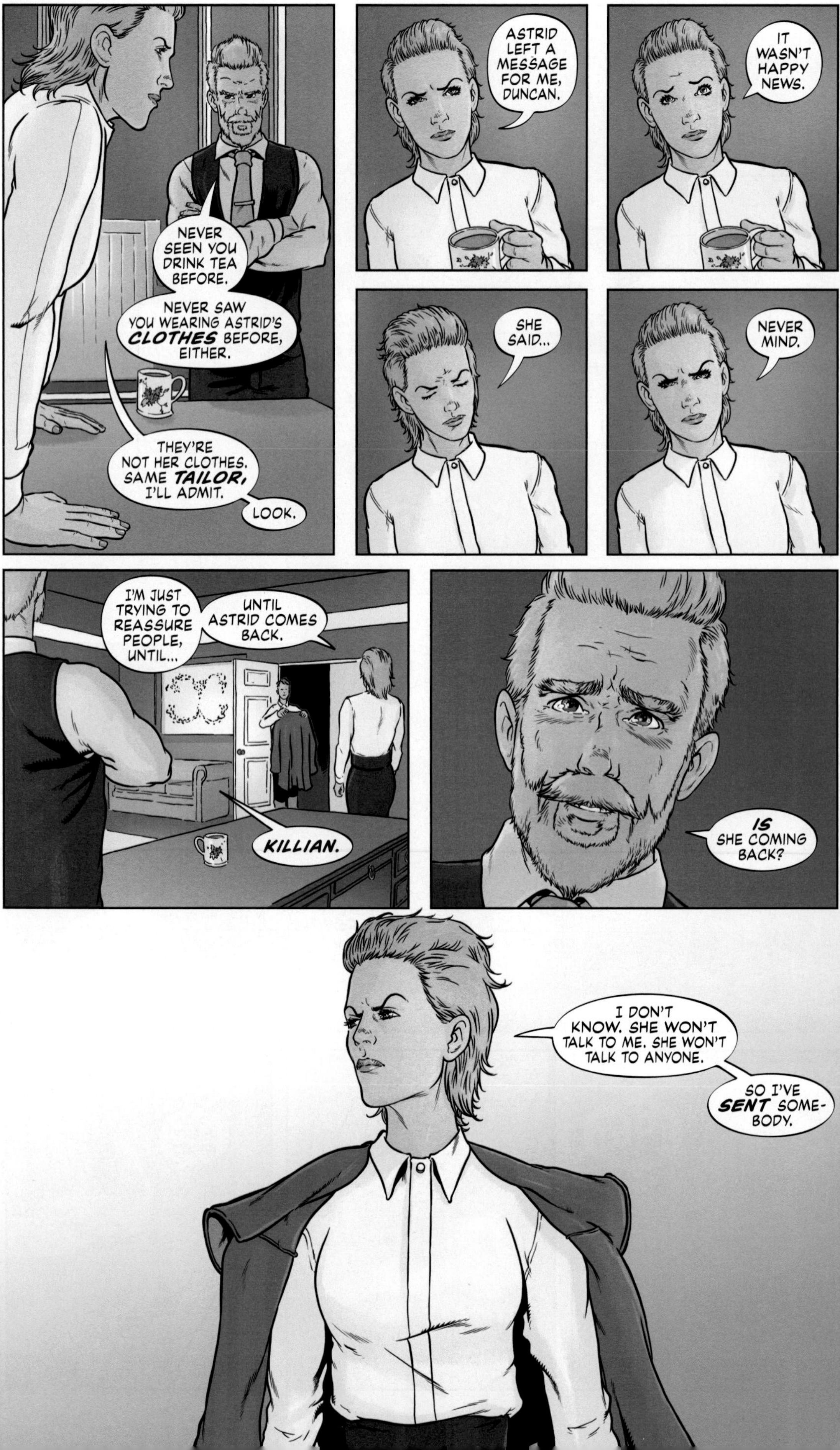
NEVER SEEN YOU DRINK TEA BEFORE.
NEVER SAW YOU WEARING ASTRID'S CLOTHES BEFORE, EITHER.
THEY'RE NOT HER CLOTHES. SAME TAILOR, I'LL ADMIT.
LOOK.
ASTRID LEFT A MESSAGE FOR ME, DUNCAN.
IT WASN'T HAPPY NEWS.
SHE SAID...
NEVER MIND.
I'M JUST TRYING TO REASSURE PEOPLE, UNTIL...
UNTIL ASTRID COMES BACK.
KILLIAN.
IS SHE COMING BACK?
I DON'T KNOW. SHE WON'T TALK TO ME. SHE WON'T TALK TO ANYONE.
SO I'VE SENT SOME-BODY.

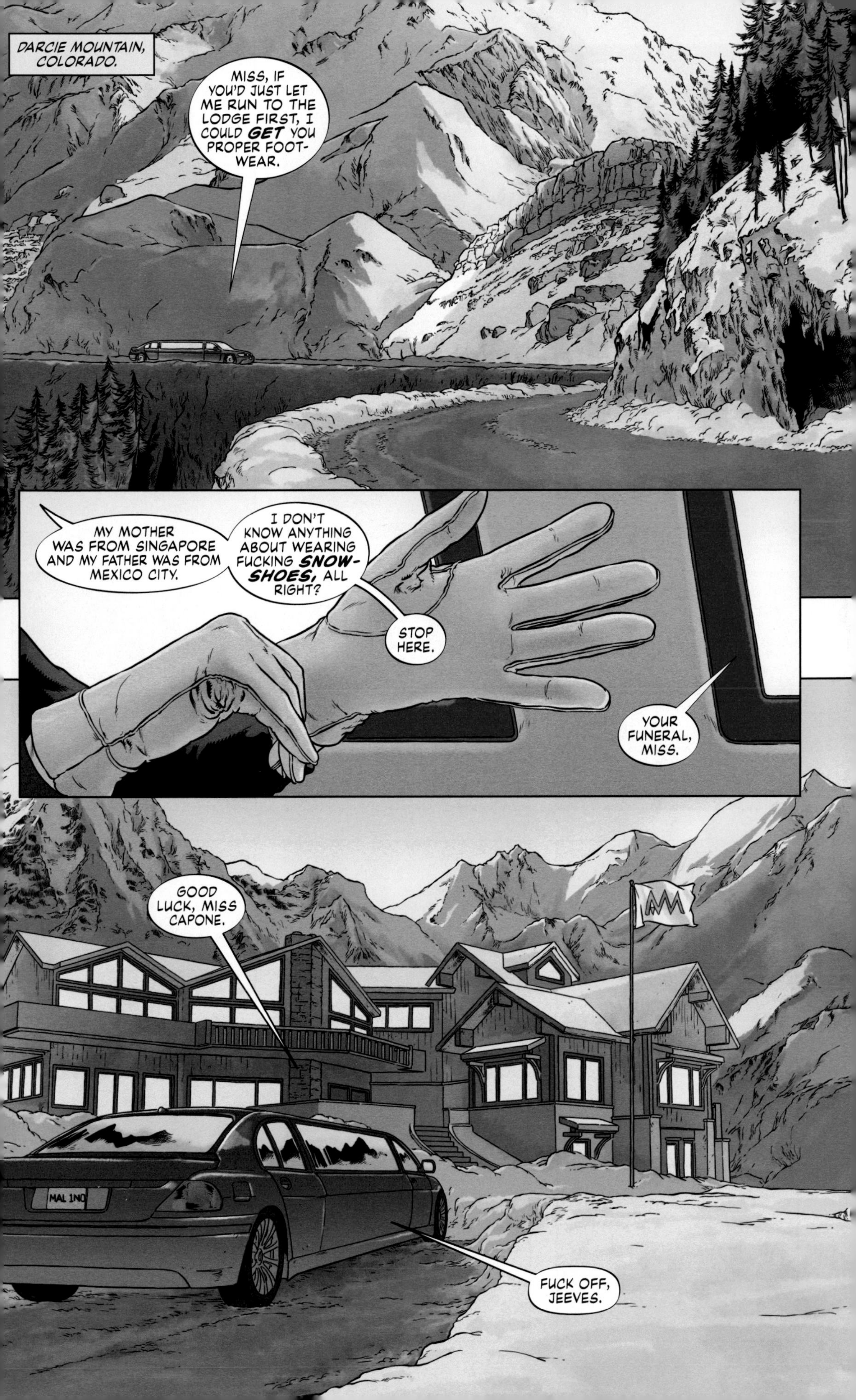
DARCIE MOUNTAIN, COLORADO.
MISS, IF YOU'D JUST LET ME RUN TO THE LODGE FIRST, I COULD GET YOU PROPER FOOT-WEAR.
MY MOTHER WAS FROM SINGAPORE AND MY FATHER WAS FROM MEXICO CITY.
I DON'T KNOW ANYTHING ABOUT WEARING FUCKING SNOW-SHOES, ALL RIGHT?
STOP HERE.
YOUR FUNERAL, MISS.
GOOD LUCK, MISS CAPONE.
MAL 1NO
FUCK OFF, JEEVES.

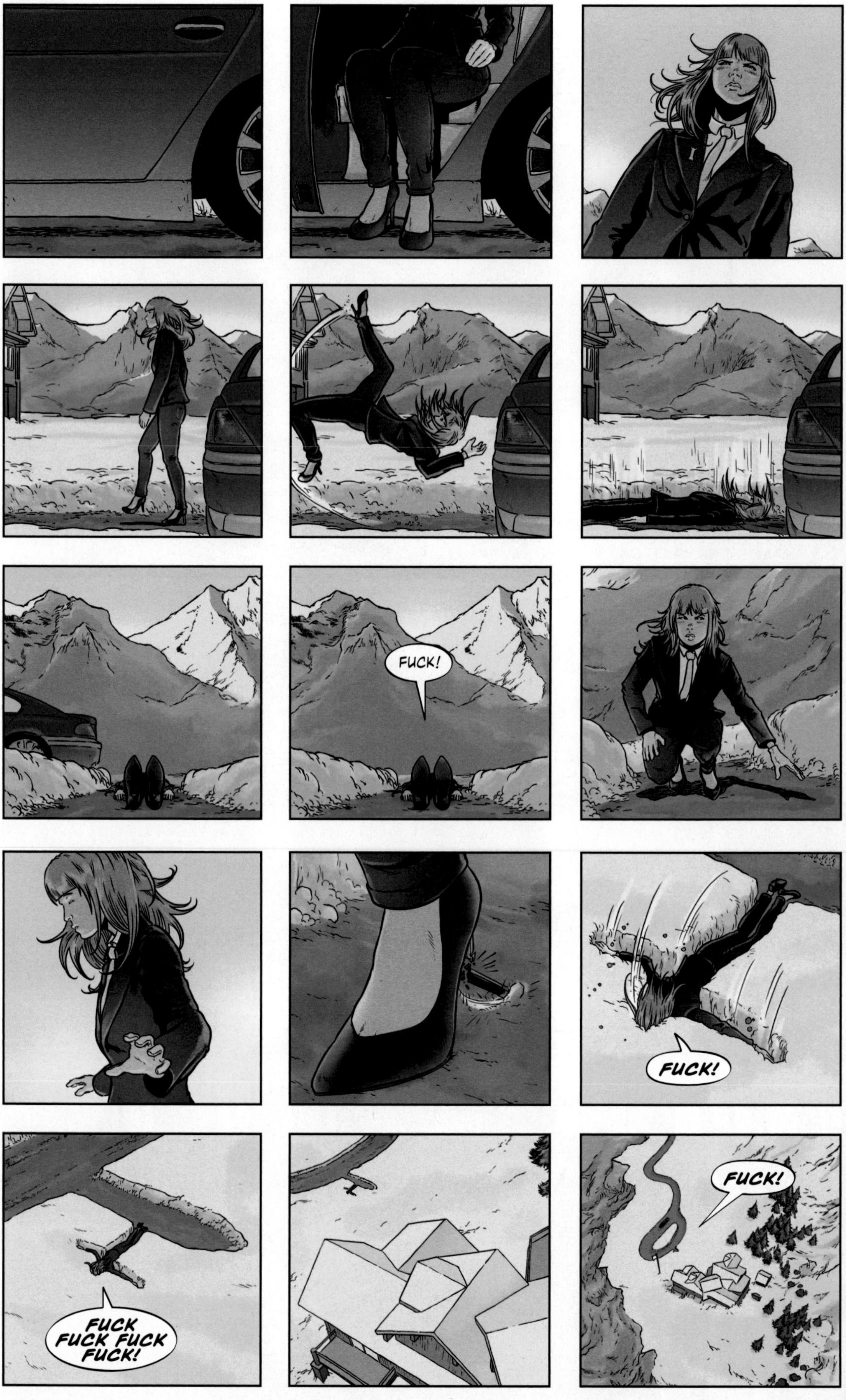
FUCK!
FUCK!
FUCK
FUCK FUCK
FUCK!
FUCK!

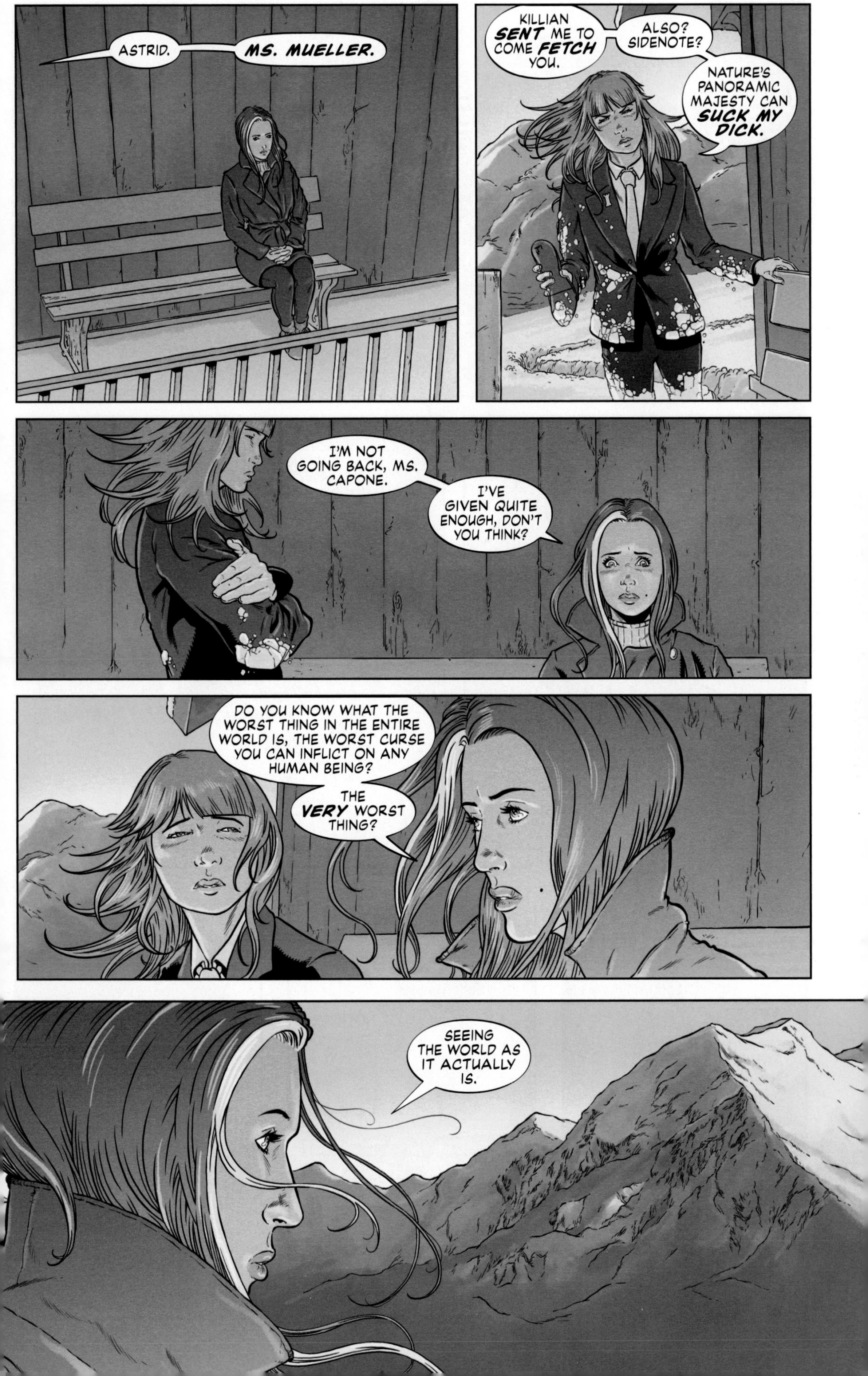
ASTRID.
MS. MUELLER.
KILLIAN SENT ME TO COME FETCH YOU.
ALSO? SIDENOTE?
NATURE'S PANORAMIC MAJESTY CAN SUCK MY DICK.
I'M NOT GOING BACK, MS. CAPONE.
I'VE GIVEN QUITE ENOUGH, DON'T YOU THINK?
DO YOU KNOW WHAT THE WORST THING IN THE ENTIRE WORLD IS, THE WORST CURSE YOU CAN INFLICT ON ANY HUMAN BEING?
THE VERY WORST THING?
SEEING THE WORLD AS IT ACTUALLY IS.

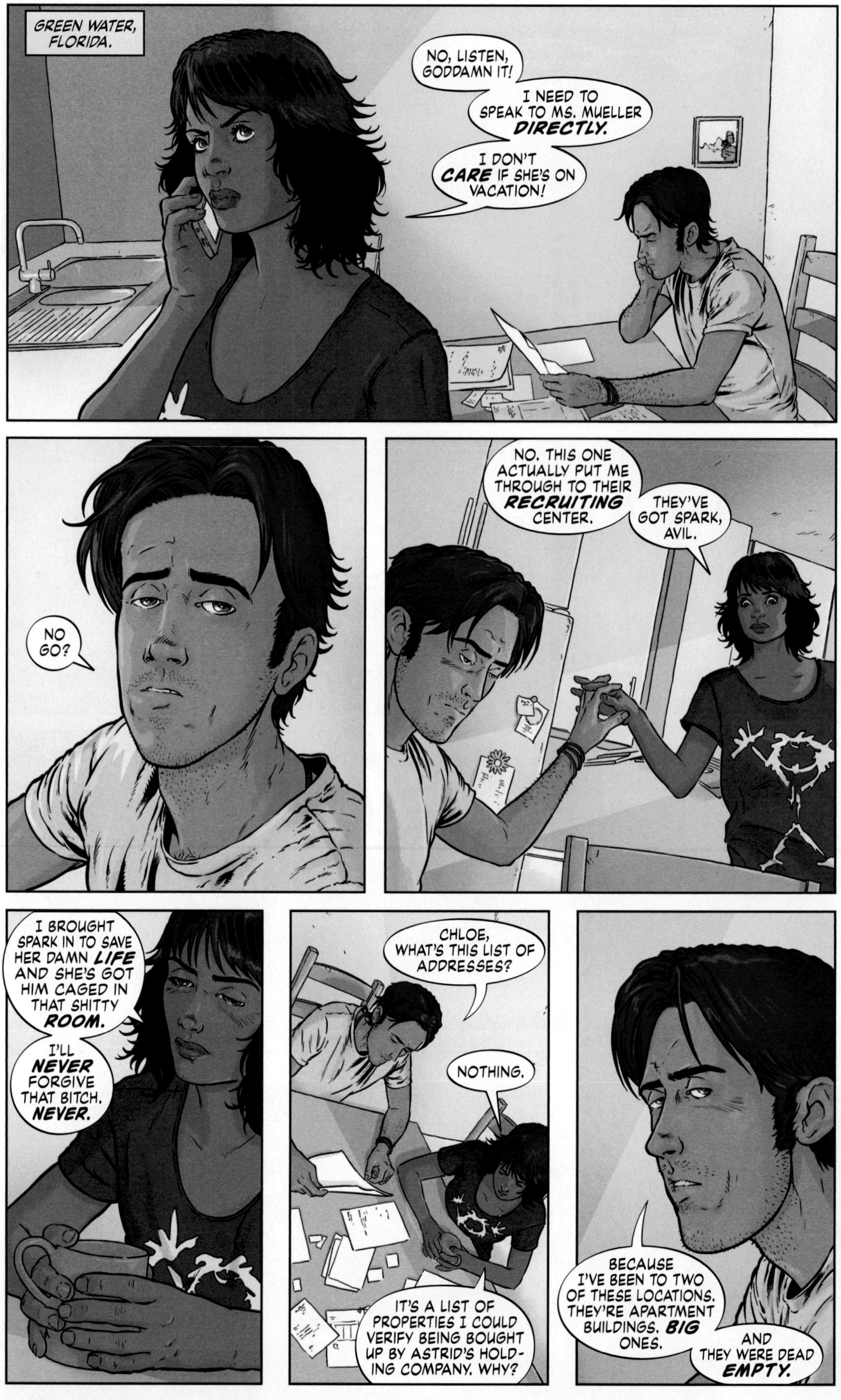
GREEN WATER, FLORIDA.
NO, LISTEN, GODDAMN IT!
I NEED TO SPEAK TO MS. MUELLER DIRECTLY.
I DON'T CARE IF SHE'S ON VACATION!
NO GO?
NO. THIS ONE ACTUALLY PUT ME THROUGH TO THEIR RECRUITING CENTER.
THEY'VE GOT SPARK, AVIL.
I BROUGHT SPARK IN TO SAVE HER DAMN LIFE AND SHE'S GOT HIM CAGED IN THAT SHITTY ROOM.
I'LL NEVER FORGIVE THAT BITCH. NEVER.
CHLOE, WHAT'S THIS LIST OF ADDRESSES?
NOTHING.
IT'S A LIST OF PROPERTIES I COULD VERIFY BEING BOUGHT UP BY ASTRID'S HOLD-ING COMPANY. WHY?
BECAUSE I'VE BEEN TO TWO OF THESE LOCATIONS. THEY'RE APARTMENT BUILDINGS. BIG ONES.
AND THEY WERE DEAD EMPTY.

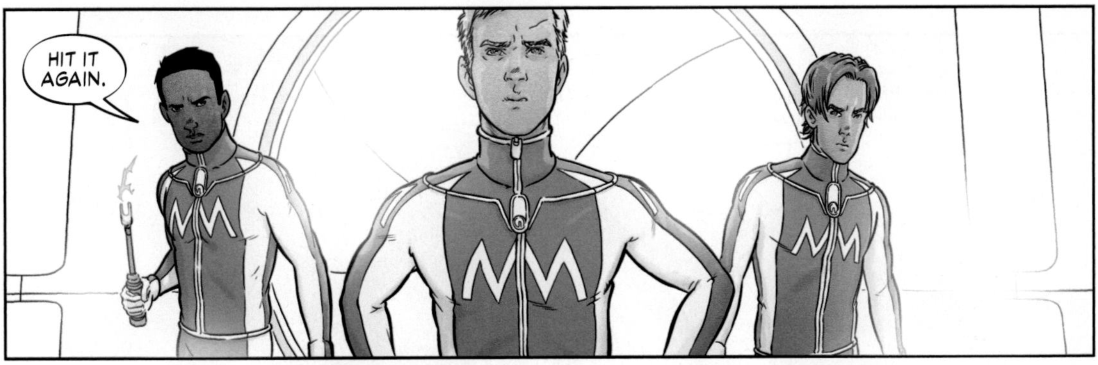
HIT IT AGAIN.

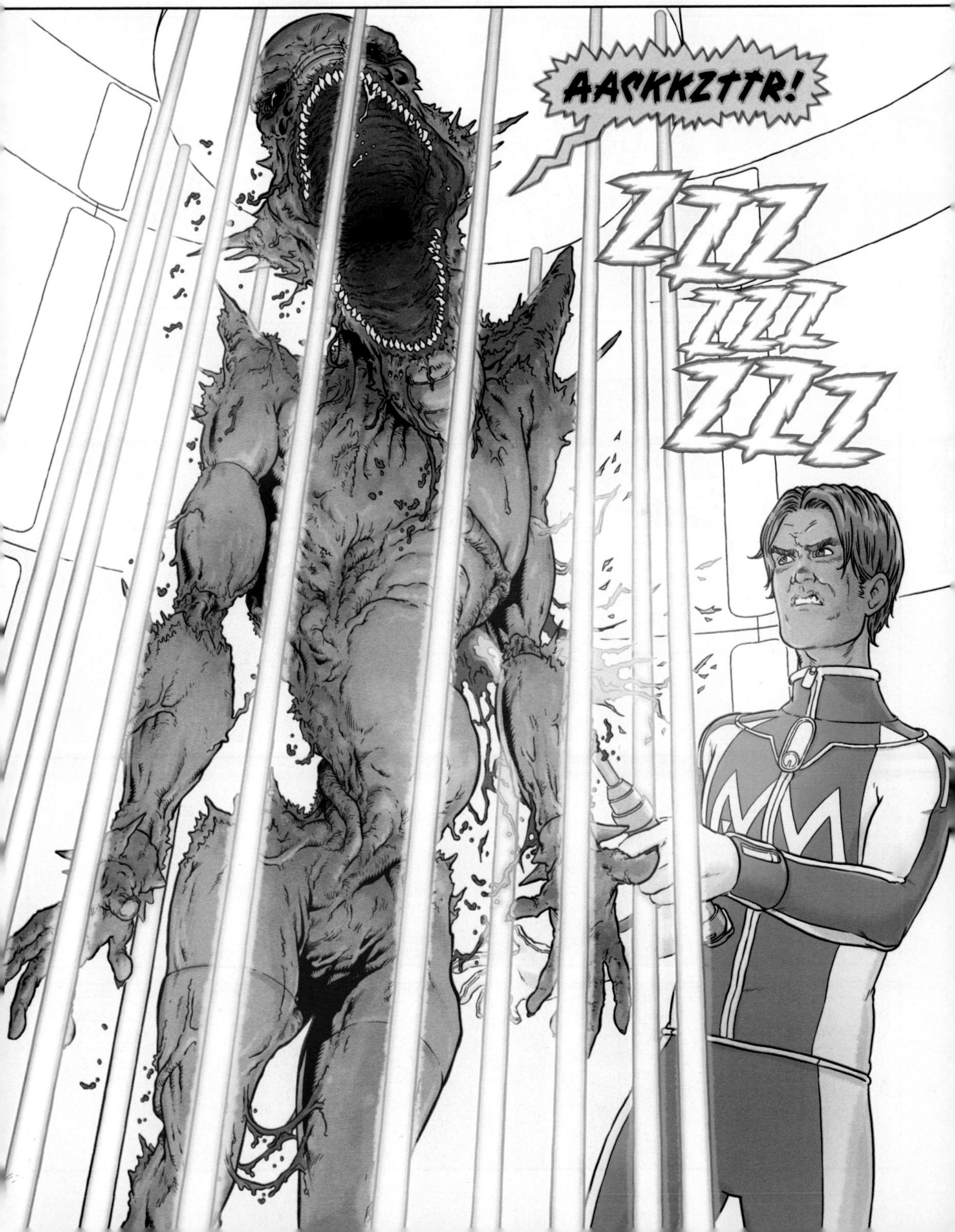
AACKKZTTR!
ZZZ
ZZZ
ZZZ

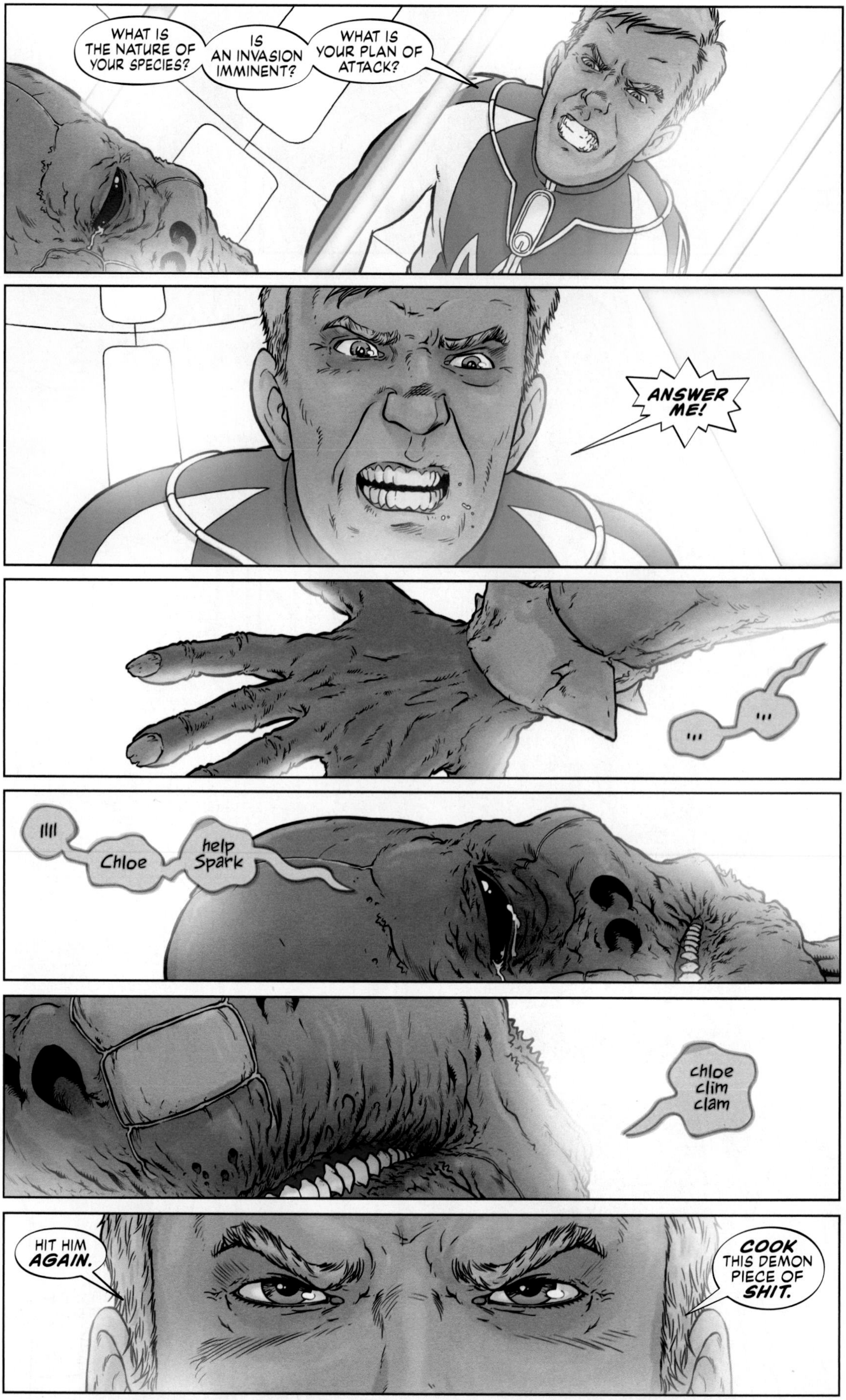
WHAT IS THE NATURE OF YOUR SPECIES?
IS AN INVASION IMMINENT?
WHAT IS YOUR PLAN OF ATTACK?
ANSWER ME!
...
...
IIII
Chloe
help Spark
chloe clim clam
HIT HIM AGAIN.
COOK THIS DEMON PIECE OF SHIT.

...

HOW MUCH OF THIS MOUNTAIN DO YOU OWN, MS. MUELLER?

EXCUSE ME?

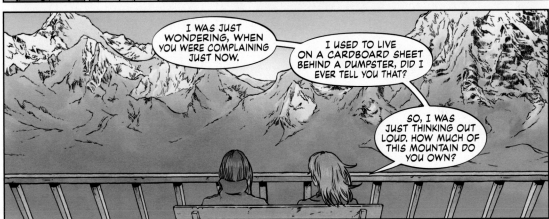

I WAS JUST WONDERING, WHEN YOU WERE COMPLAINING JUST NOW.

I USED TO LIVE ON A CARDBOARD SHEET BEHIND A DUMPSTER, DID I EVER TELL YOU THAT?

SO, I WAS JUST THINKING OUT LOUD. HOW MUCH OF THIS MOUNTAIN DO YOU OWN?

I HAVE NO IDEA, MS. CAPONE.

ALL OF IT, I EXPECT.

ARE WE COMPARING TRAGEDIES THIS MORNING?

NO, GODDAMN IT.

IT WAS ONE OF YOUR FOLLOWERS. HE TOLD ME YOUR MESSAGE, RIGHT THERE BEHIND THE DUMPSTER.

THAT I DIDN'T **HAVE** TO LIVE THAT LIFE.

YOU SAID TAKING CARE OF YOURSELF WAS **JOB ONE.**

I NEEDED TO HEAR THAT, I NEEDED YOU TO **SAY** IT.

YOU NEVER APOLOGIZE, YOU NEVER LET ANYONE ELSE'S HORSESHIT STICK TO YOU.

WHERE **IS** THAT WOMAN?

THAT WOMAN WAS SHOT THROUGH THE HEART BY HER BROTHER.

AND FINDS HERSELF UNABLE TO CRAWL FROM THAT DUMPSTER, SOMEHOW.

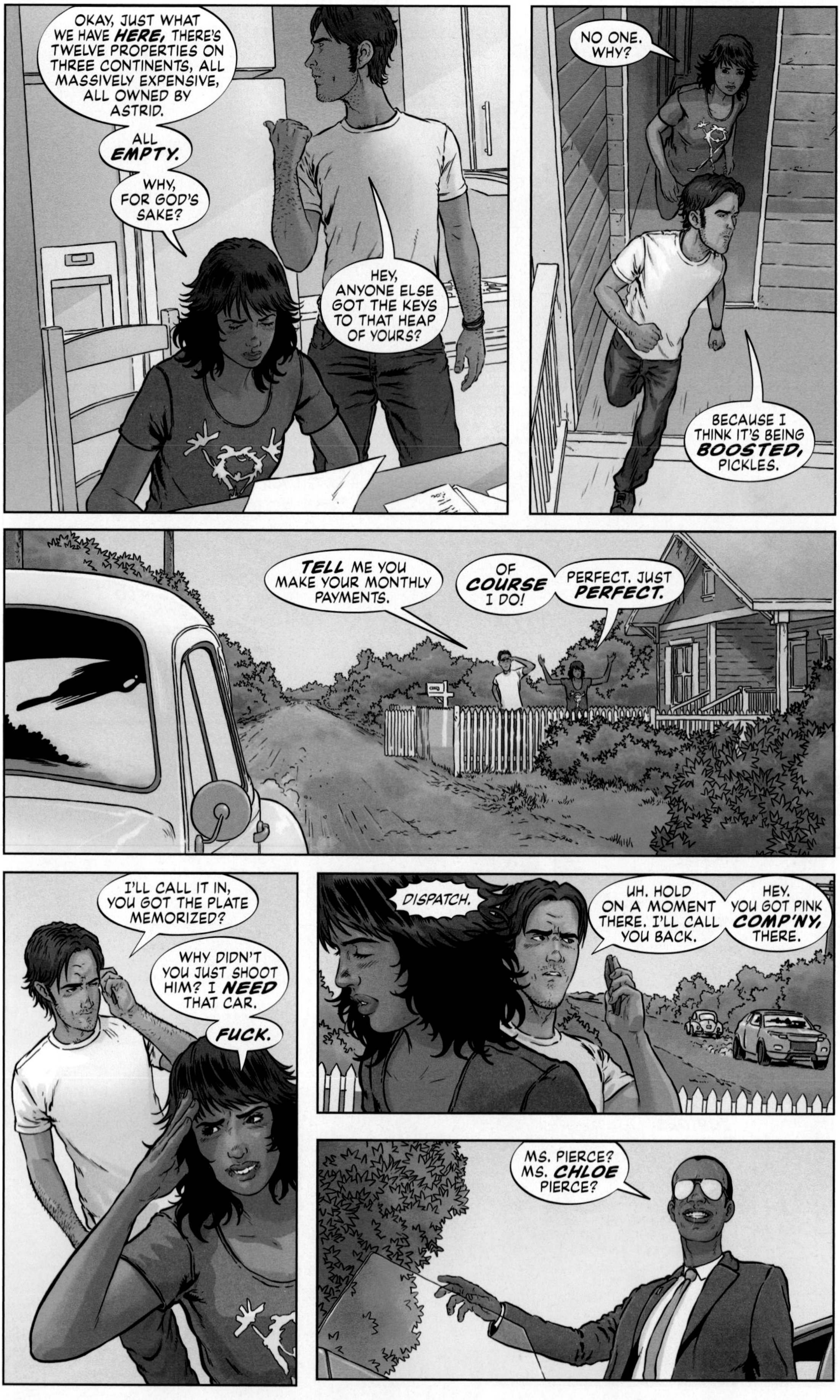
OKAY, JUST WHAT WE HAVE HERE, THERE'S TWELVE PROPERTIES ON THREE CONTINENTS, ALL MASSIVELY EXPENSIVE, ALL OWNED BY ASTRID.
ALL EMPTY.
WHY, FOR GOD'S SAKE?
HEY, ANYONE ELSE GOT THE KEYS TO THAT HEAP OF YOURS?
NO ONE. WHY?
BECAUSE I THINK IT'S BEING BOOSTED, PICKLES.
TELL ME YOU MAKE YOUR MONTHLY PAYMENTS.
OF COURSE I DO!
PERFECT. JUST PERFECT.
I'LL CALL IT IN, YOU GOT THE PLATE MEMORIZED?
WHY DIDN'T YOU JUST SHOOT HIM? I NEED THAT CAR.
FUCK.
DISPATCH.
UH. HOLD ON A MOMENT THERE. I'LL CALL YOU BACK.
HEY. YOU GOT PINK COMP'NY, THERE.
MS. PIERCE? MS. CHLOE PIERCE?

MY NAME IS GARVIN.

I'M HERE TO EXPRESS THE SINCERE *APPRECIATION* OF THE ASTRID MUELLER FOUNDATION FOR YOUR RECENT HEROIC ACTIONS ON OUR LEADER'S BEHALF.

ACTING DIRECTOR KILLIAN REED SENDS HER *PERSONAL* REGARDS.

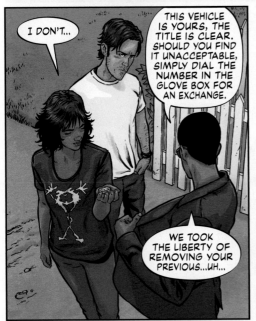

I DON'T...

THIS VEHICLE IS YOURS, THE TITLE IS CLEAR. SHOULD YOU FIND IT UNACCEPTABLE, SIMPLY DIAL THE NUMBER IN THE GLOVE BOX FOR AN EXCHANGE.

WE TOOK THE LIBERTY OF REMOVING YOUR PREVIOUS...UH...

...*VEHICLE.*

SECONDLY, WE WISH TO PROVIDE AN HONORARIUM.

TO SUPPORT YOUR WRITING?

THIS CARD HAS *NO* LIMIT, ESSENTIALLY, MISS.

LOOK, I CAN'T JUST...

IF YOU THINK THAT...

IF *SHE* THINKS I'M JUST GOING TO *FORGET* WHAT SHE DID...

THESE ARE NOT BRIBES, MS. PIERCE.

THEY ARE *GIFTS.*

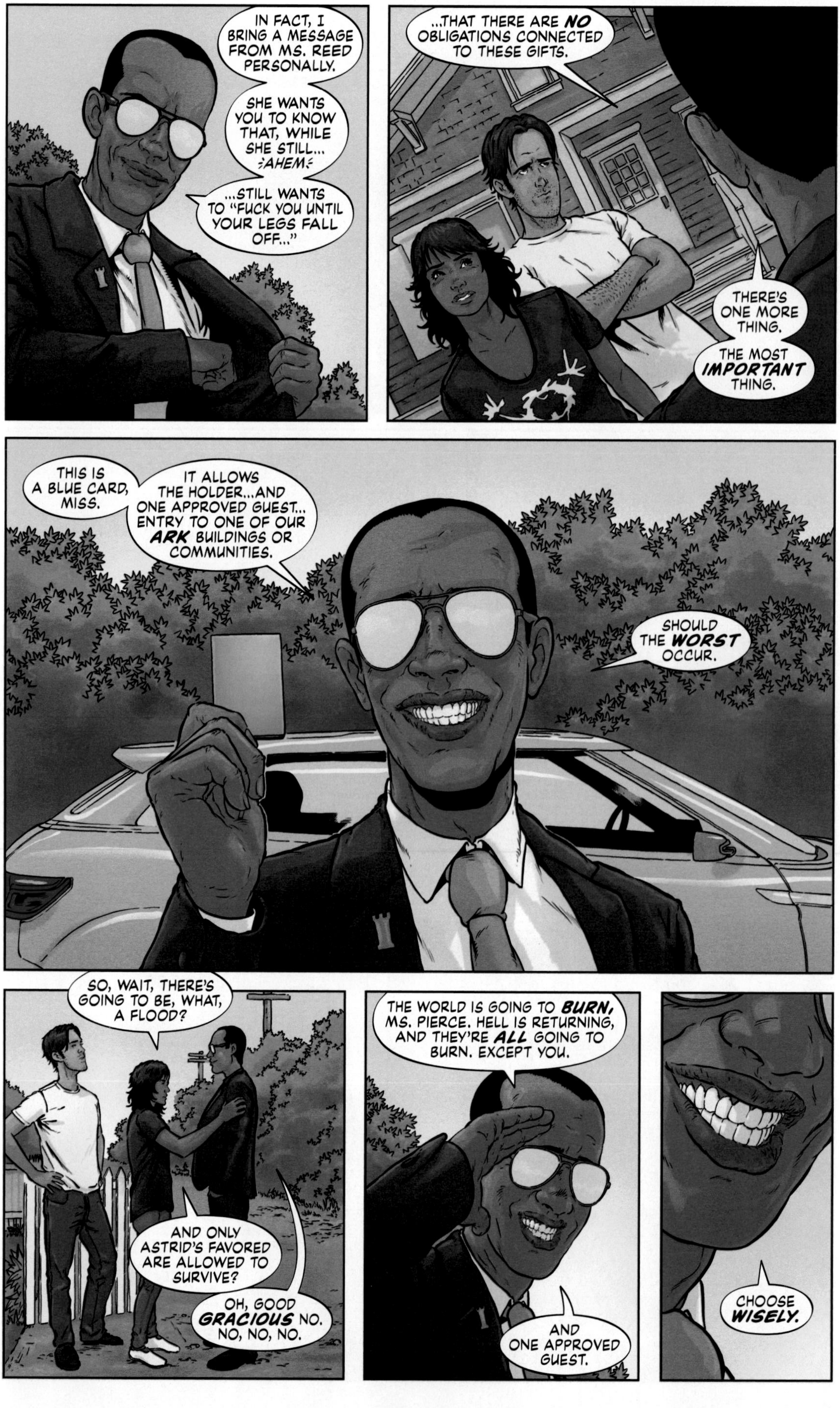
IN FACT, I BRING A MESSAGE FROM MS. REED PERSONALLY.
SHE WANTS YOU TO KNOW THAT, WHILE SHE STILL...
AHEM
...STILL WANTS TO "FUCK YOU UNTIL YOUR LEGS FALL OFF..."
...THAT THERE ARE NO OBLIGATIONS CONNECTED TO THESE GIFTS.
THERE'S ONE MORE THING.
THE MOST IMPORTANT THING.
THIS IS A BLUE CARD, MISS.
IT ALLOWS THE HOLDER...AND ONE APPROVED GUEST... ENTRY TO ONE OF OUR ARK BUILDINGS OR COMMUNITIES.
SHOULD THE WORST OCCUR.
SO, WAIT, THERE'S GOING TO BE, WHAT, A FLOOD?
AND ONLY ASTRID'S FAVORED ARE ALLOWED TO SURVIVE?
OH, GOOD GRACIOUS NO. NO, NO, NO.
THE WORLD IS GOING TO BURN, MS. PIERCE. HELL IS RETURNING, AND THEY'RE ALL GOING TO BURN. EXCEPT YOU.
AND ONE APPROVED GUEST.
CHOOSE WISELY.

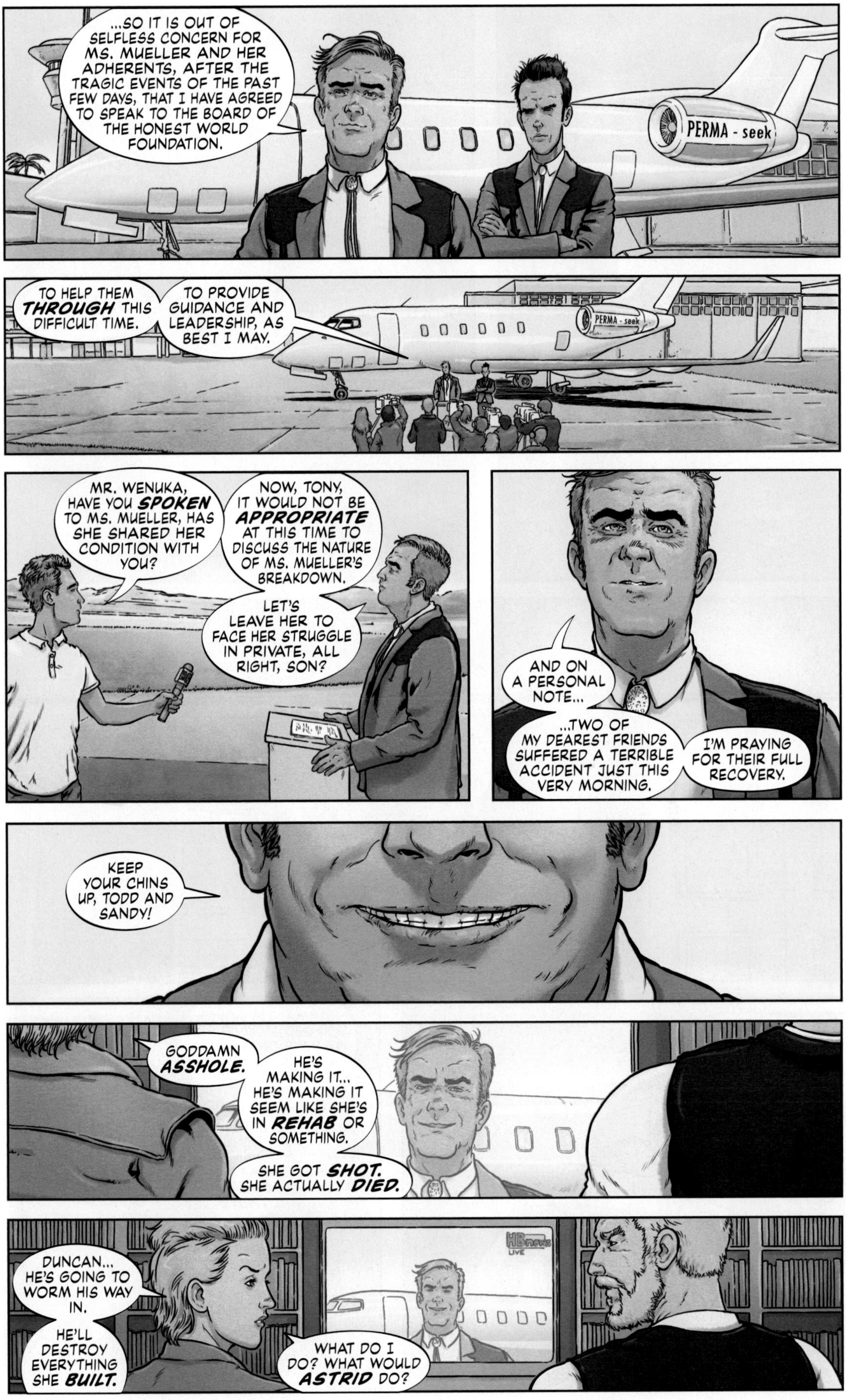
...SO IT IS OUT OF SELFLESS CONCERN FOR MS. MUELLER AND HER ADHERENTS, AFTER THE TRAGIC EVENTS OF THE PAST FEW DAYS, THAT I HAVE AGREED TO SPEAK TO THE BOARD OF THE HONEST WORLD FOUNDATION.
PERMA - seek
TO HELP THEM THROUGH THIS DIFFICULT TIME.
TO PROVIDE GUIDANCE AND LEADERSHIP, AS BEST I MAY.
PERMA - seek
MR. WENUKA, HAVE YOU SPOKEN TO MS. MUELLER, HAS SHE SHARED HER CONDITION WITH YOU?
NOW, TONY, IT WOULD NOT BE APPROPRIATE AT THIS TIME TO DISCUSS THE NATURE OF MS. MUELLER'S BREAKDOWN.
LET'S LEAVE HER TO FACE HER STRUGGLE IN PRIVATE, ALL RIGHT, SON?
AND ON A PERSONAL NOTE...
...TWO OF MY DEAREST FRIENDS SUFFERED A TERRIBLE ACCIDENT JUST THIS VERY MORNING.
I'M PRAYING FOR THEIR FULL RECOVERY.
KEEP YOUR CHINS UP, TODD AND SANDY!
GODDAMN ASSHOLE.
HE'S MAKING IT... HE'S MAKING IT SEEM LIKE SHE'S IN REHAB OR SOMETHING.
SHE GOT SHOT. SHE ACTUALLY DIED.
HB news
LIVE
DUNCAN... HE'S GOING TO WORM HIS WAY IN.
HE'LL DESTROY EVERYTHING SHE BUILT.
WHAT DO I DO? WHAT WOULD ASTRID DO?

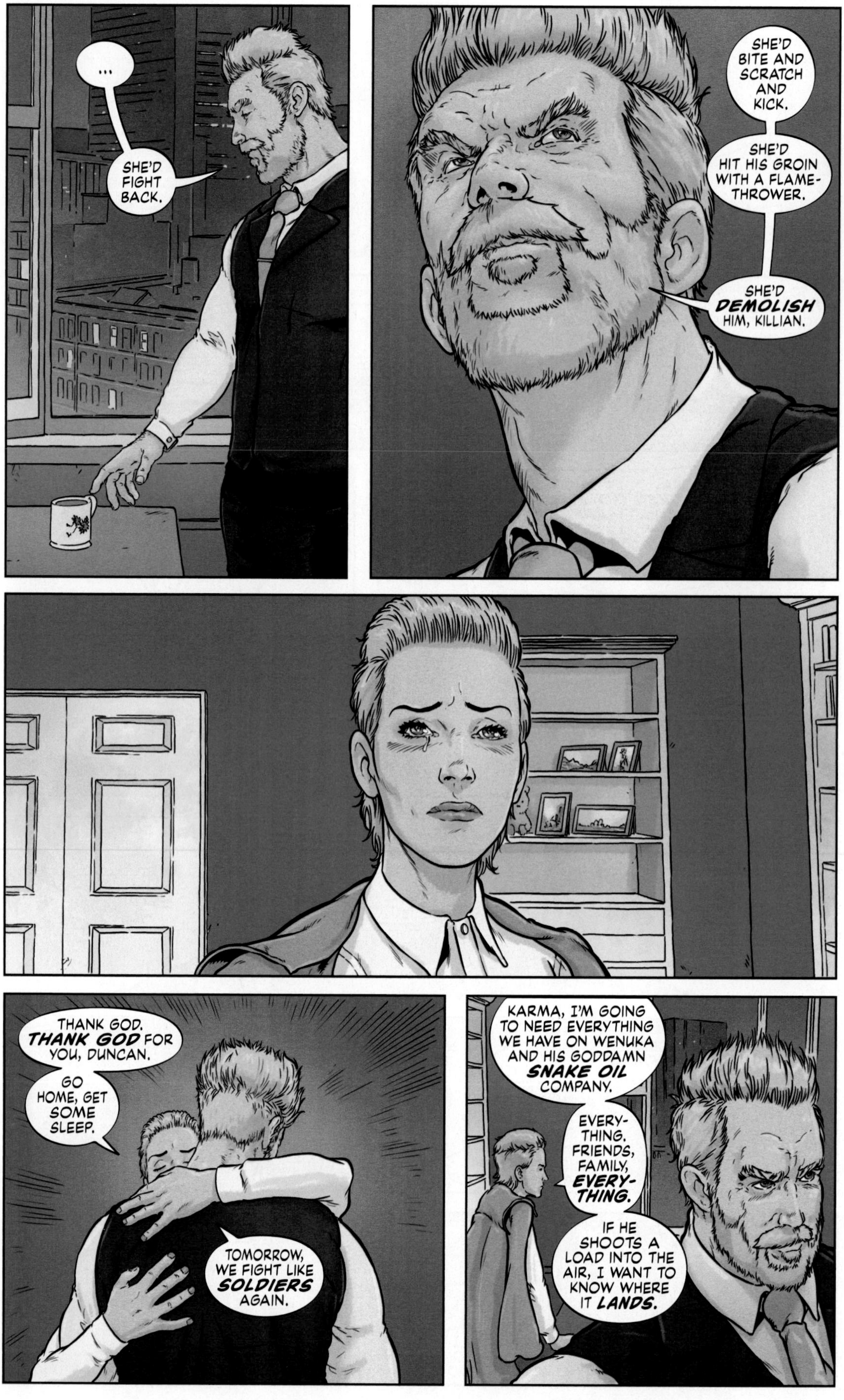
...
SHE'D FIGHT BACK.
SHE'D BITE AND SCRATCH AND KICK.
SHE'D HIT HIS GROIN WITH A FLAME-THROWER.
SHE'D **DEMOLISH** HIM, KILLIAN.
THANK GOD. **THANK GOD** FOR YOU, DUNCAN.
GO HOME, GET SOME SLEEP.
TOMORROW, WE FIGHT LIKE **SOLDIERS** AGAIN.
KARMA, I'M GOING TO NEED EVERYTHING WE HAVE ON WENUKA AND HIS GODDAMN **SNAKE OIL** COMPANY.
EVERY-THING. FRIENDS, FAMILY, **EVERY-THING.**
IF HE SHOOTS A LOAD INTO THE AIR, I WANT TO KNOW WHERE IT **LANDS.**

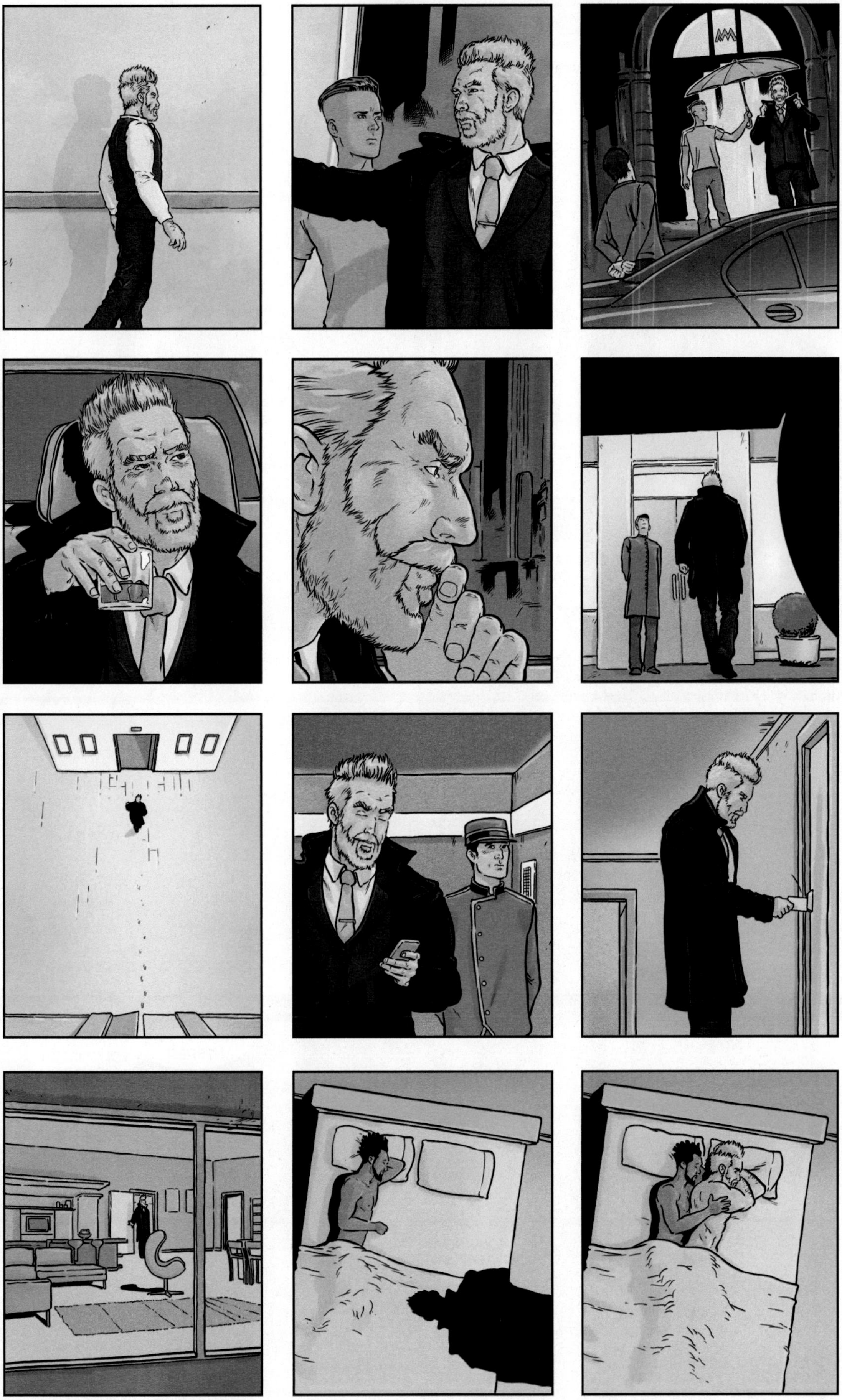

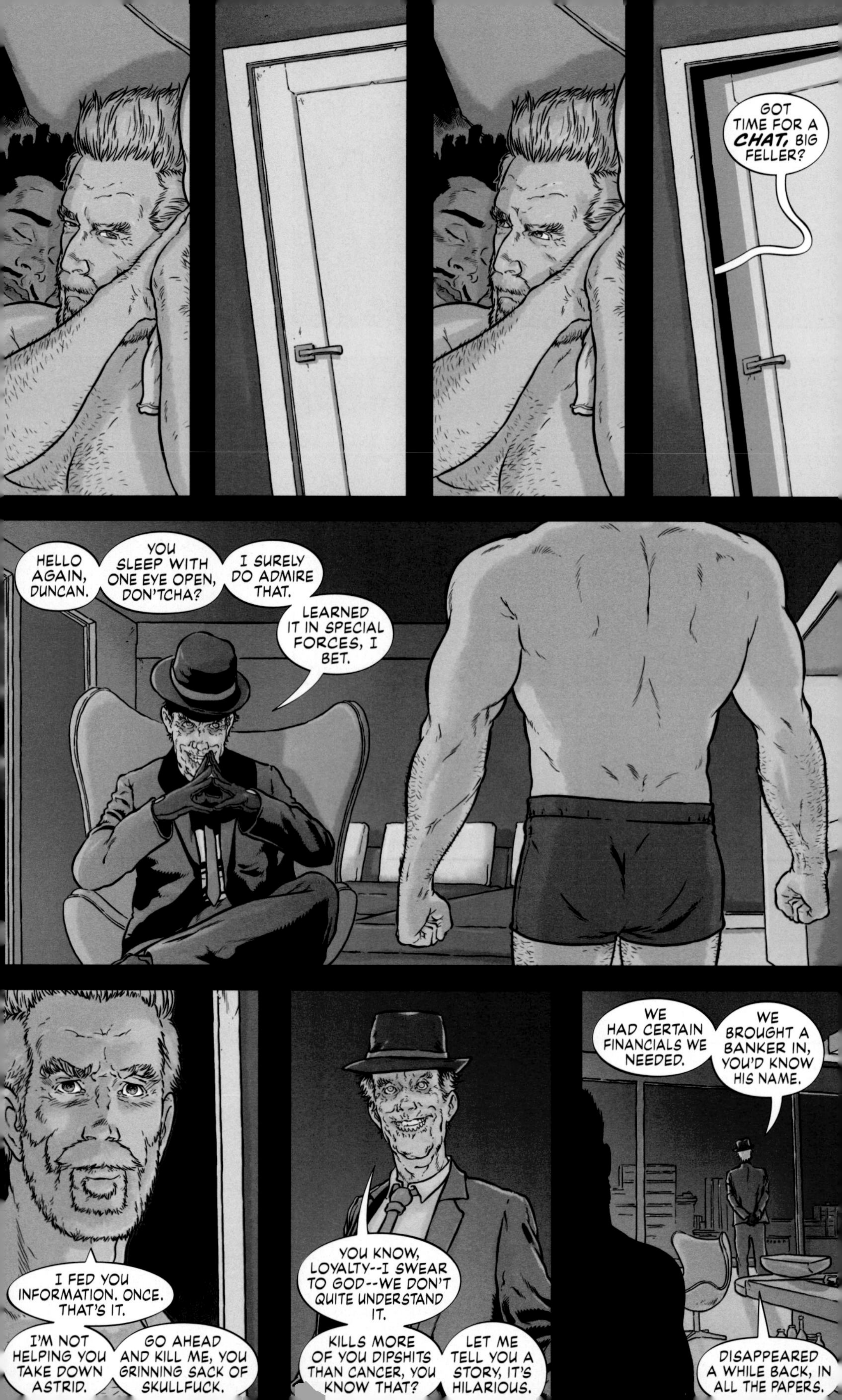
GOT TIME FOR A *CHAT,* BIG FELLER?
HELLO AGAIN, DUNCAN.
YOU SLEEP WITH ONE EYE OPEN, DON'TCHA?
I SURELY DO ADMIRE THAT.
LEARNED IT IN SPECIAL FORCES, I BET.
I FED YOU INFORMATION. ONCE. THAT'S IT.
I'M NOT HELPING YOU TAKE DOWN ASTRID.
GO AHEAD AND KILL ME, YOU GRINNING SACK OF SKULLFUCK.
YOU KNOW, LOYALTY--I SWEAR TO GOD--WE DON'T QUITE UNDERSTAND IT.
KILLS MORE OF YOU DIPSHITS THAN CANCER, YOU KNOW THAT?
LET ME TELL YOU A STORY, IT'S HILARIOUS.
WE HAD CERTAIN FINANCIALS WE NEEDED.
WE BROUGHT A BANKER IN, YOU'D KNOW HIS NAME.
DISAPPEARED A WHILE BACK, IN ALL THE PAPERS.

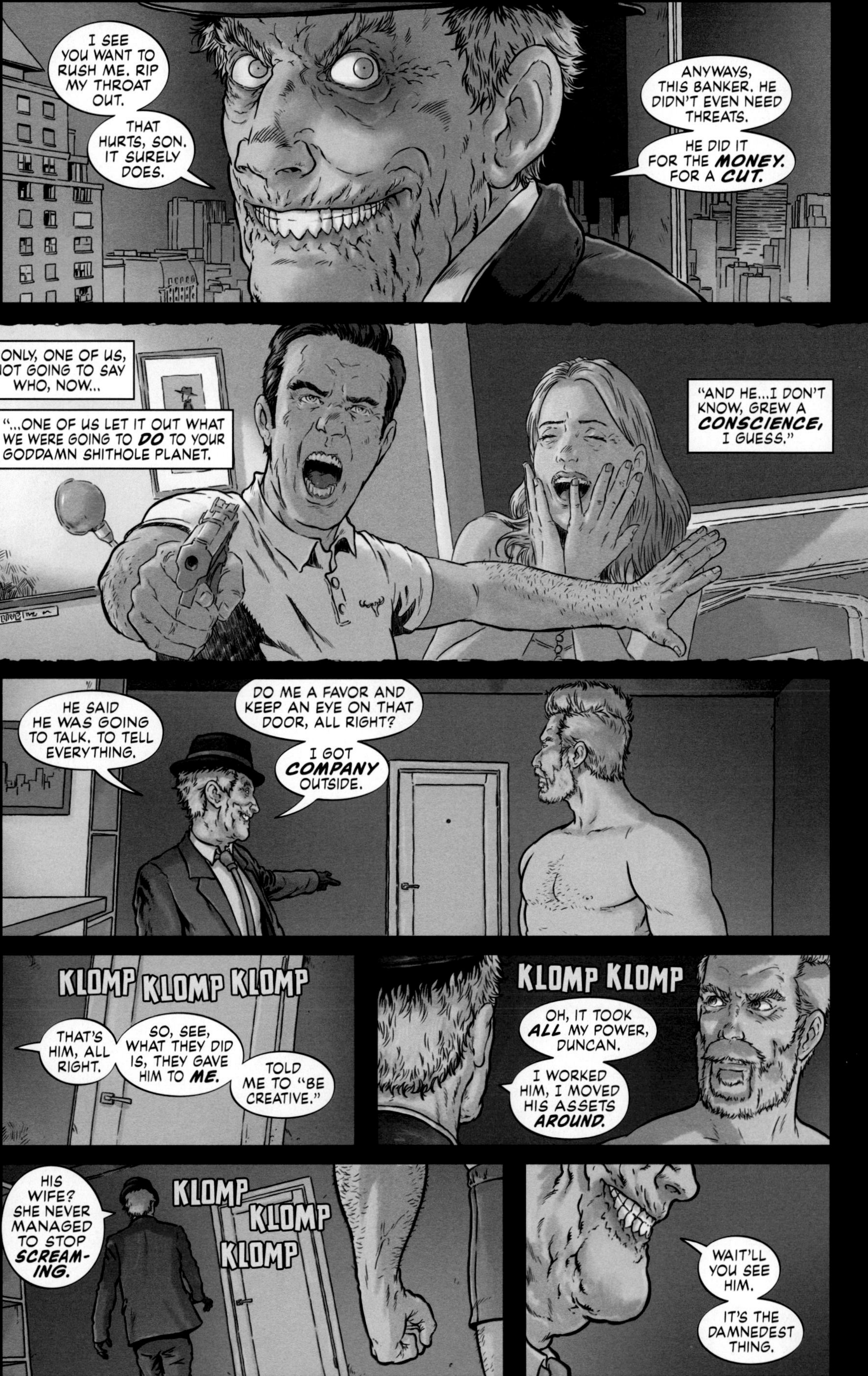
I SEE YOU WANT TO RUSH ME. RIP MY THROAT OUT.
THAT HURTS, SON. IT SURELY DOES.
ANYWAYS, THIS BANKER. HE DIDN'T EVEN NEED THREATS.
HE DID IT FOR THE **MONEY.** FOR A **CUT.**
"ONLY, ONE OF US, NOT GOING TO SAY WHO, NOW...
"...ONE OF US LET IT OUT WHAT WE WERE GOING TO **DO** TO YOUR GODDAMN SHITHOLE PLANET.
"AND HE...I DON'T KNOW, GREW A **CONSCIENCE,** I GUESS."
HE SAID HE WAS GOING TO TALK. TO TELL EVERYTHING.
DO ME A FAVOR AND KEEP AN EYE ON THAT DOOR, ALL RIGHT?
I GOT **COMPANY** OUTSIDE.
KLOMP KLOMP KLOMP
THAT'S HIM, ALL RIGHT.
SO, SEE, WHAT THEY DID IS, THEY GAVE HIM TO **ME.**
TOLD ME TO "BE CREATIVE."
KLOMP KLOMP
OH, IT TOOK **ALL** MY POWER, DUNCAN.
I WORKED HIM, I MOVED HIS ASSETS **AROUND.**
HIS WIFE? SHE NEVER MANAGED TO STOP **SCREAM-ING.**
KLOMP
KLOMP
KLOMP
WAIT'LL YOU SEE HIM.
IT'S THE DAMNEDEST THING.

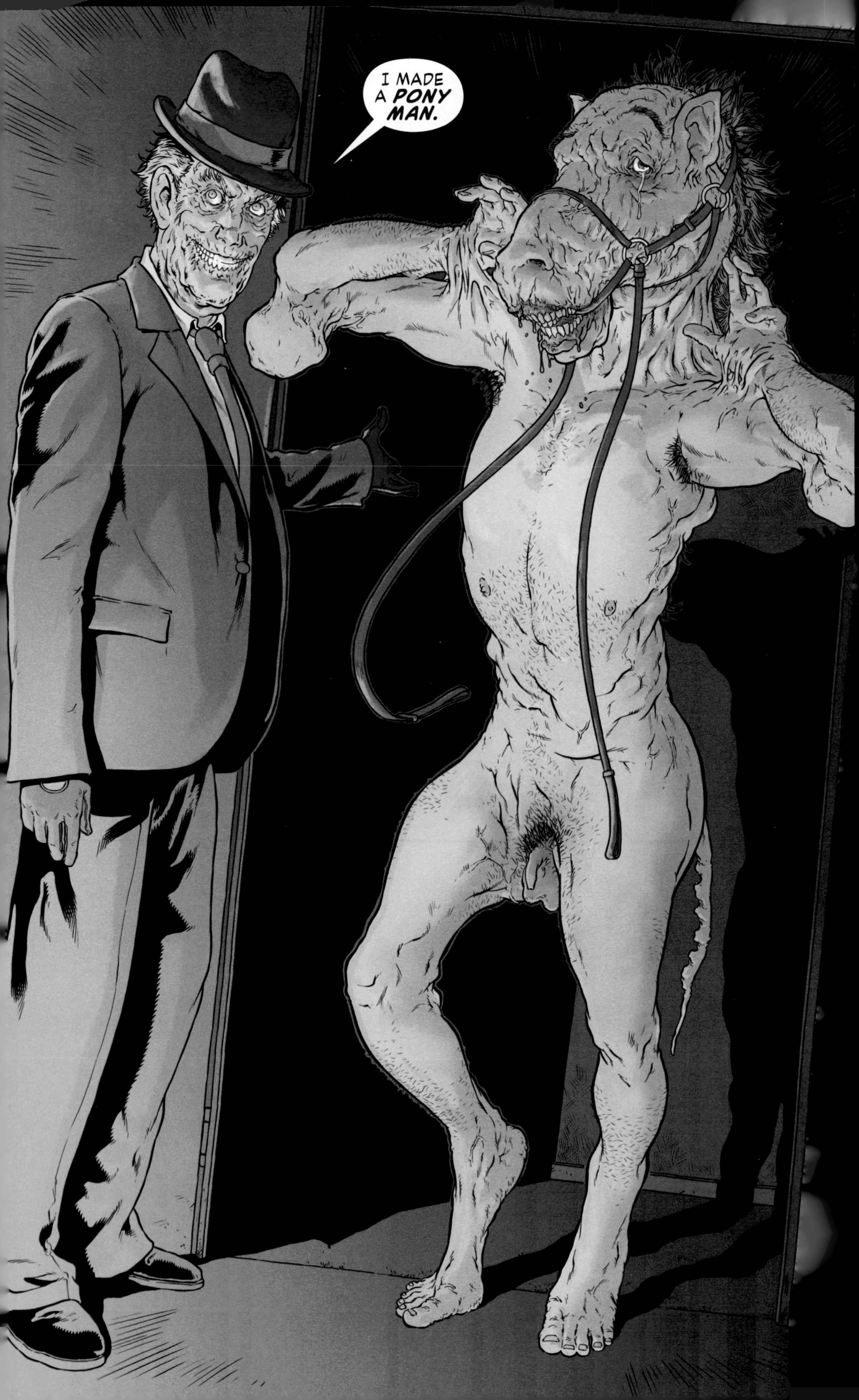
I MADE A PONY MAN.

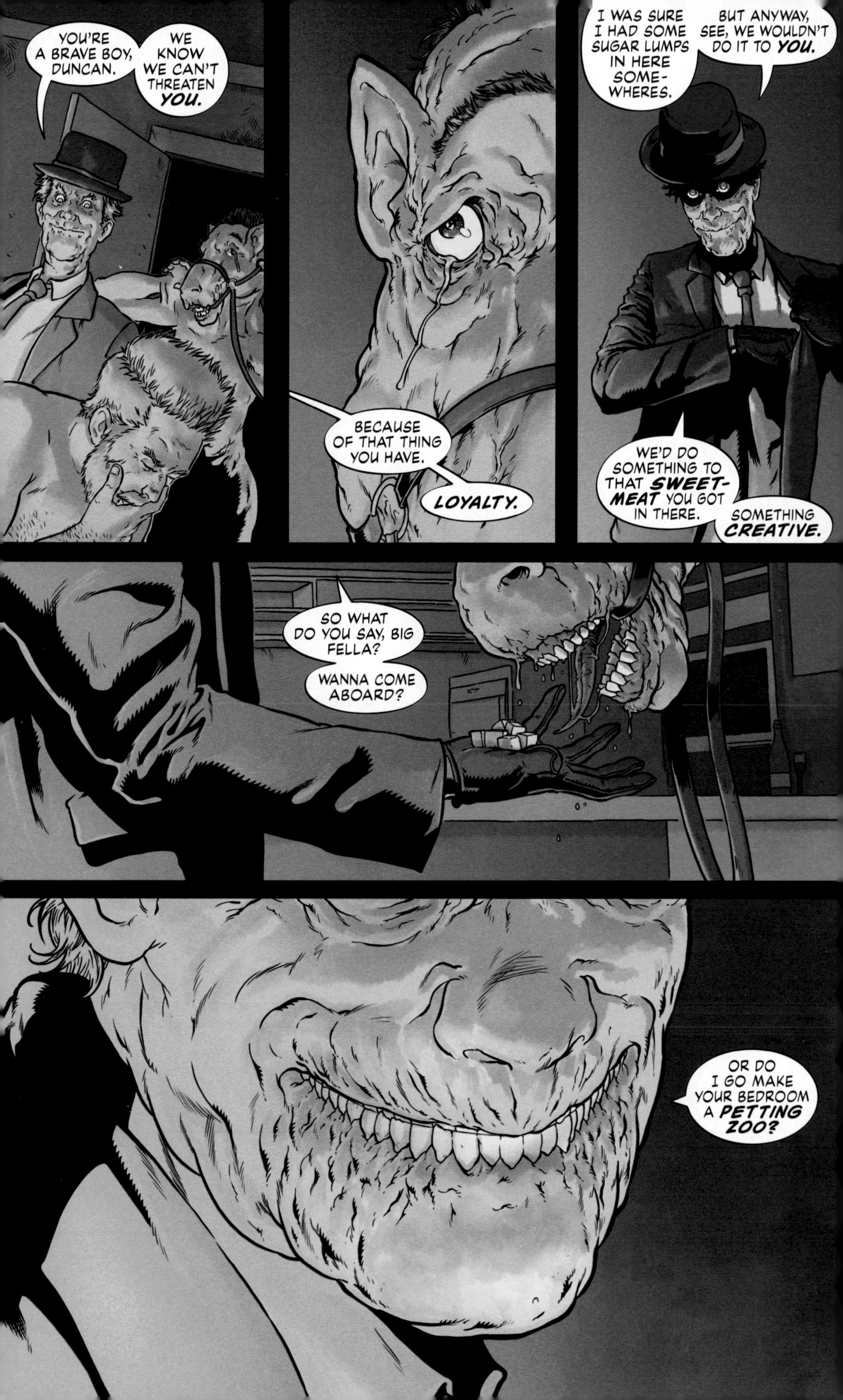
YOU'RE A BRAVE BOY, DUNCAN.
WE KNOW WE CAN'T THREATEN *YOU.*
BECAUSE OF THAT THING YOU HAVE.
LOYALTY.
I WAS SURE I HAD SOME SUGAR LUMPS IN HERE SOME-WHERES.
BUT ANYWAY, SEE, WE WOULDN'T DO IT TO *YOU.*
WE'D DO SOMETHING TO THAT *SWEET-MEAT* YOU GOT IN THERE.
SOMETHING *CREATIVE.*
SO WHAT DO YOU SAY, BIG FELLA?
WANNA COME ABOARD?
OR DO I GO MAKE YOUR BEDROOM A *PETTING ZOO?*

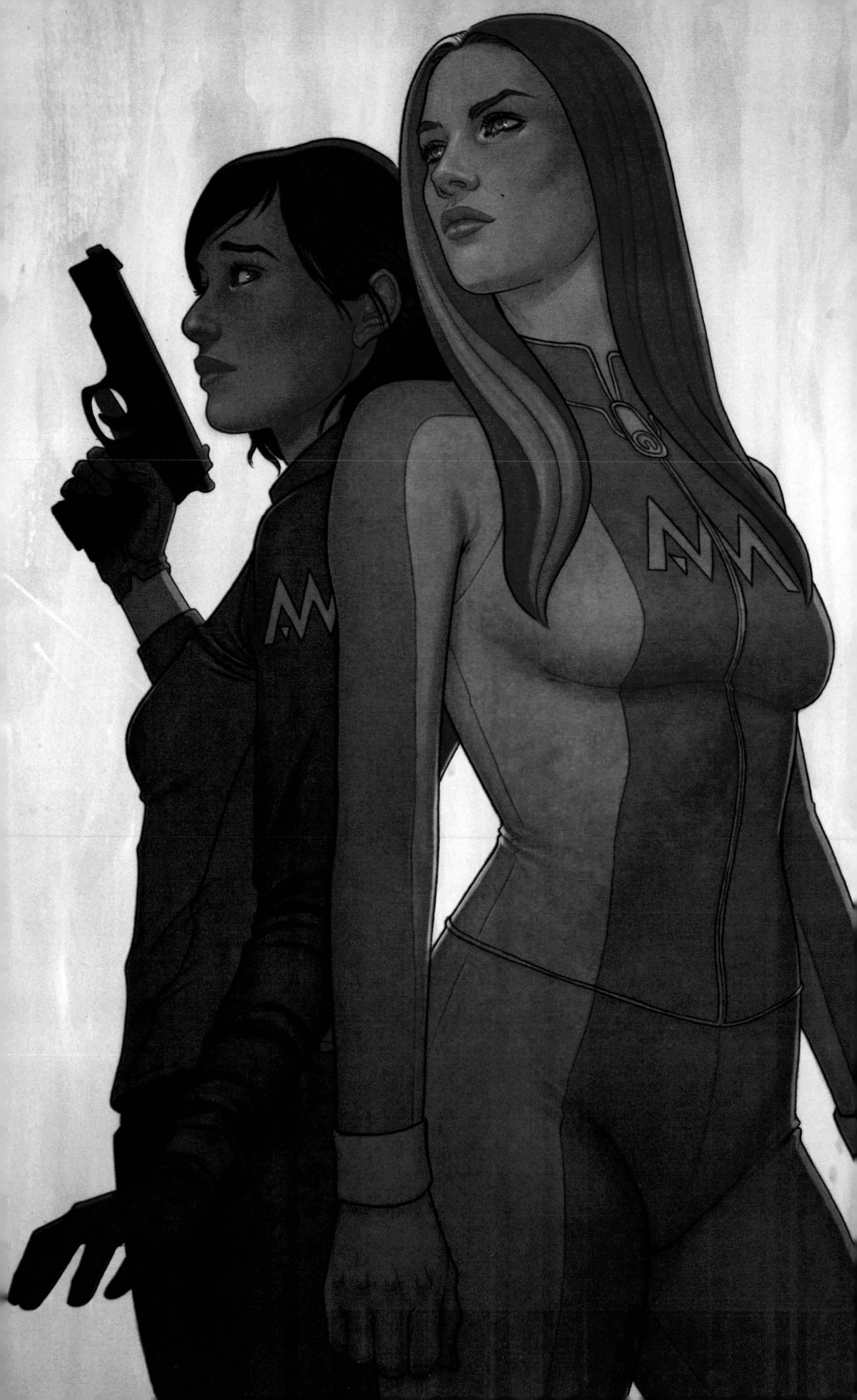

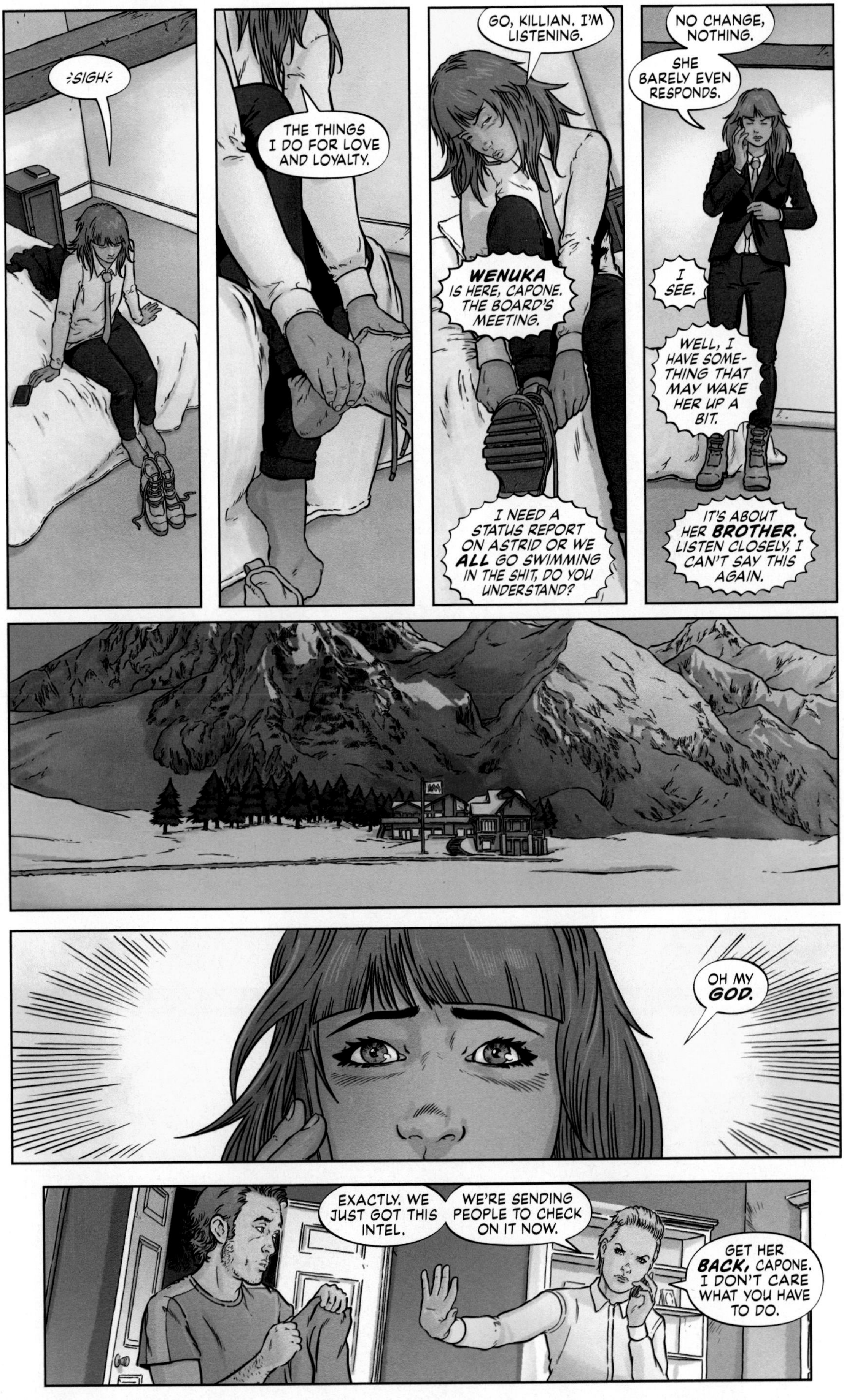

:SIGH:
THE THINGS I DO FOR LOVE AND LOYALTY.
GO, KILLIAN. I'M LISTENING.
WENUKA IS HERE, CAPONE. THE BOARD'S MEETING.
I NEED A STATUS REPORT ON ASTRID OR WE ALL GO SWIMMING IN THE SHIT, DO YOU UNDERSTAND?
NO CHANGE, NOTHING.
SHE BARELY EVEN RESPONDS.
I SEE.
WELL, I HAVE SOME-THING THAT MAY WAKE HER UP A BIT.
IT'S ABOUT HER BROTHER. LISTEN CLOSELY, I CAN'T SAY THIS AGAIN.
OH MY GOD.
EXACTLY. WE JUST GOT THIS INTEL.
WE'RE SENDING PEOPLE TO CHECK ON IT NOW.
GET HER BACK, CAPONE. I DON'T CARE WHAT YOU HAVE TO DO.

RED INVENTORY

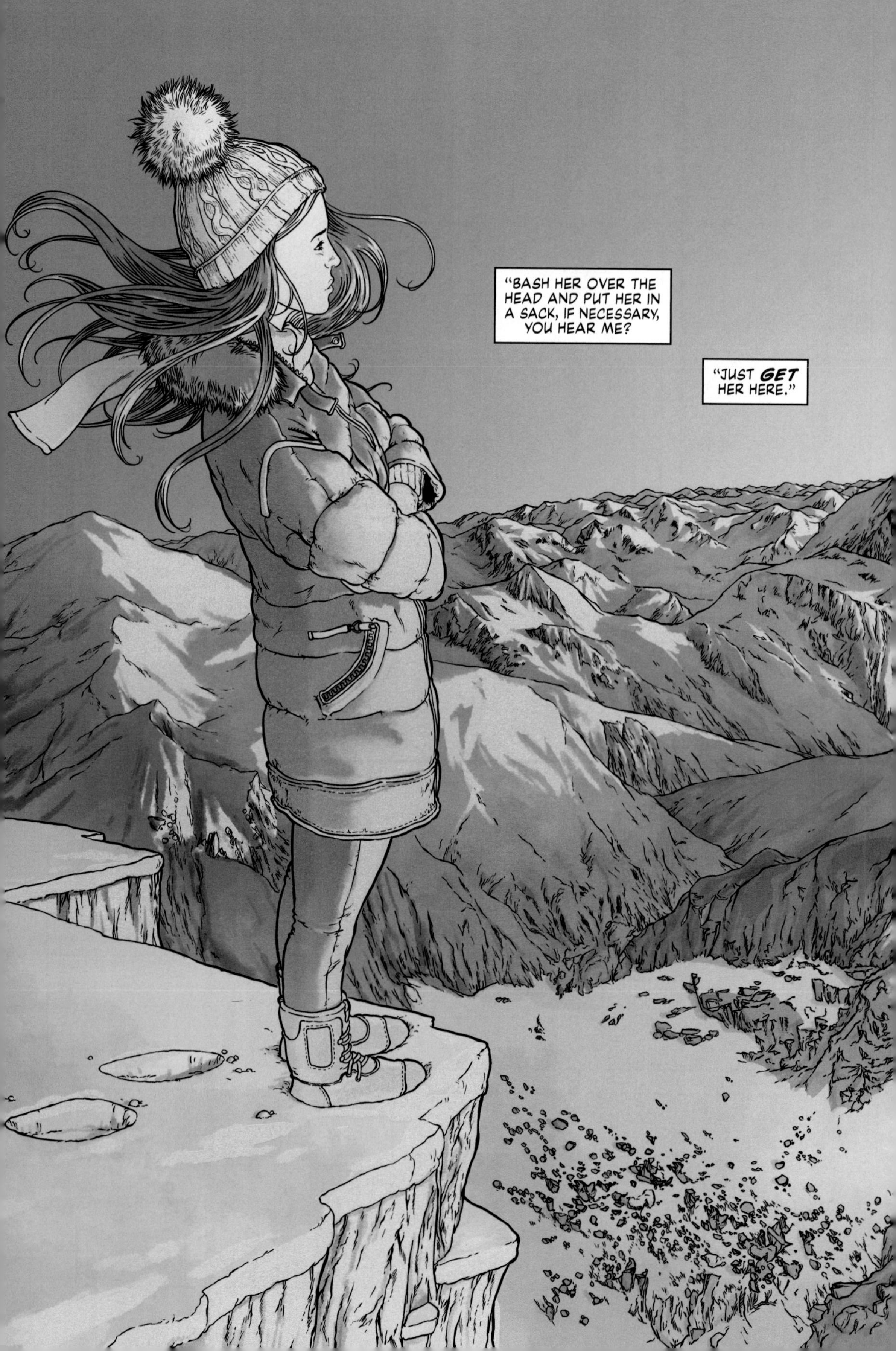
"BASH HER OVER THE HEAD AND PUT HER IN A SACK, IF NECESSARY, YOU HEAR ME?
"JUST **GET** HER HERE."

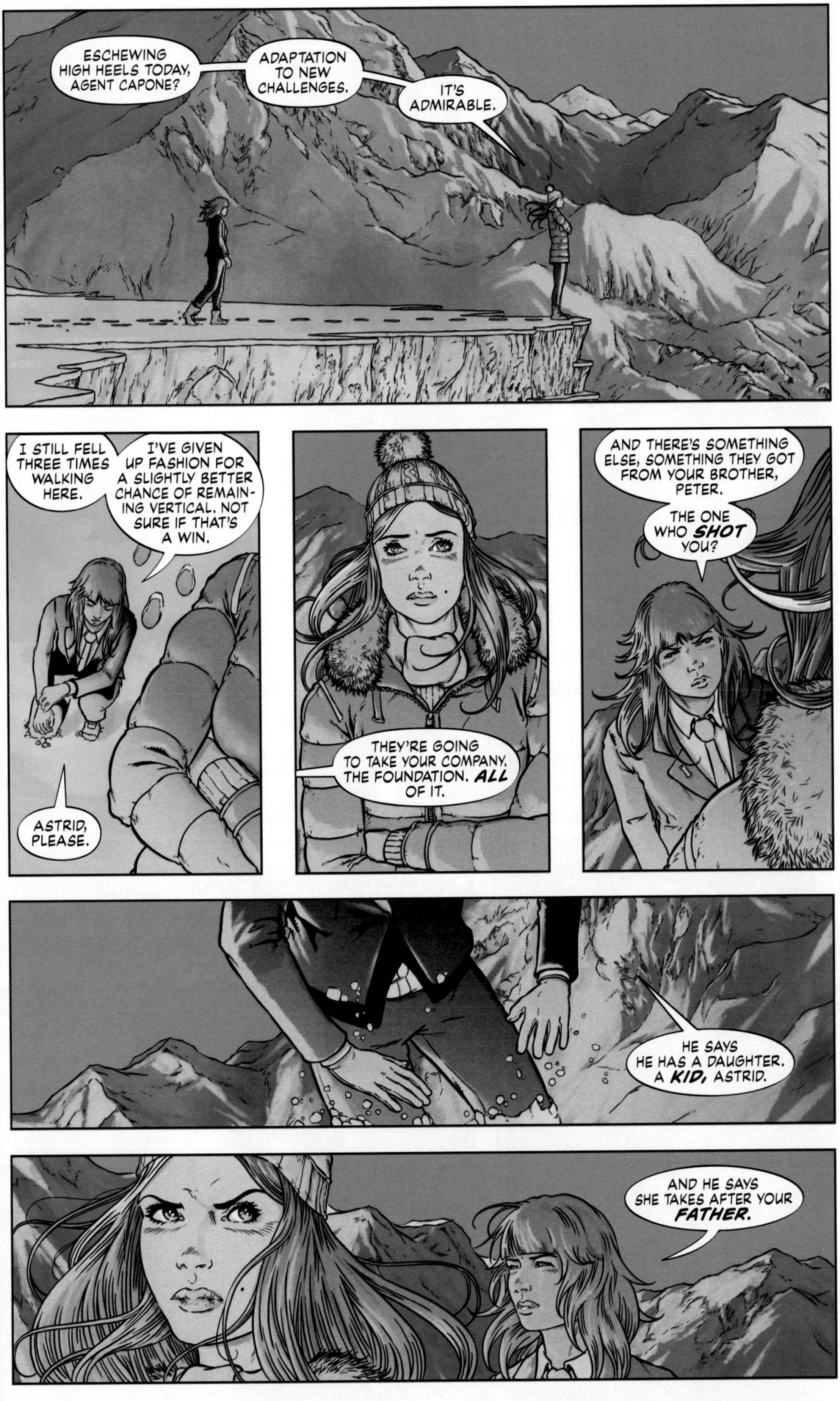
ESCHEWING HIGH HEELS TODAY, AGENT CAPONE?
ADAPTATION TO NEW CHALLENGES.
IT'S ADMIRABLE.
I STILL FELL THREE TIMES WALKING HERE.
I'VE GIVEN UP FASHION FOR A SLIGHTLY BETTER CHANCE OF REMAINING VERTICAL. NOT SURE IF THAT'S A WIN.
ASTRID, PLEASE.
THEY'RE GOING TO TAKE YOUR COMPANY. THE FOUNDATION. ALL OF IT.
AND THERE'S SOMETHING ELSE, SOMETHING THEY GOT FROM YOUR BROTHER, PETER.
THE ONE WHO SHOT YOU?
HE SAYS HE HAS A DAUGHTER. A KID, ASTRID.
AND HE SAYS SHE TAKES AFTER YOUR FATHER.

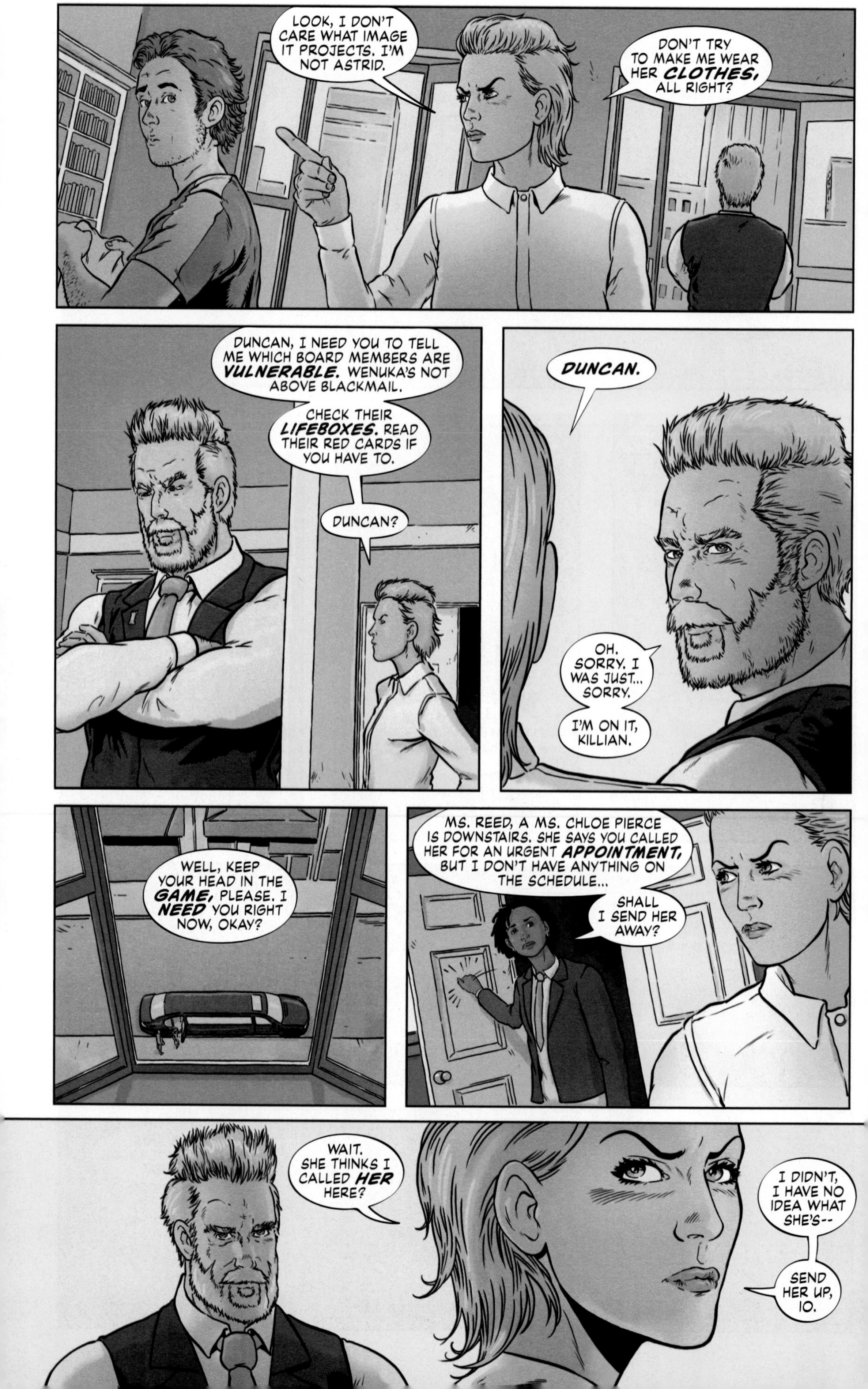
LOOK, I DON'T CARE WHAT IMAGE IT PROJECTS. I'M NOT ASTRID.
DON'T TRY TO MAKE ME WEAR HER *CLOTHES,* ALL RIGHT?
DUNCAN, I NEED YOU TO TELL ME WHICH BOARD MEMBERS ARE *VULNERABLE.* WENUKA'S NOT ABOVE BLACKMAIL.
CHECK THEIR *LIFEBOXES.* READ THEIR RED CARDS IF YOU HAVE TO.
DUNCAN?
DUNCAN.
OH. SORRY. I WAS JUST... SORRY.
I'M ON IT, KILLIAN.
WELL, KEEP YOUR HEAD IN THE *GAME,* PLEASE. I *NEED* YOU RIGHT NOW, OKAY?
MS. REED, A MS. CHLOE PIERCE IS DOWNSTAIRS. SHE SAYS YOU CALLED HER FOR AN URGENT *APPOINTMENT,* BUT I DON'T HAVE ANYTHING ON THE SCHEDULE...
SHALL I SEND HER AWAY?
WAIT. SHE THINKS I CALLED *HER* HERE?
I DIDN'T, I HAVE NO IDEA WHAT SHE'S--
SEND HER UP, IO.

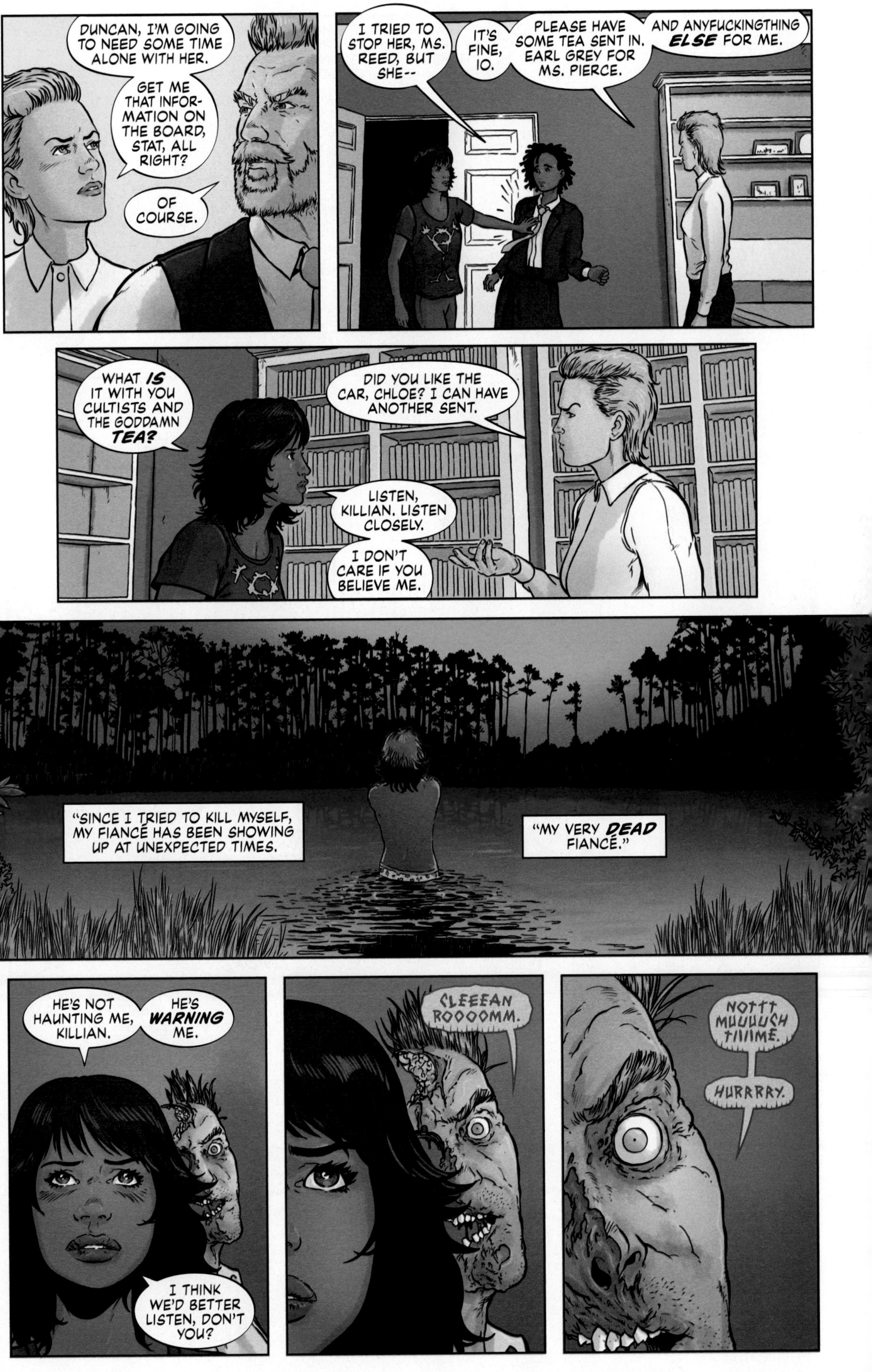
DUNCAN, I'M GOING TO NEED SOME TIME ALONE WITH HER.
GET ME THAT INFORMATION ON THE BOARD, STAT, ALL RIGHT?
OF COURSE.
I TRIED TO STOP HER, MS. REED, BUT SHE--
IT'S FINE, IO.
PLEASE HAVE SOME TEA SENT IN. EARL GREY FOR MS. PIERCE.
AND ANYFUCKINGTHING ELSE FOR ME.
WHAT IS IT WITH YOU CULTISTS AND THE GODDAMN TEA?
DID YOU LIKE THE CAR, CHLOE? I CAN HAVE ANOTHER SENT.
LISTEN, KILLIAN. LISTEN CLOSELY.
I DON'T CARE IF YOU BELIEVE ME.
"SINCE I TRIED TO KILL MYSELF, MY FIANCÉ HAS BEEN SHOWING UP AT UNEXPECTED TIMES.
"MY VERY DEAD FIANCÉ."
HE'S NOT HAUNTING ME, KILLIAN.
HE'S WARNING ME.
I THINK WE'D BETTER LISTEN, DON'T YOU?
CLEEEAN ROOOOMM.
NOTTT MUUUUCH TIIIIME.
HURRRRY.

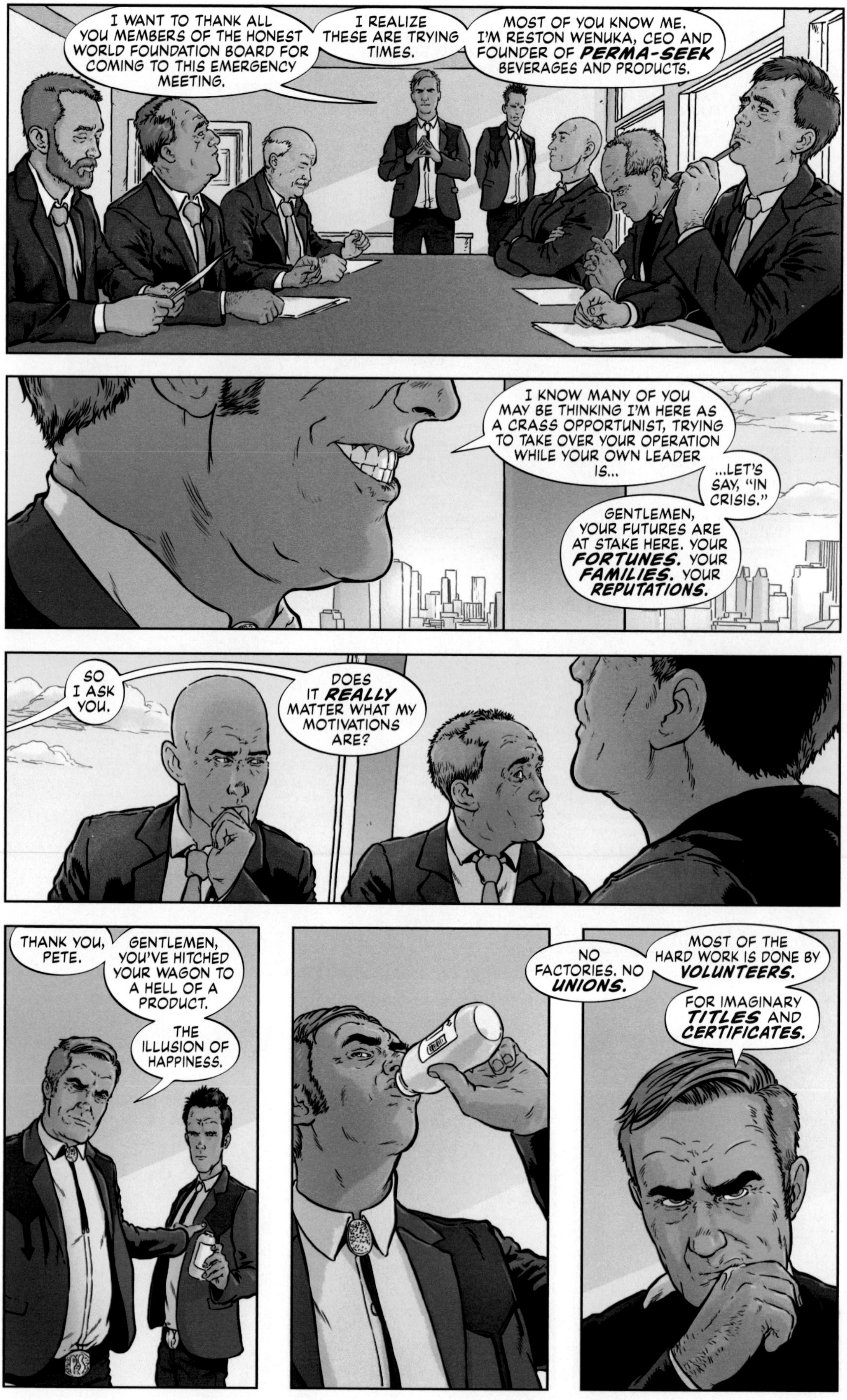
I WANT TO THANK ALL YOU MEMBERS OF THE HONEST WORLD FOUNDATION BOARD FOR COMING TO THIS EMERGENCY MEETING.
I REALIZE THESE ARE TRYING TIMES.
MOST OF YOU KNOW ME. I'M RESTON WENUKA, CEO AND FOUNDER OF PERMA-SEEK BEVERAGES AND PRODUCTS.
I KNOW MANY OF YOU MAY BE THINKING I'M HERE AS A CRASS OPPORTUNIST, TRYING TO TAKE OVER YOUR OPERATION WHILE YOUR OWN LEADER IS...
...LET'S SAY, "IN CRISIS."
GENTLEMEN, YOUR FUTURES ARE AT STAKE HERE. YOUR FORTUNES. YOUR FAMILIES. YOUR REPUTATIONS.
SO I ASK YOU.
DOES IT REALLY MATTER WHAT MY MOTIVATIONS ARE?
THANK YOU, PETE.
GENTLEMEN, YOU'VE HITCHED YOUR WAGON TO A HELL OF A PRODUCT.
THE ILLUSION OF HAPPINESS.
NO FACTORIES. NO UNIONS.
MOST OF THE HARD WORK IS DONE BY VOLUNTEERS.
FOR IMAGINARY TITLES AND CERTIFICATES.

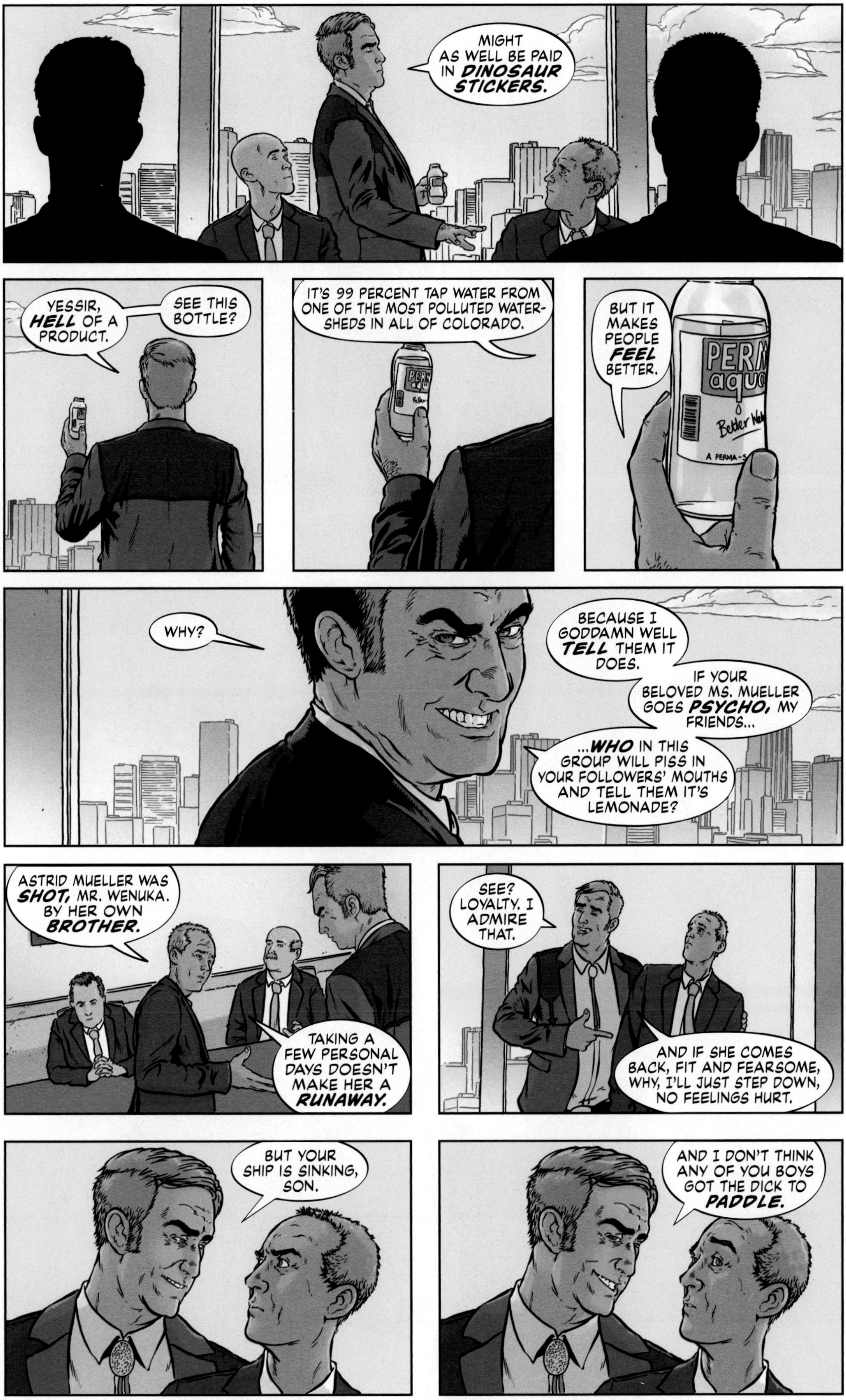

MIGHT AS WELL BE PAID IN DINOSAUR STICKERS.
YESSIR, HELL OF A PRODUCT.
SEE THIS BOTTLE?
IT'S 99 PERCENT TAP WATER FROM ONE OF THE MOST POLLUTED WATER-SHEDS IN ALL OF COLORADO.
PERMA aqua
BUT IT MAKES PEOPLE FEEL BETTER.
WHY?
BECAUSE I GODDAMN WELL TELL THEM IT DOES.
IF YOUR BELOVED MS. MUELLER GOES PSYCHO, MY FRIENDS...
...WHO IN THIS GROUP WILL PISS IN YOUR FOLLOWERS' MOUTHS AND TELL THEM IT'S LEMONADE?
ASTRID MUELLER WAS SHOT, MR. WENUKA. BY HER OWN BROTHER.
TAKING A FEW PERSONAL DAYS DOESN'T MAKE HER A RUNAWAY.
SEE? LOYALTY. I ADMIRE THAT.
AND IF SHE COMES BACK, FIT AND FEARSOME, WHY, I'LL JUST STEP DOWN, NO FEELINGS HURT.
BUT YOUR SHIP IS SINKING, SON.
AND I DON'T THINK ANY OF YOU BOYS GOT THE DICK TO PADDLE.

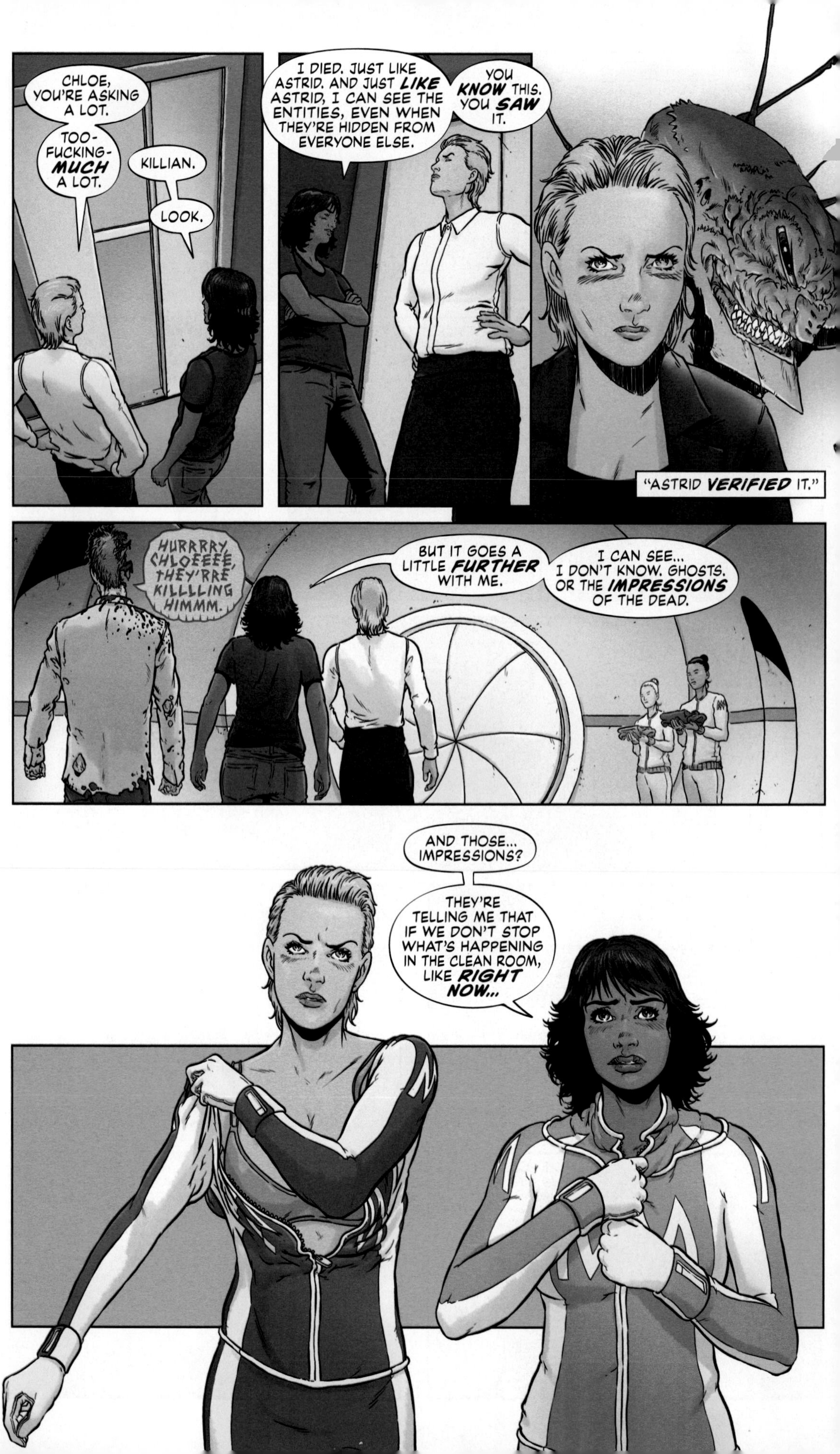

CHLOE, YOU'RE ASKING A LOT.
TOO-FUCKING-MUCH A LOT.
KILLIAN.
LOOK.
I DIED. JUST LIKE ASTRID. AND JUST LIKE ASTRID, I CAN SEE THE ENTITIES, EVEN WHEN THEY'RE HIDDEN FROM EVERYONE ELSE.
YOU KNOW THIS. YOU SAW IT.
"ASTRID VERIFIED IT."
HURRRRY, CHLOEEEEE, THEY'RRE KILLLLING HIMMMM.
BUT IT GOES A LITTLE FURTHER WITH ME.
I CAN SEE... I DON'T KNOW. GHOSTS. OR THE IMPRESSIONS OF THE DEAD.
AND THOSE... IMPRESSIONS?
THEY'RE TELLING ME THAT IF WE DON'T STOP WHAT'S HAPPENING IN THE CLEAN ROOM, LIKE RIGHT NOW...

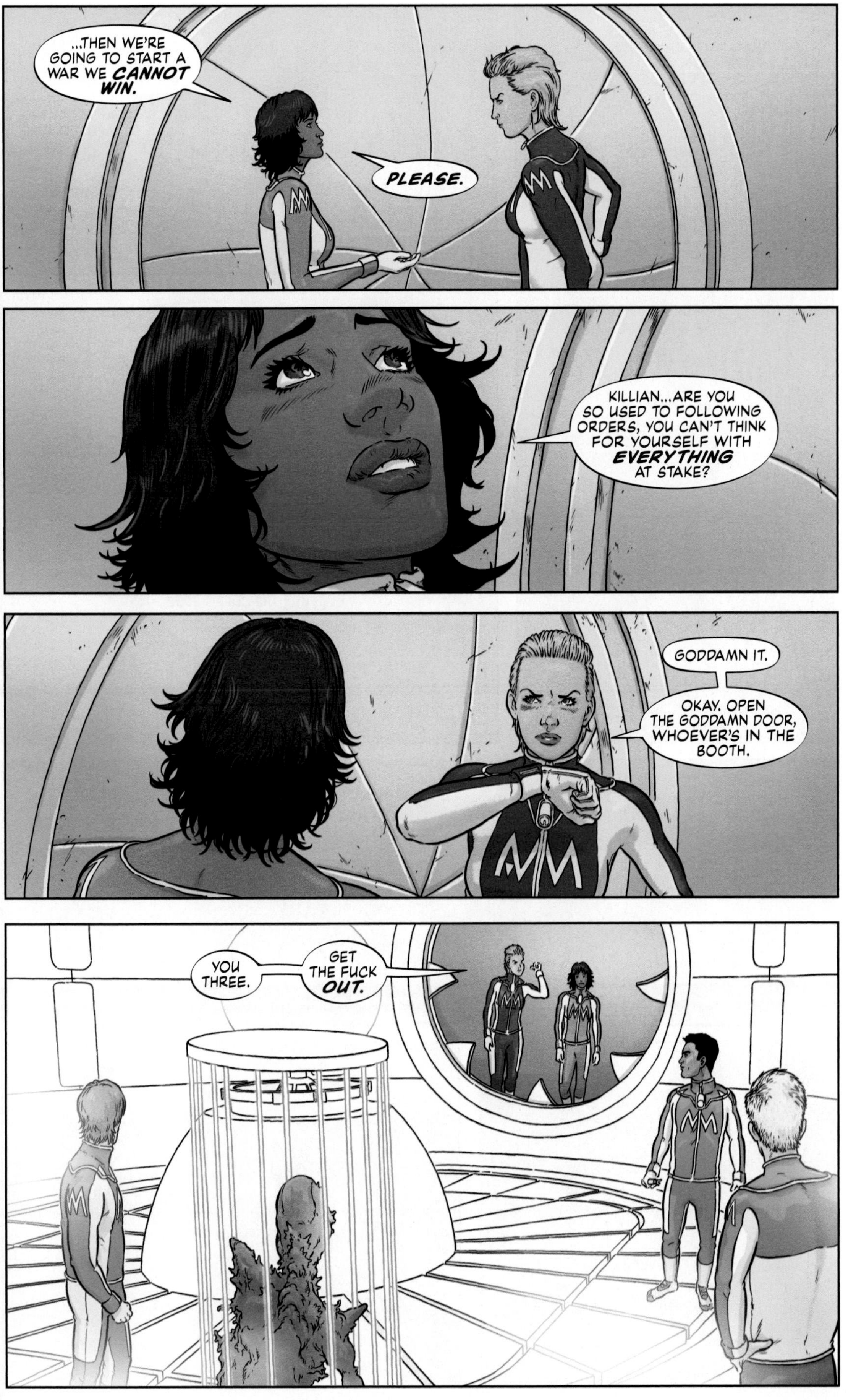
...THEN WE'RE GOING TO START A WAR WE CANNOT WIN.
PLEASE.
KILLIAN...ARE YOU SO USED TO FOLLOWING ORDERS, YOU CAN'T THINK FOR YOURSELF WITH EVERYTHING AT STAKE?
GODDAMN IT.
OKAY. OPEN THE GODDAMN DOOR, WHOEVER'S IN THE BOOTH.
YOU THREE.
GET THE FUCK OUT.

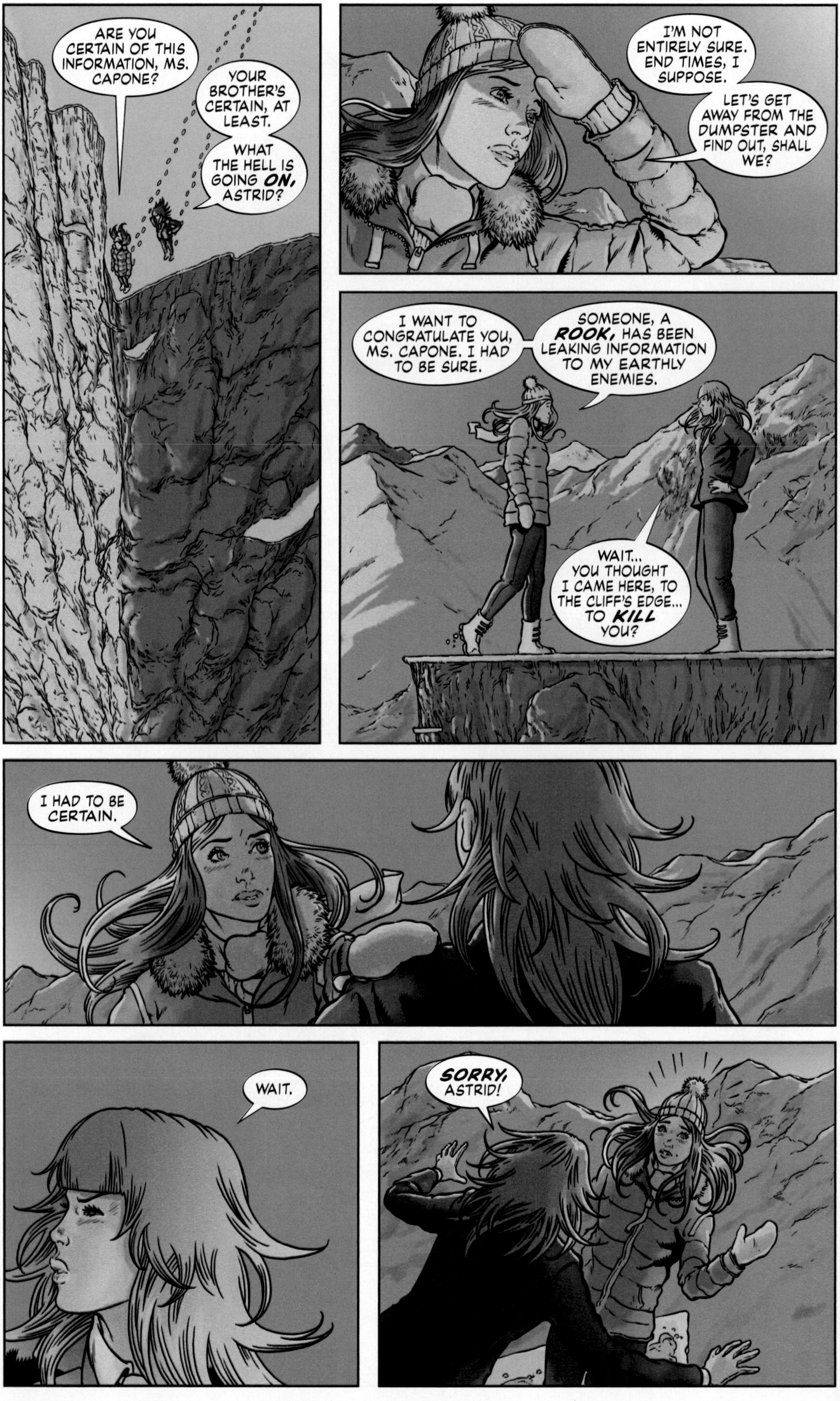
ARE YOU CERTAIN OF THIS INFORMATION, MS. CAPONE?
YOUR BROTHER'S CERTAIN, AT LEAST.
WHAT THE HELL IS GOING ON, ASTRID?
I'M NOT ENTIRELY SURE. END TIMES, I SUPPOSE.
LET'S GET AWAY FROM THE DUMPSTER AND FIND OUT, SHALL WE?
I WANT TO CONGRATULATE YOU, MS. CAPONE. I HAD TO BE SURE.
SOMEONE, A ROOK, HAS BEEN LEAKING INFORMATION TO MY EARTHLY ENEMIES.
WAIT... YOU THOUGHT I CAME HERE, TO THE CLIFF'S EDGE... TO KILL YOU?
I HAD TO BE CERTAIN.
WAIT.
SORRY, ASTRID!

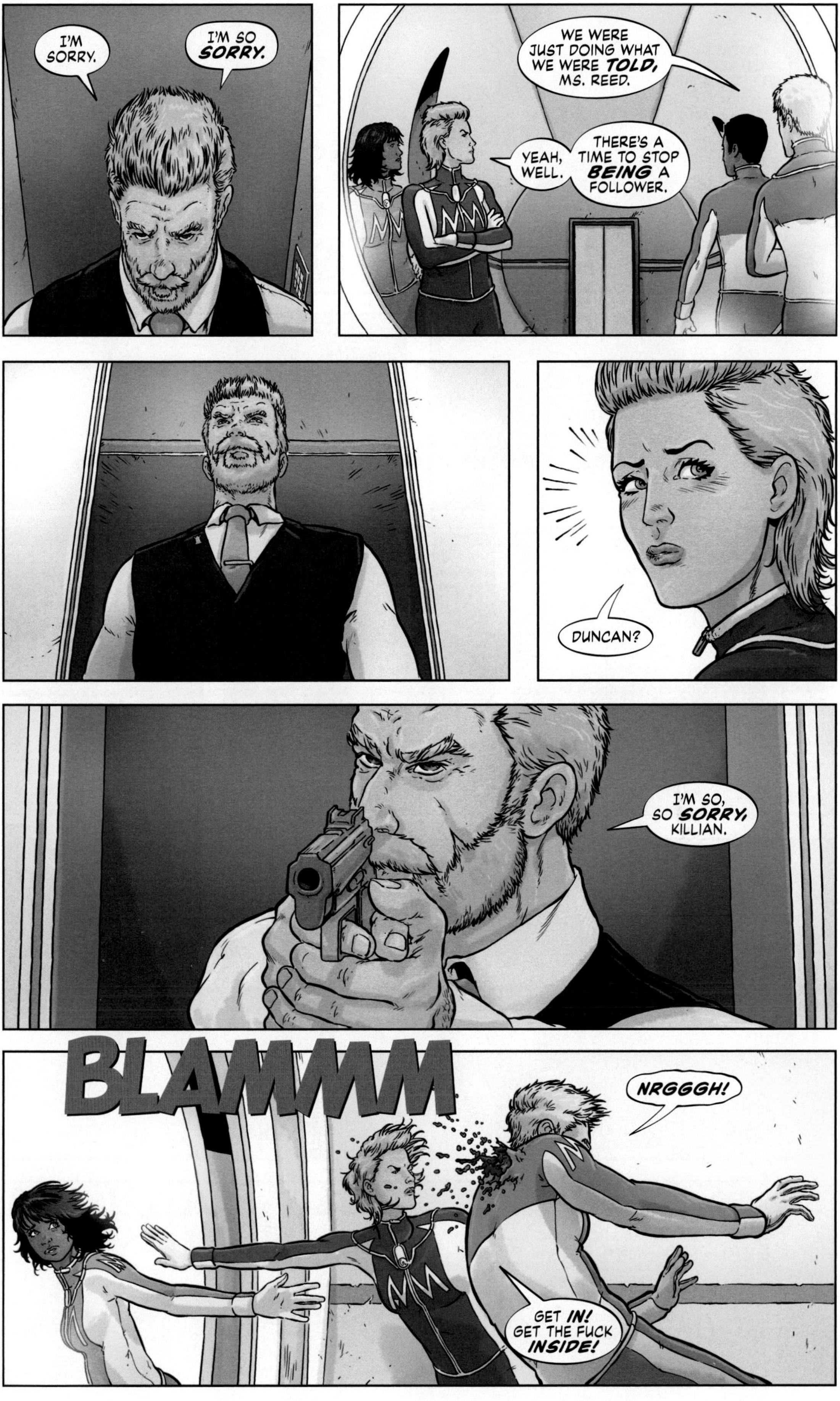
I'M SORRY.
I'M SO SORRY.
WE WERE JUST DOING WHAT WE WERE TOLD, MS. REED.
YEAH, WELL.
THERE'S A TIME TO STOP BEING A FOLLOWER.
DUNCAN?
I'M SO, SO SORRY, KILLIAN.
BLAMMM
NRGGGH!
GET IN! GET THE FUCK INSIDE!

WOULD YOU LET ME UP, PLEASE, MS. CAPONE?

SHUT UP. QUIET.

KRACKK

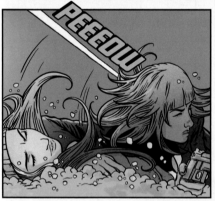

PEEEOW

WAS THAT BY CHANCE A--

A SNIPER, YES.

STAY DOWN.

:SNIFF:

IT'S ALL SHIT. EVERY-THING'S GONE TO SHIT.

I DON'T WISH TO QUESTION YOUR JUDGMENT, BUT ARE YOU CERTAIN YOU SHOULD BE STANDING--

ASTRID.

HUSH.

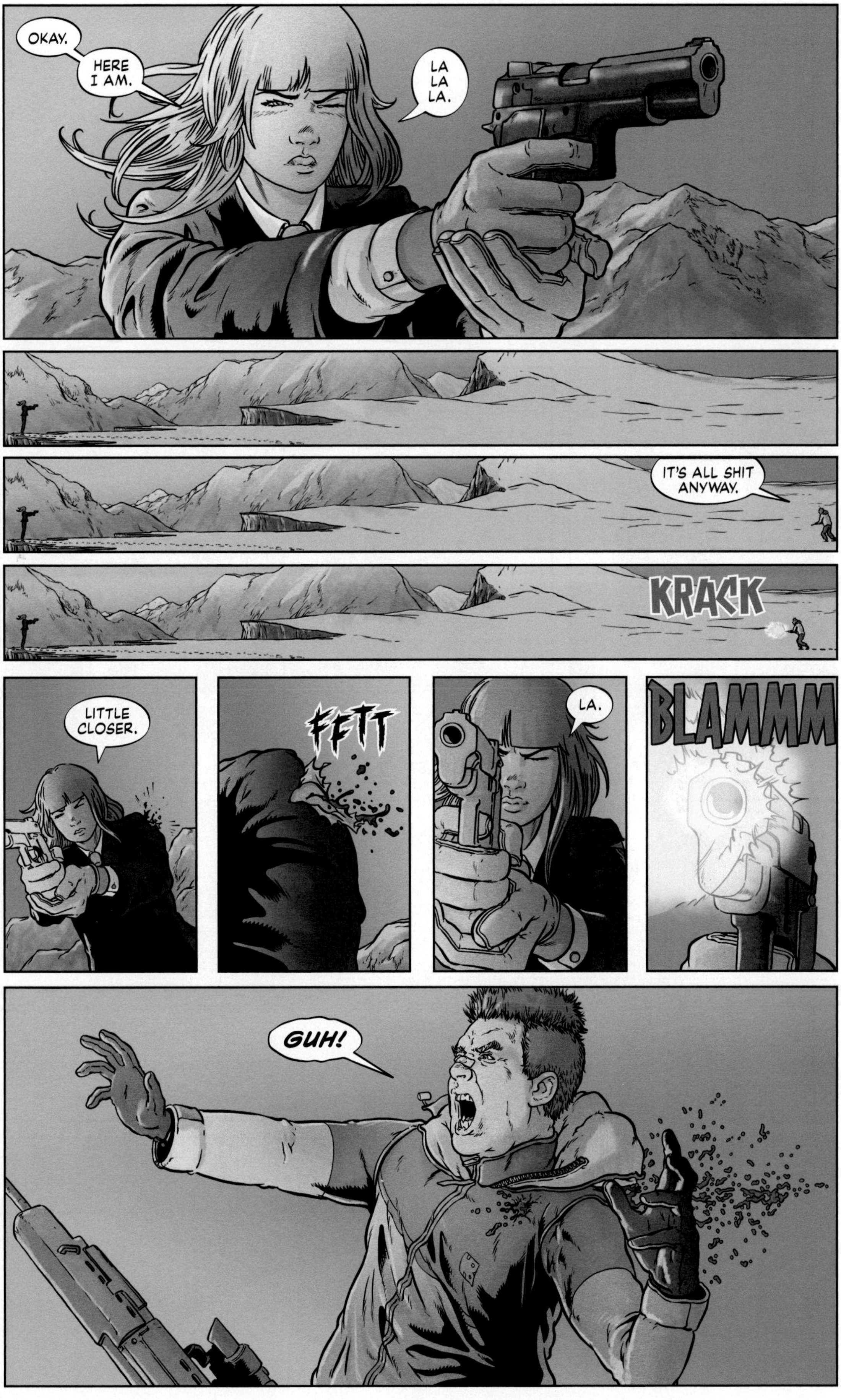

OKAY.
HERE I AM.
LA LA LA.
IT'S ALL SHIT ANYWAY.
KRACK
LITTLE CLOSER.
FFTT
LA.
BLAMMM
GUH!

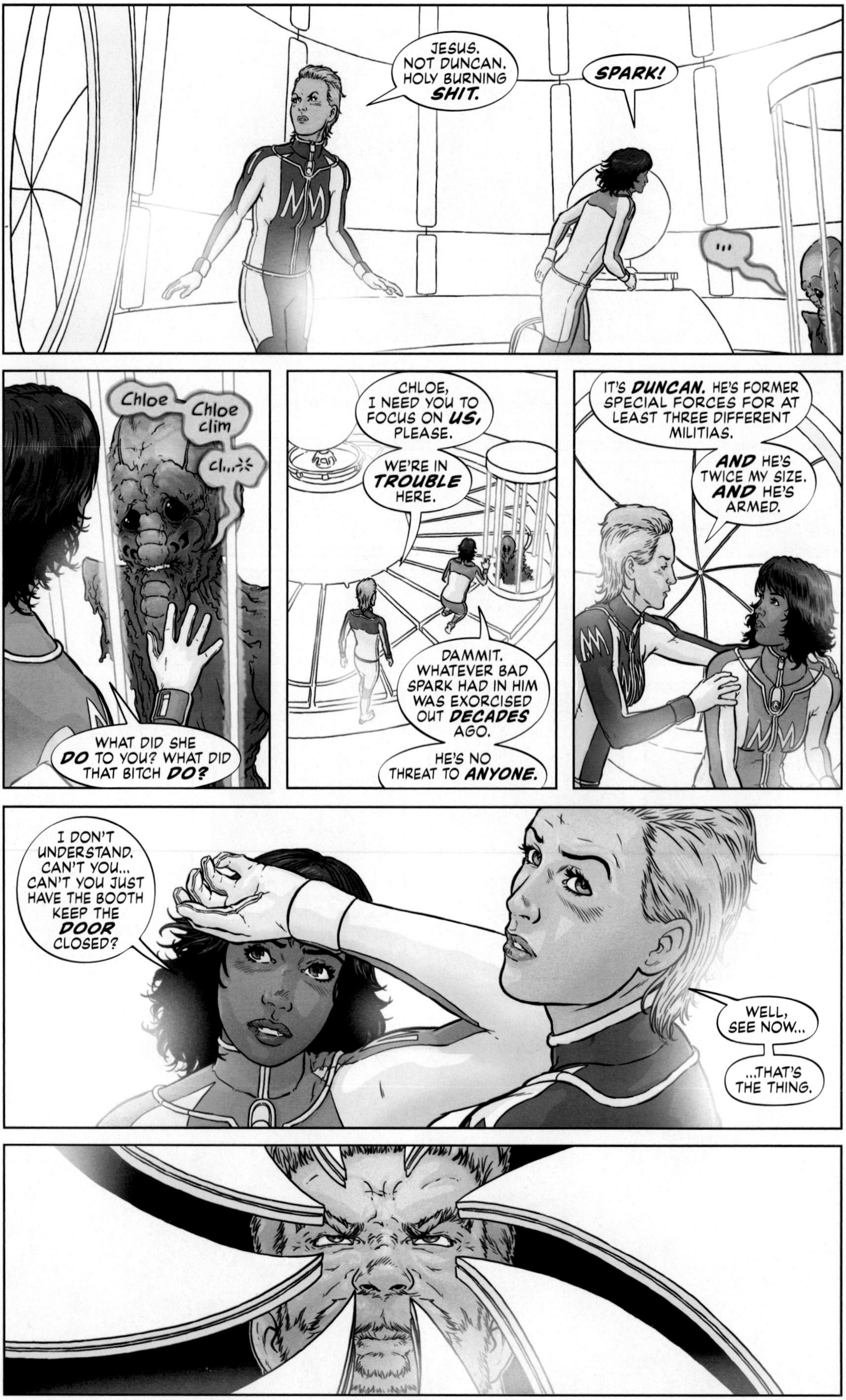
JESUS. NOT DUNCAN. HOLY BURNING SHIT.
SPARK!
...
Chloe
Chloe clim
Cl...
WHAT DID SHE DO TO YOU? WHAT DID THAT BITCH DO?
CHLOE, I NEED YOU TO FOCUS ON US, PLEASE.
WE'RE IN TROUBLE HERE.
DAMMIT. WHATEVER BAD SPARK HAD IN HIM WAS EXORCISED OUT DECADES AGO.
HE'S NO THREAT TO ANYONE.
IT'S DUNCAN. HE'S FORMER SPECIAL FORCES FOR AT LEAST THREE DIFFERENT MILITIAS.
AND HE'S TWICE MY SIZE. AND HE'S ARMED.
I DON'T UNDERSTAND. CAN'T YOU... CAN'T YOU JUST HAVE THE BOOTH KEEP THE DOOR CLOSED?
WELL, SEE NOW...
...THAT'S THE THING.

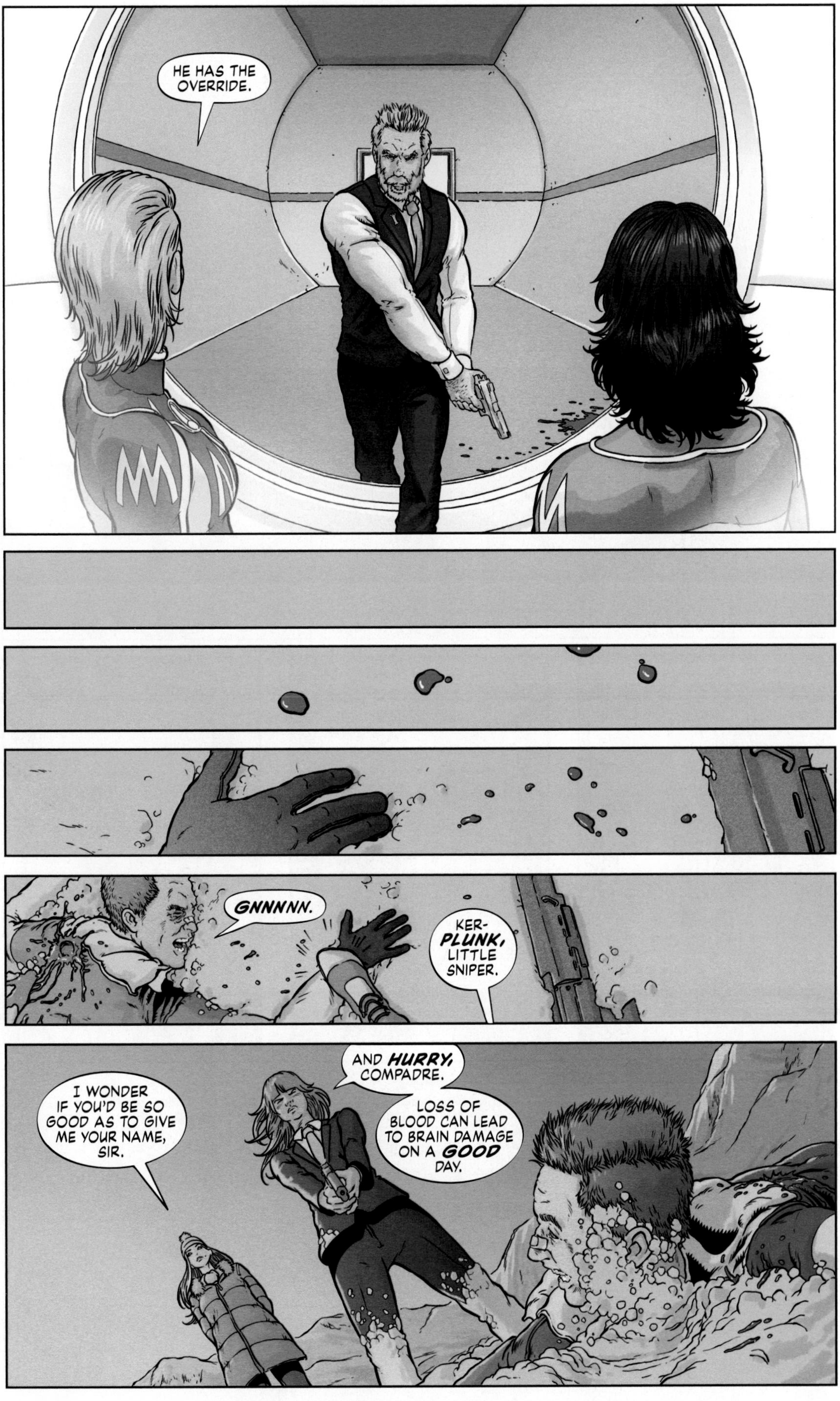
HE HAS THE OVERRIDE.
GNNNNN.
KER-PLUNK, LITTLE SNIPER.
I WONDER IF YOU'D BE SO GOOD AS TO GIVE ME YOUR NAME, SIR.
AND HURRY, COMPADRE.
LOSS OF BLOOD CAN LEAD TO BRAIN DAMAGE ON A GOOD DAY.

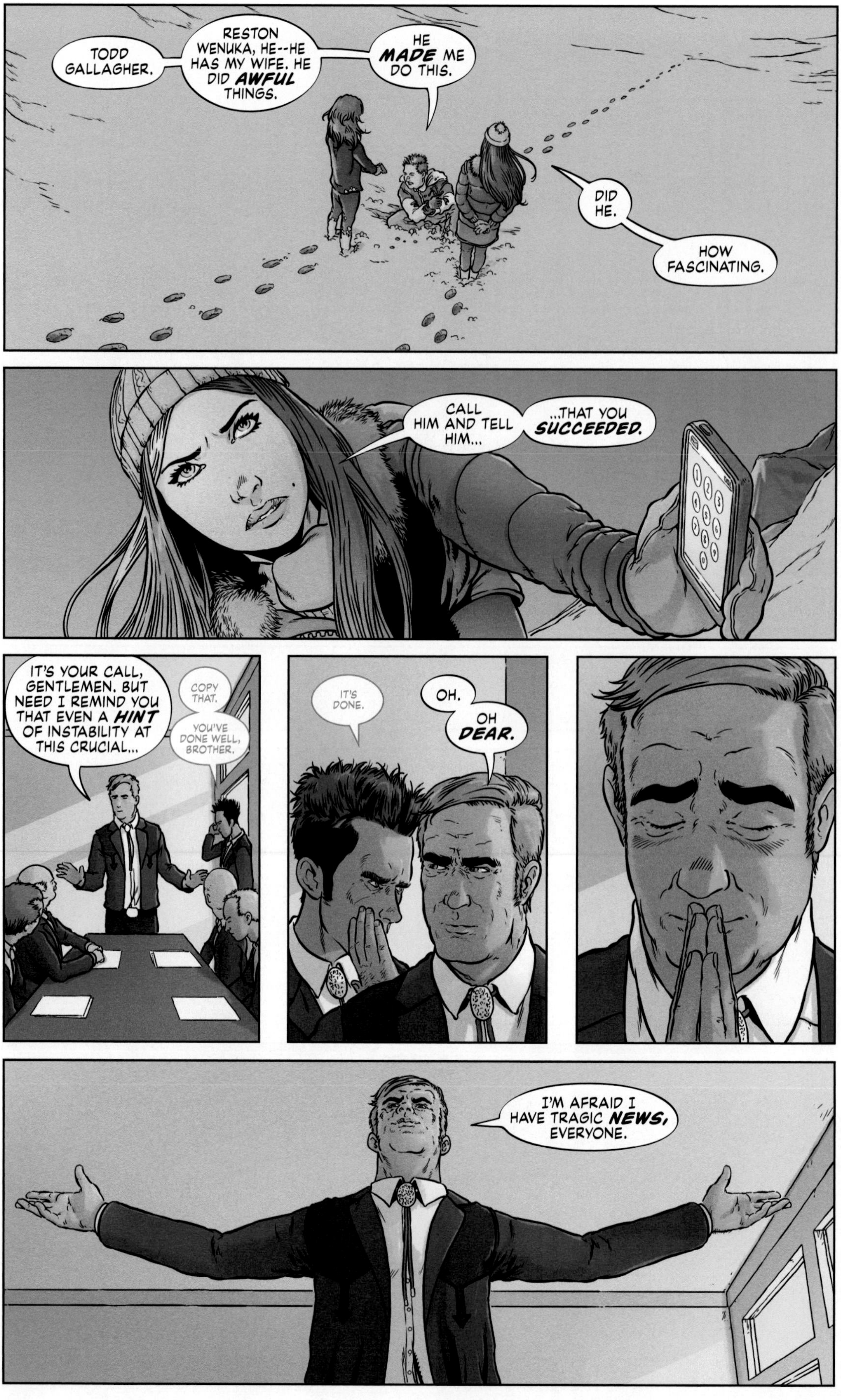
TODD GALLAGHER.
RESTON WENUKA, HE--HE HAS MY WIFE. HE DID AWFUL THINGS.
HE MADE ME DO THIS.
DID HE.
HOW FASCINATING.
CALL HIM AND TELL HIM...
...THAT YOU SUCCEEDED.
IT'S YOUR CALL, GENTLEMEN. BUT NEED I REMIND YOU THAT EVEN A HINT OF INSTABILITY AT THIS CRUCIAL...
COPY THAT.
YOU'VE DONE WELL, BROTHER.
IT'S DONE.
OH.
OH DEAR.
I'M AFRAID I HAVE TRAGIC NEWS, EVERYONE.

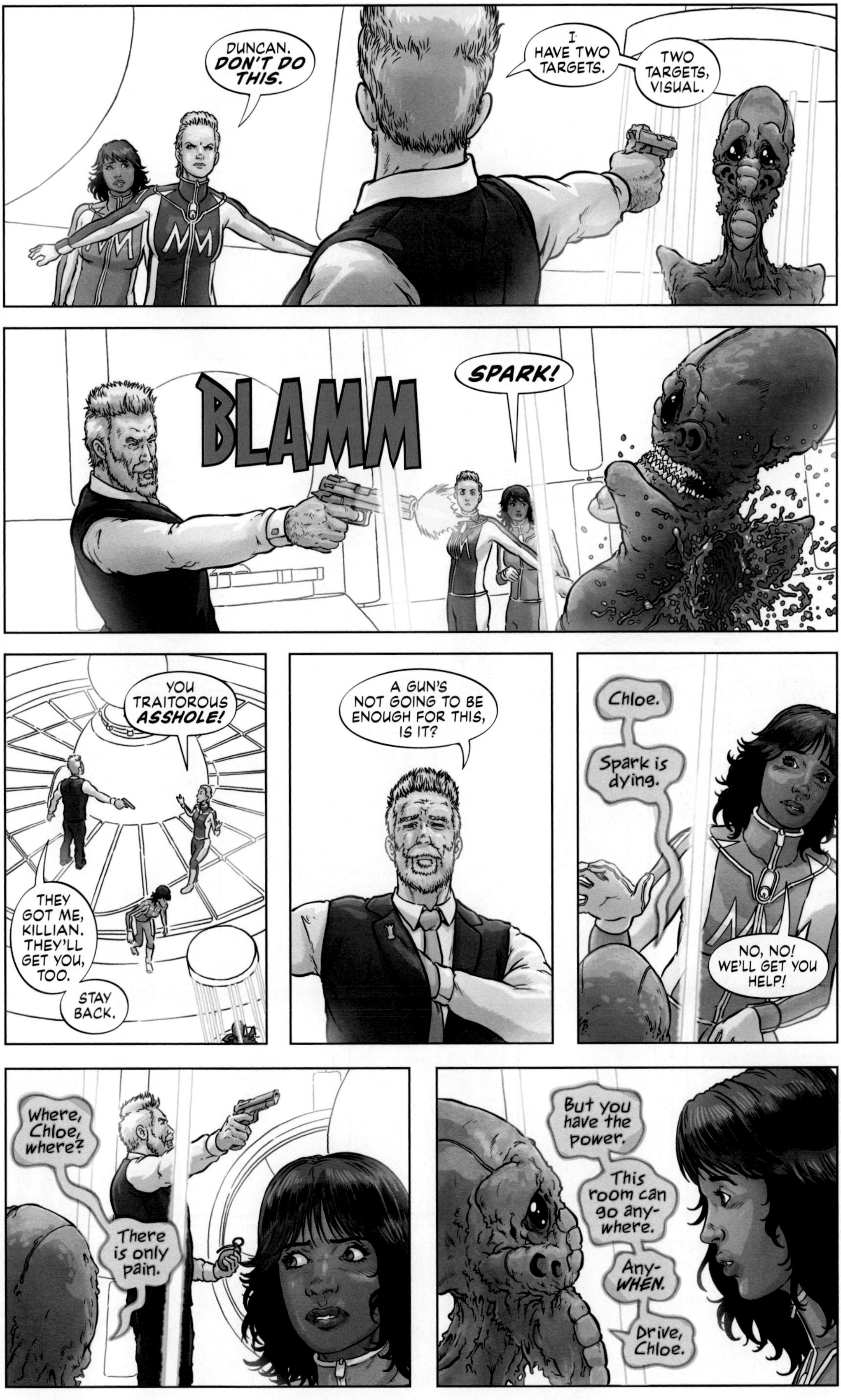
DUNCAN. **DON'T DO THIS.**
I- HAVE TWO TARGETS.
TWO TARGETS, VISUAL.
BLAMM
SPARK!
YOU TRAITOROUS **ASSHOLE!**
THEY GOT ME, KILLIAN. THEY'LL GET YOU, TOO.
STAY BACK.
A GUN'S NOT GOING TO BE ENOUGH FOR THIS, IS IT?
Chloe.
Spark is dying.
NO, NO! WE'LL GET YOU HELP!
Where, Chloe, where?
There is only pain.
But you have the power.
This room can go anywhere.
Any-**WHEN.**
Drive, Chloe.

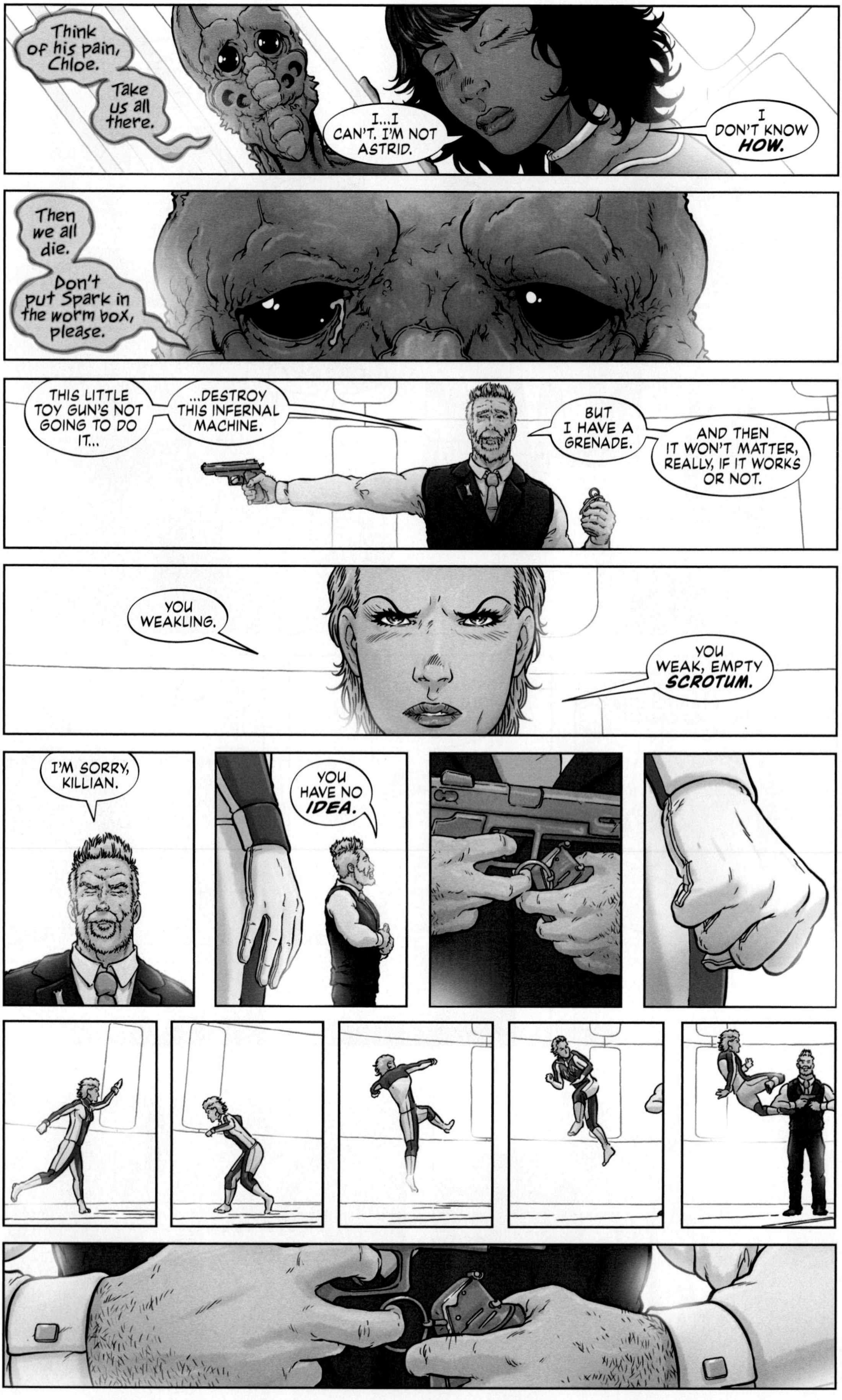
Think of his pain, Chloe.
Take us all there.
I...I CAN'T. I'M NOT ASTRID.
I DON'T KNOW *HOW.*
Then we all die.
Don't put Spark in the worm box, please.
THIS LITTLE TOY GUN'S NOT GOING TO DO IT...
...DESTROY THIS INFERNAL MACHINE.
BUT I HAVE A GRENADE.
AND THEN IT WON'T MATTER, REALLY, IF IT WORKS OR NOT.
YOU WEAKLING.
YOU WEAK, EMPTY *SCROTUM.*
I'M SORRY, KILLIAN.
YOU HAVE NO *IDEA.*

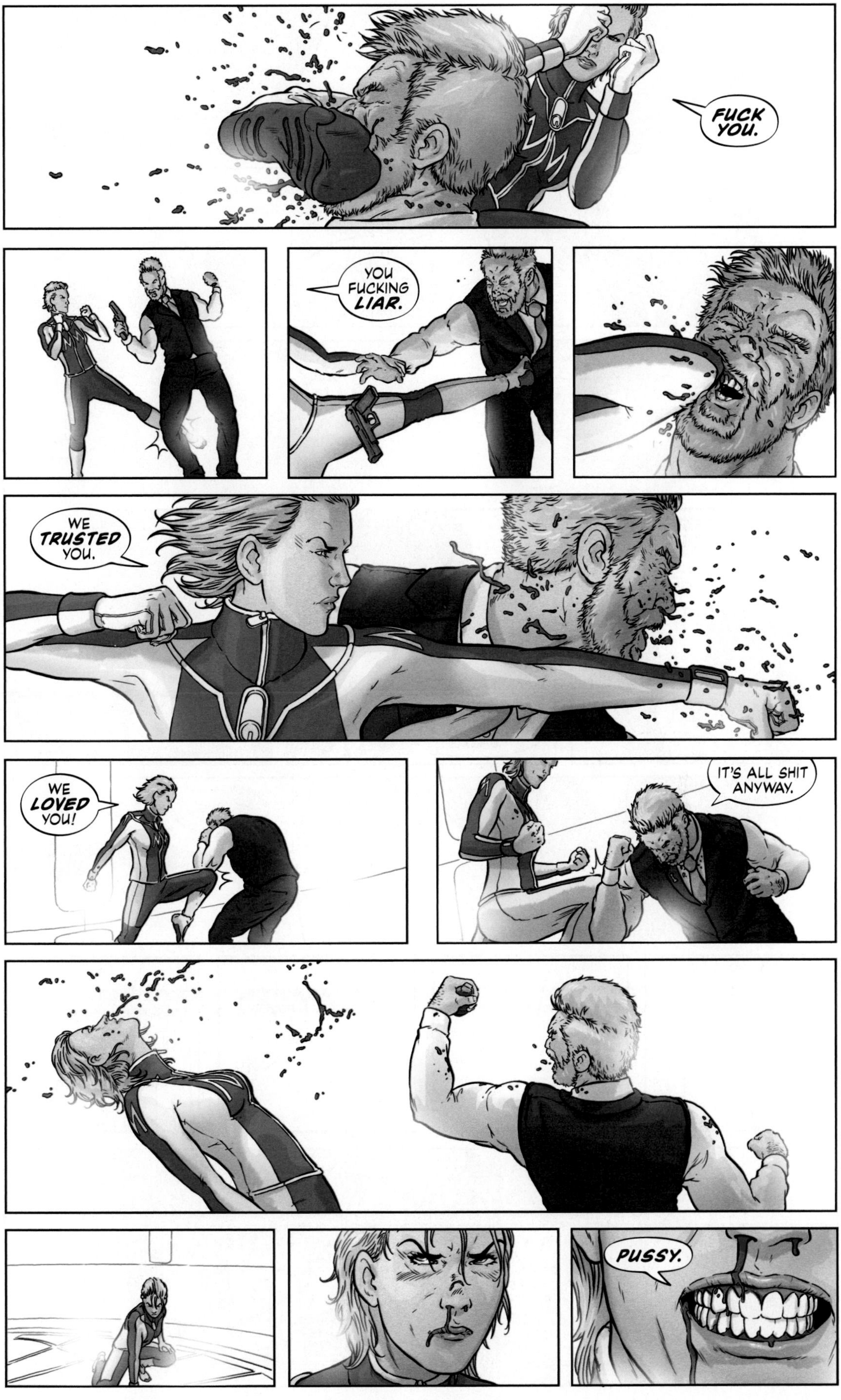
FUCK YOU.
YOU FUCKING LIAR.
WE TRUSTED YOU.
WE LOVED YOU!
IT'S ALL SHIT ANYWAY.
PUSSY.

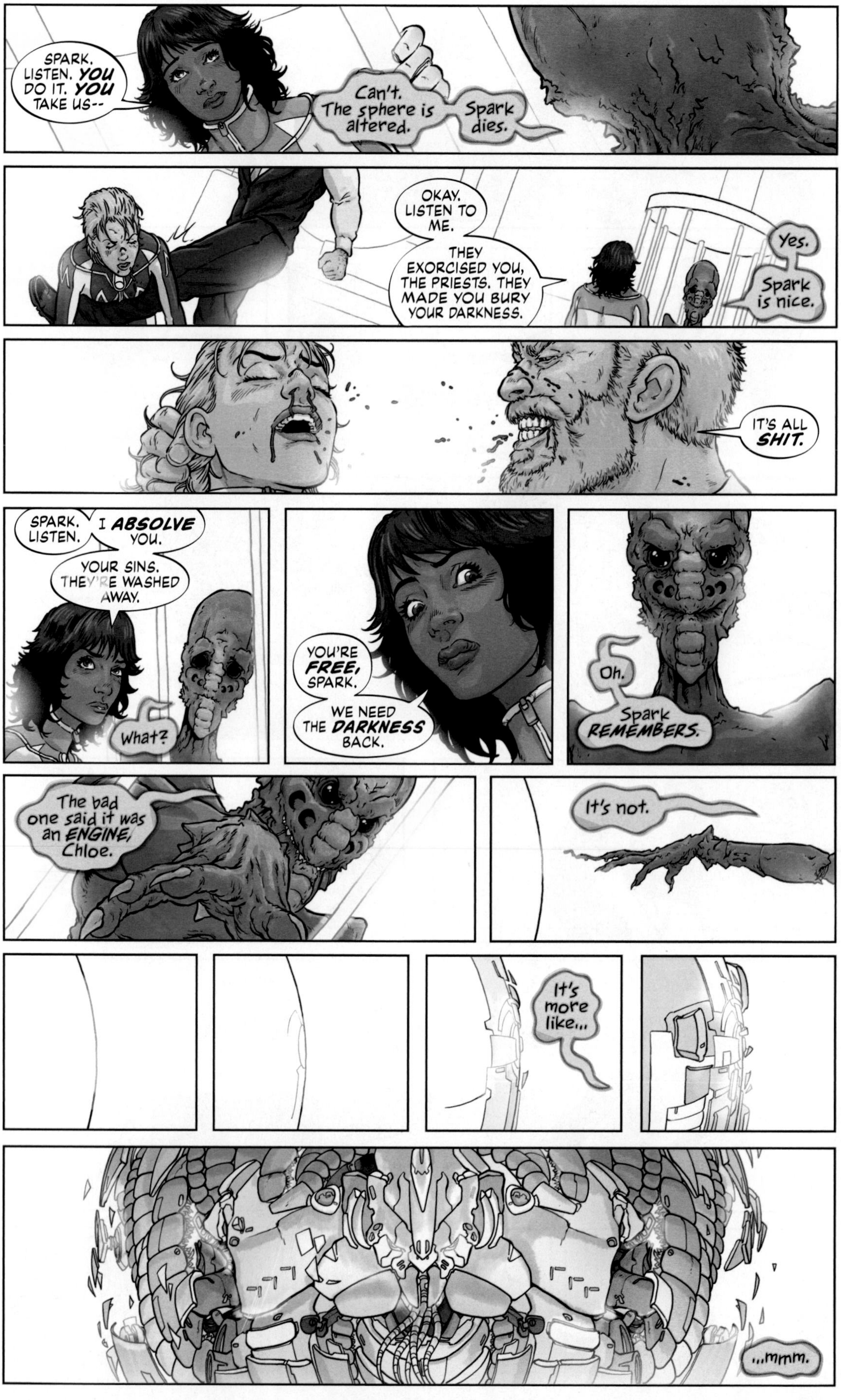
SPARK. LISTEN. YOU DO IT. YOU TAKE US--
Can't. The sphere is altered.
Spark dies.
OKAY. LISTEN TO ME.
THEY EXORCISED YOU, THE PRIESTS. THEY MADE YOU BURY YOUR DARKNESS.
Yes.
Spark is nice.
IT'S ALL SHIT.
SPARK. LISTEN.
I ABSOLVE YOU.
YOUR SINS. THEY'RE WASHED AWAY.
What?
YOU'RE FREE, SPARK.
WE NEED THE DARKNESS BACK.
Oh.
Spark REMEMBERS.
The bad one said it was an ENGINE, Chloe.
It's not.
It's more like...
...mmm.

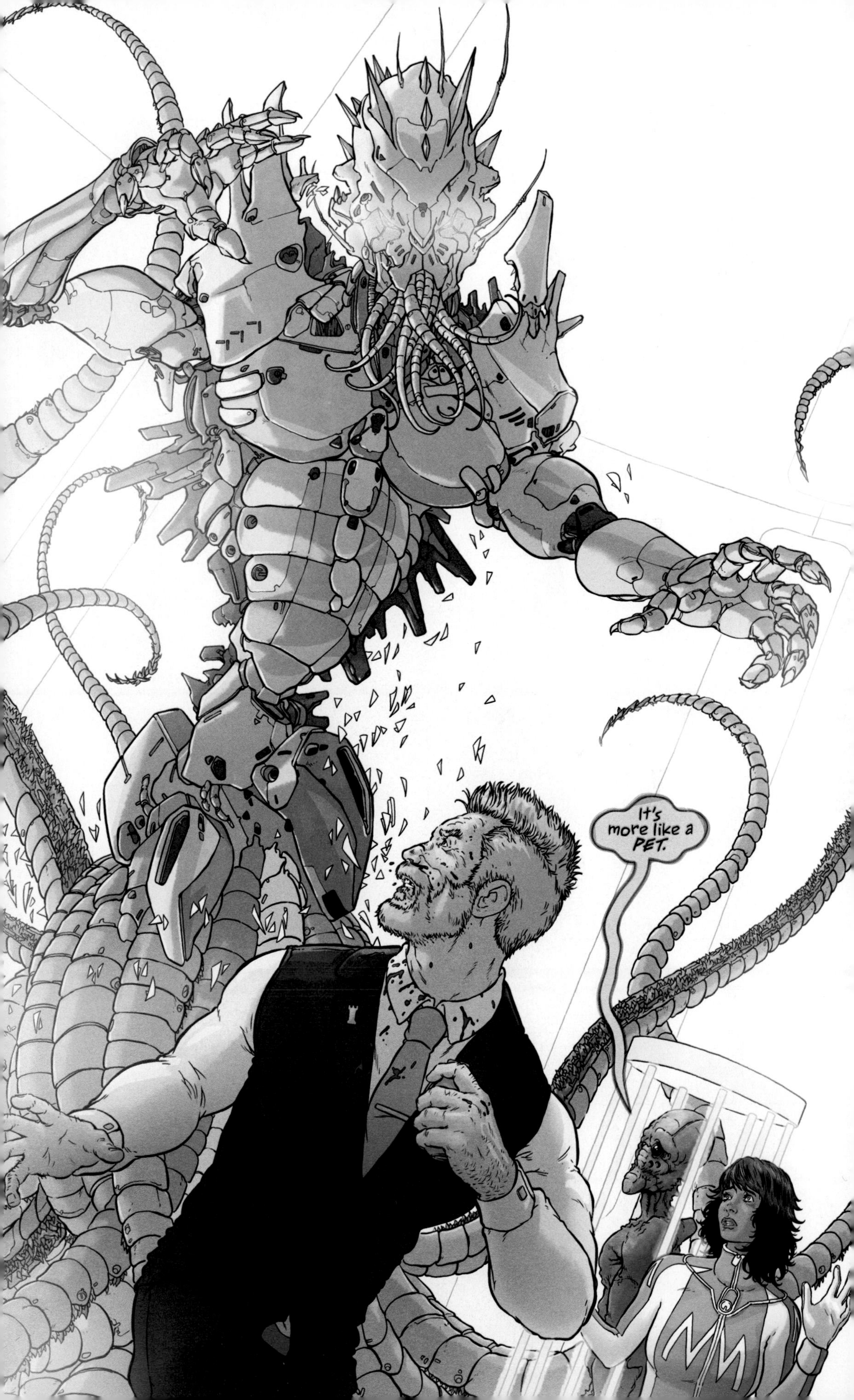
It's more like a PET.

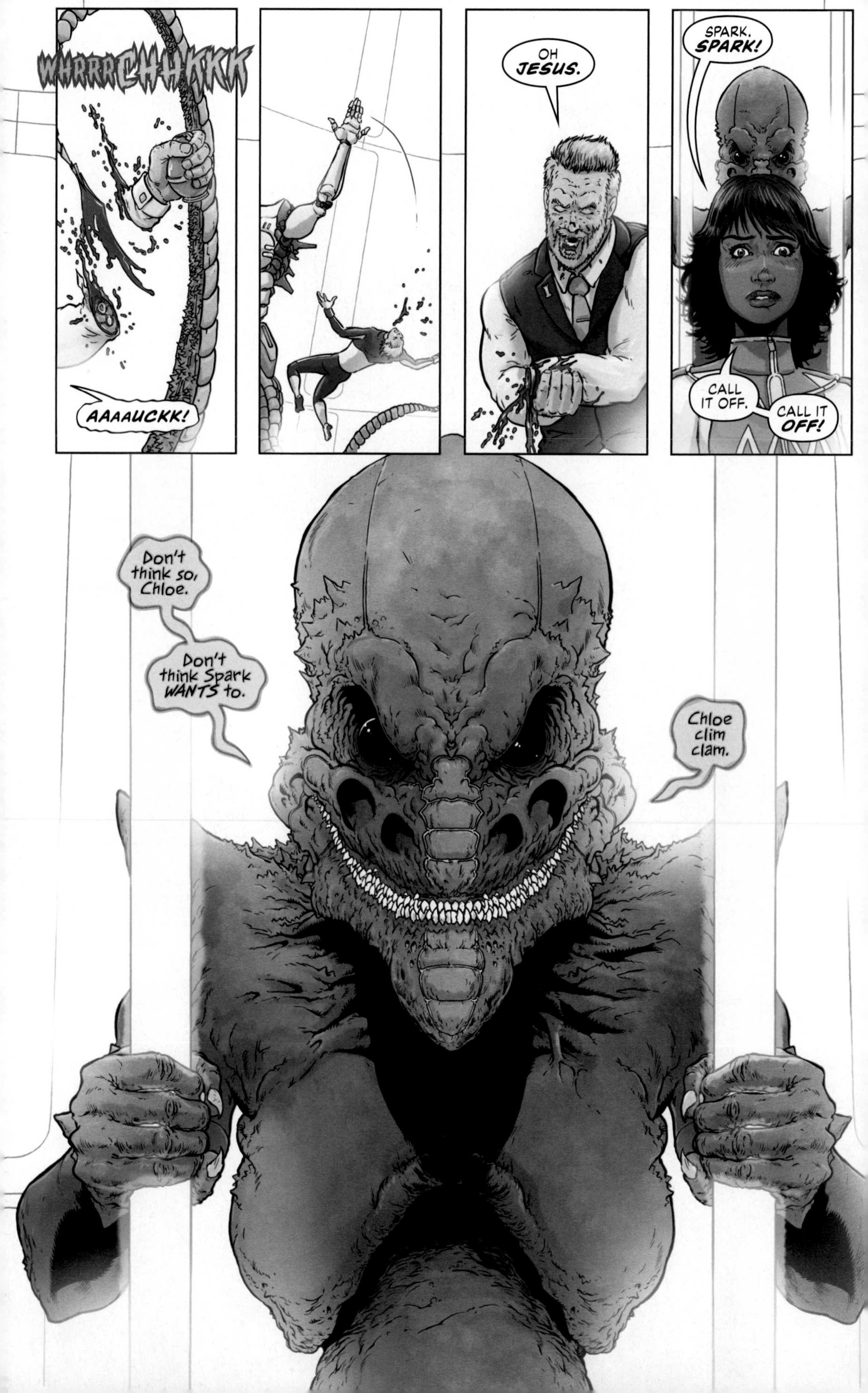
WHRRRCHHKKK
AAAAUCKK!
OH JESUS.
SPARK. SPARK!
CALL IT OFF.
CALL IT OFF!
Don't think so, Chloe.
Don't think Spark WANTS to.
Chloe clim clam.

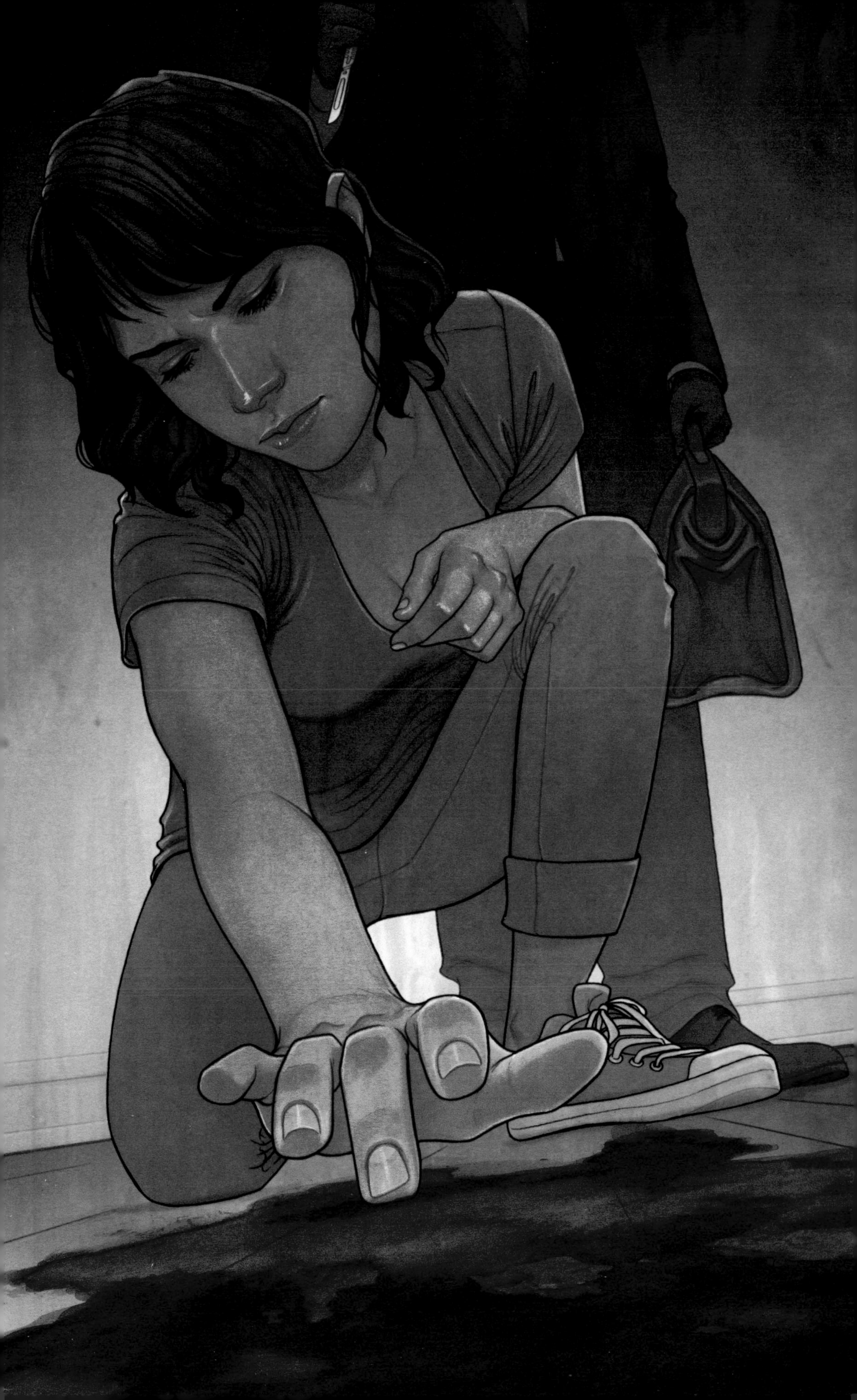

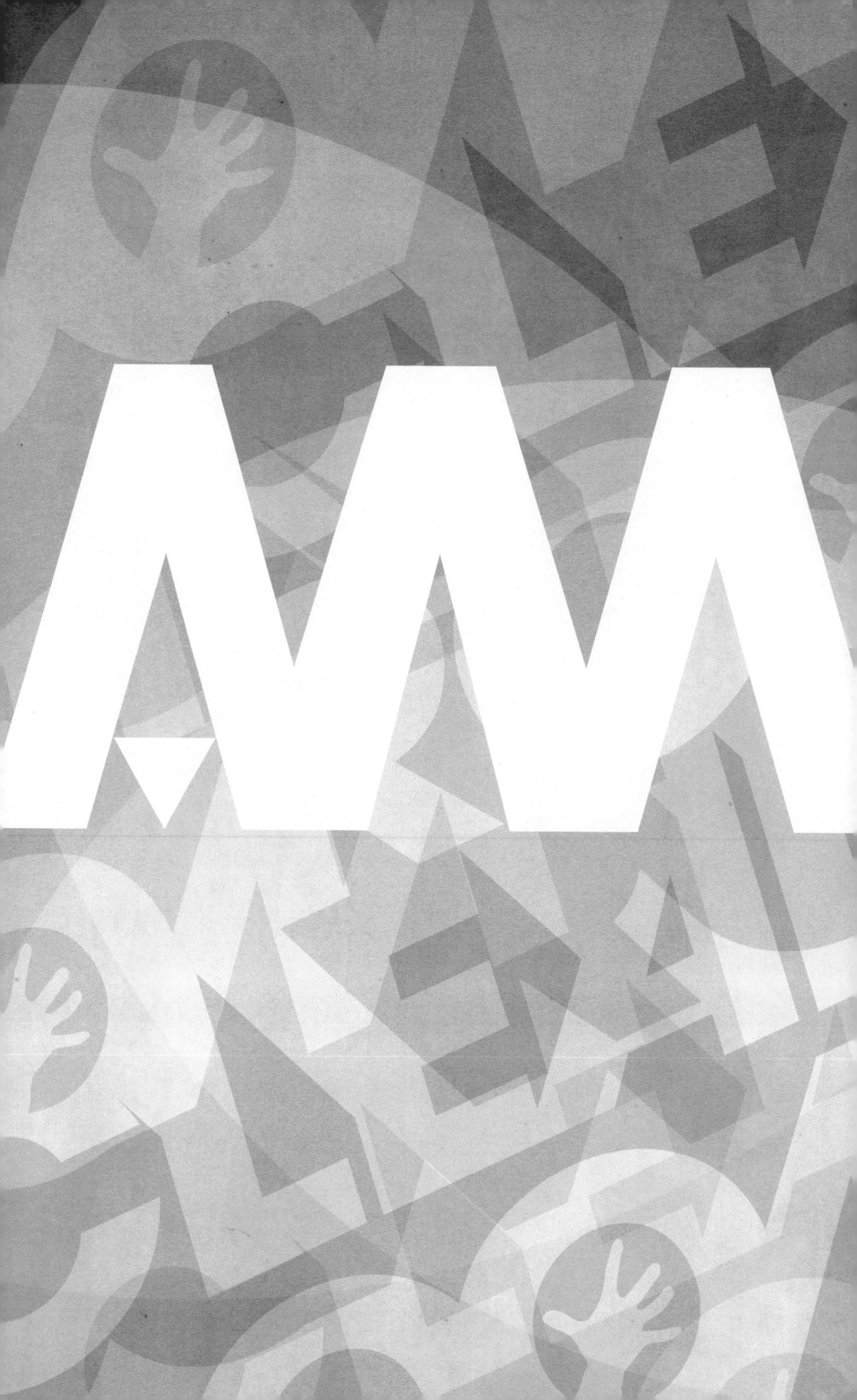

EINBAHNSTRAßE, GERMANY, 23 YEARS AGO.

‹IS THIS YOUR WAY OF DEALING WITH A PROBLEM, ASTRID?›*

‹REFUSING TO SPEAK TO YOUR THERAPIST?›

‹IT WASN'T MY IDEA TO BE HERE, DR. LEHMANN.›

*Translated from German. --Editor

‹I SEE NO REASON FOR EXCESSIVE FORMALITY.›

‹YOU MAY REFER TO ME AS INGRID.›

‹WHAT *ARE* YOU HERE FOR, YOUNG LADY, DO YOU IMAGINE?›

‹WELL, I EXPECT IT'S BECAUSE MY FAMILY BELIEVES I STABBED MY FATHER.›

‹BUT YOU DISAGREE.›

‹I DO.›

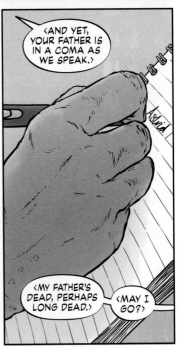

‹AND YET, YOUR FATHER IS IN A COMA AS WE SPEAK.›

‹MY FATHER'S DEAD, PERHAPS LONG DEAD.›

‹MAY I GO?›

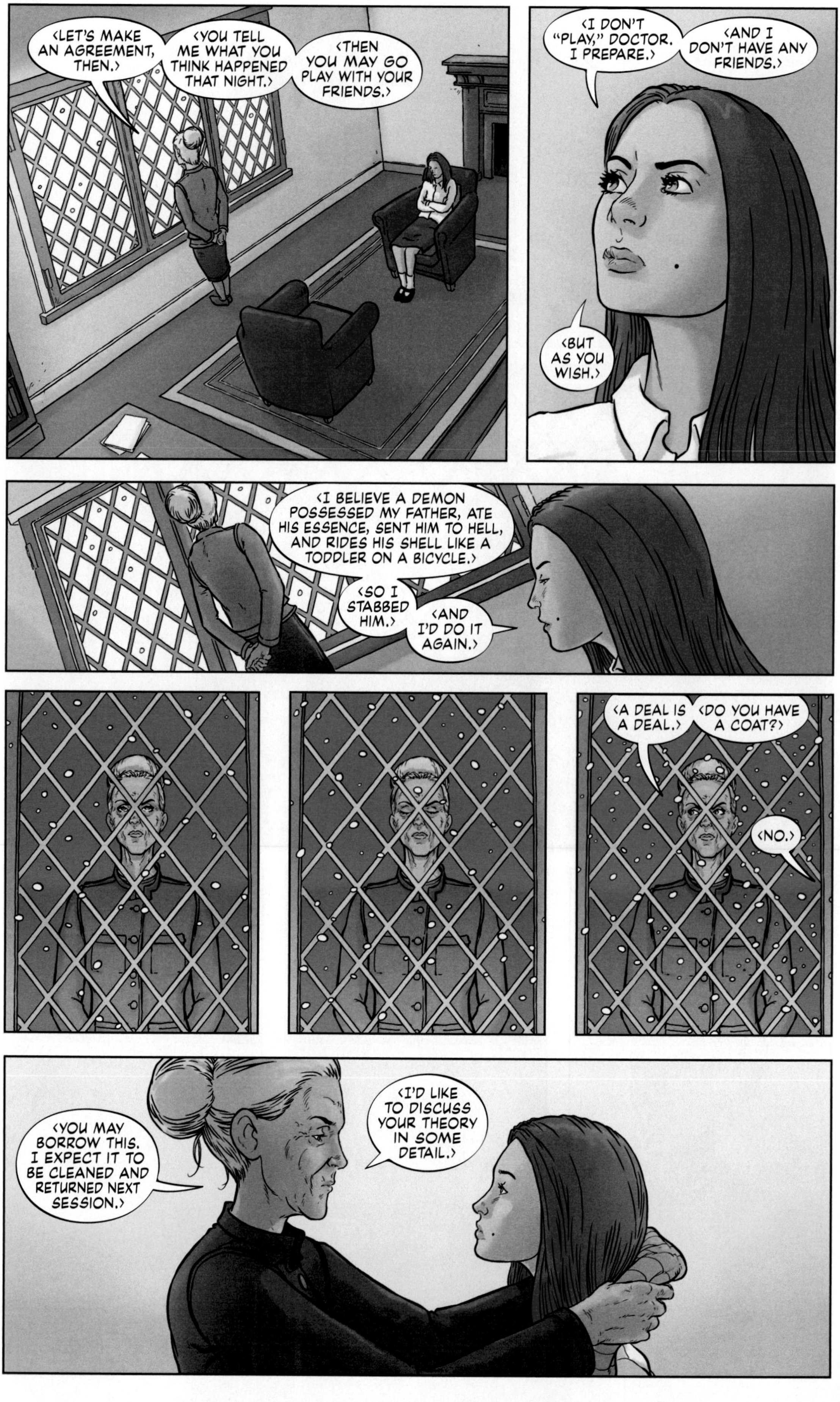
‹LET'S MAKE AN AGREEMENT, THEN.›
‹YOU TELL ME WHAT YOU THINK HAPPENED THAT NIGHT.›
‹THEN YOU MAY GO PLAY WITH YOUR FRIENDS.›
‹I DON'T "PLAY," DOCTOR. I PREPARE.›
‹AND I DON'T HAVE ANY FRIENDS.›
‹BUT AS YOU WISH.›
‹I BELIEVE A DEMON POSSESSED MY FATHER, ATE HIS ESSENCE, SENT HIM TO HELL, AND RIDES HIS SHELL LIKE A TODDLER ON A BICYCLE.›
‹SO I STABBED HIM.›
‹AND I'D DO IT AGAIN.›
‹A DEAL IS A DEAL.›
‹DO YOU HAVE A COAT?›
‹NO.›
‹YOU MAY BORROW THIS. I EXPECT IT TO BE CLEANED AND RETURNED NEXT SESSION.›
‹I'D LIKE TO DISCUSS YOUR THEORY IN SOME DETAIL.›

THE DAMNED LAY DYING

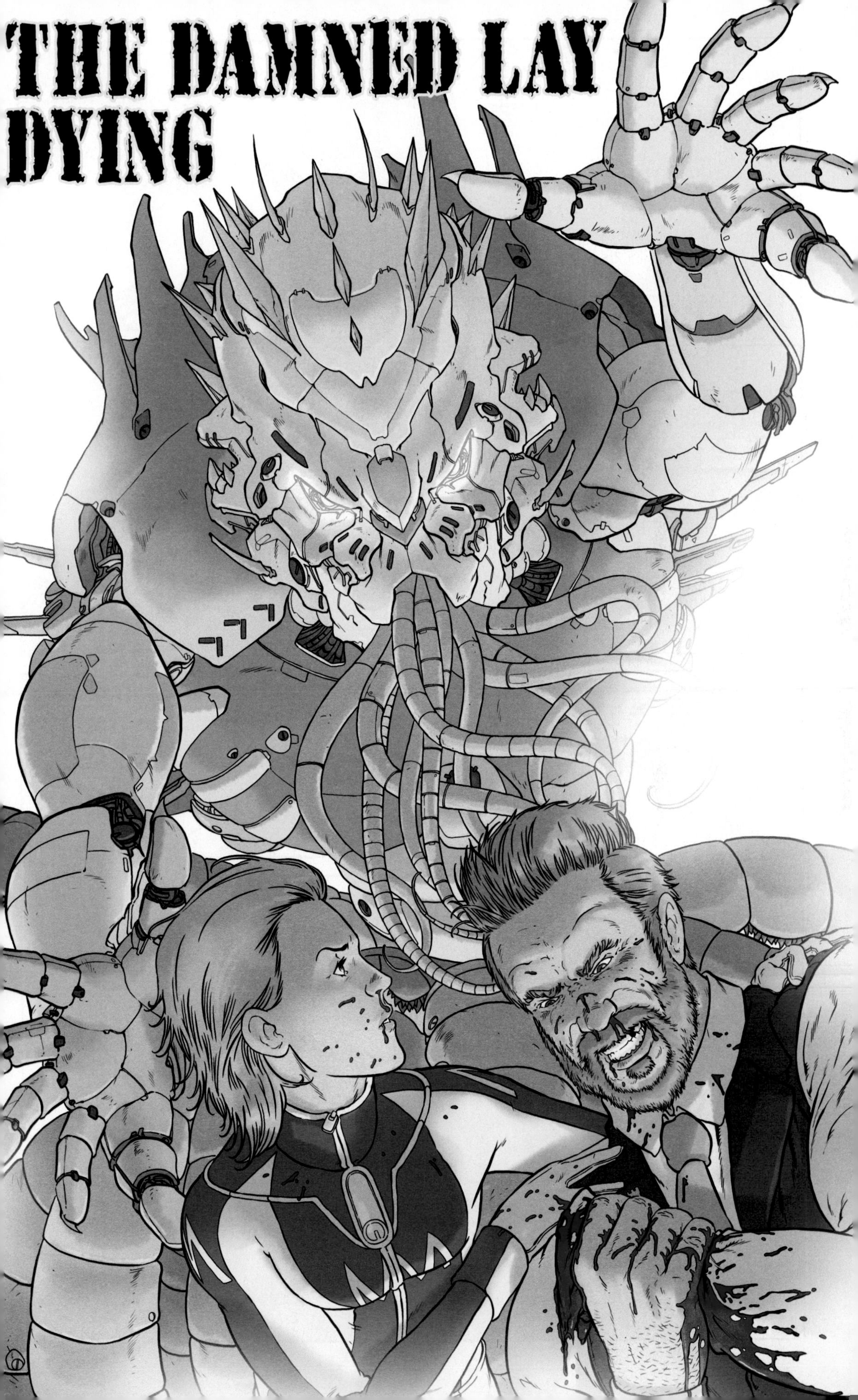

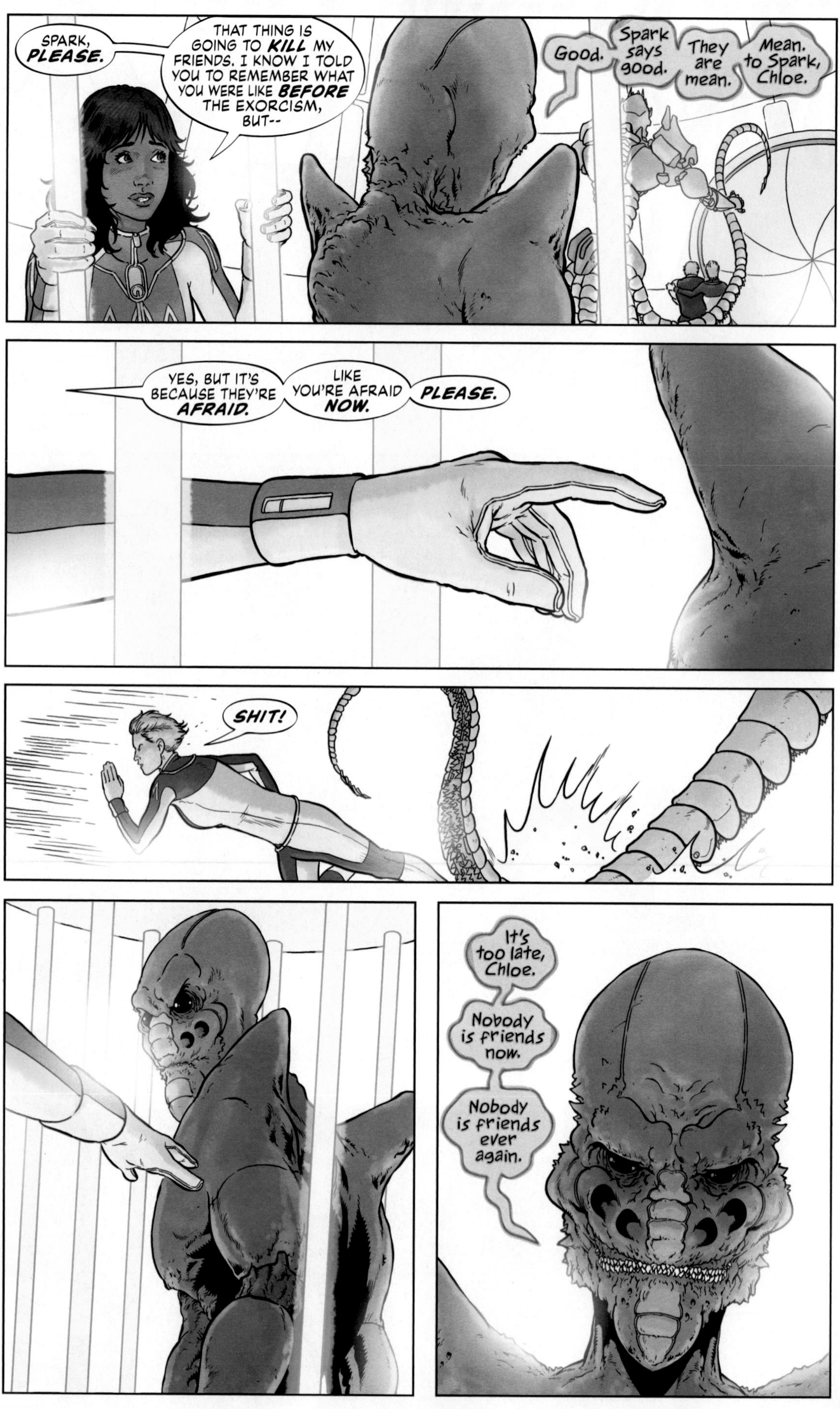
SPARK, PLEASE.
THAT THING IS GOING TO KILL MY FRIENDS. I KNOW I TOLD YOU TO REMEMBER WHAT YOU WERE LIKE BEFORE THE EXORCISM, BUT--
Good.
Spark says good.
They are mean.
Mean. to Spark, Chloe.
YES, BUT IT'S BECAUSE THEY'RE AFRAID.
LIKE YOU'RE AFRAID NOW.
PLEASE.
SHIT!
It's too late, Chloe.
Nobody is friends now.
Nobody is friends ever again.

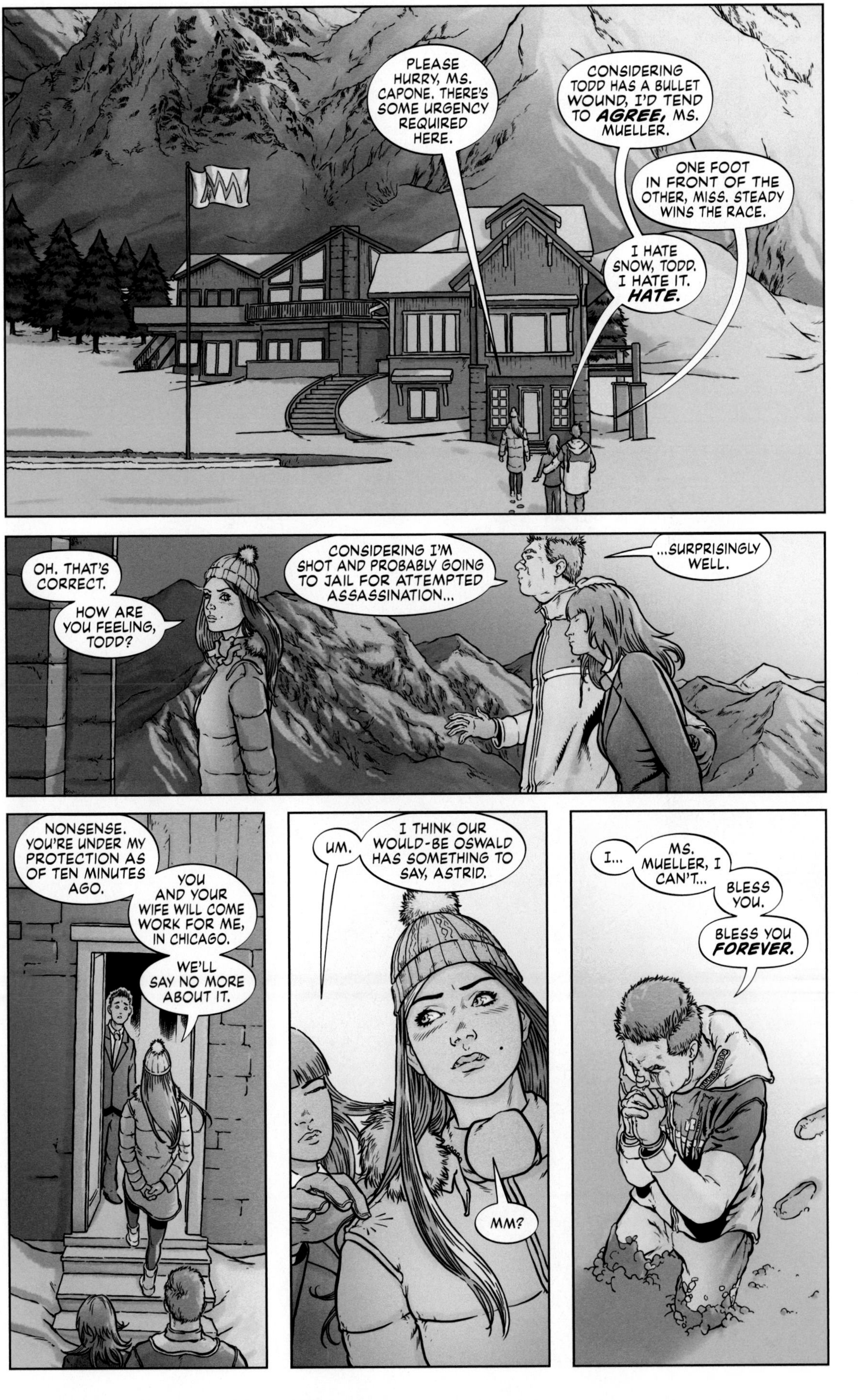
PLEASE HURRY, MS. CAPONE. THERE'S SOME URGENCY REQUIRED HERE.
CONSIDERING TODD HAS A BULLET WOUND, I'D TEND TO AGREE, MS. MUELLER.
ONE FOOT IN FRONT OF THE OTHER, MISS. STEADY WINS THE RACE.
I HATE SNOW, TODD. I HATE IT. HATE.
OH. THAT'S CORRECT.
HOW ARE YOU FEELING, TODD?
CONSIDERING I'M SHOT AND PROBABLY GOING TO JAIL FOR ATTEMPTED ASSASSINATION...
...SURPRISINGLY WELL.
NONSENSE. YOU'RE UNDER MY PROTECTION AS OF TEN MINUTES AGO.
YOU AND YOUR WIFE WILL COME WORK FOR ME, IN CHICAGO.
WE'LL SAY NO MORE ABOUT IT.
UM.
I THINK OUR WOULD-BE OSWALD HAS SOMETHING TO SAY, ASTRID.
MM?
I...
MS. MUELLER, I CAN'T...
BLESS YOU.
BLESS YOU FOREVER.

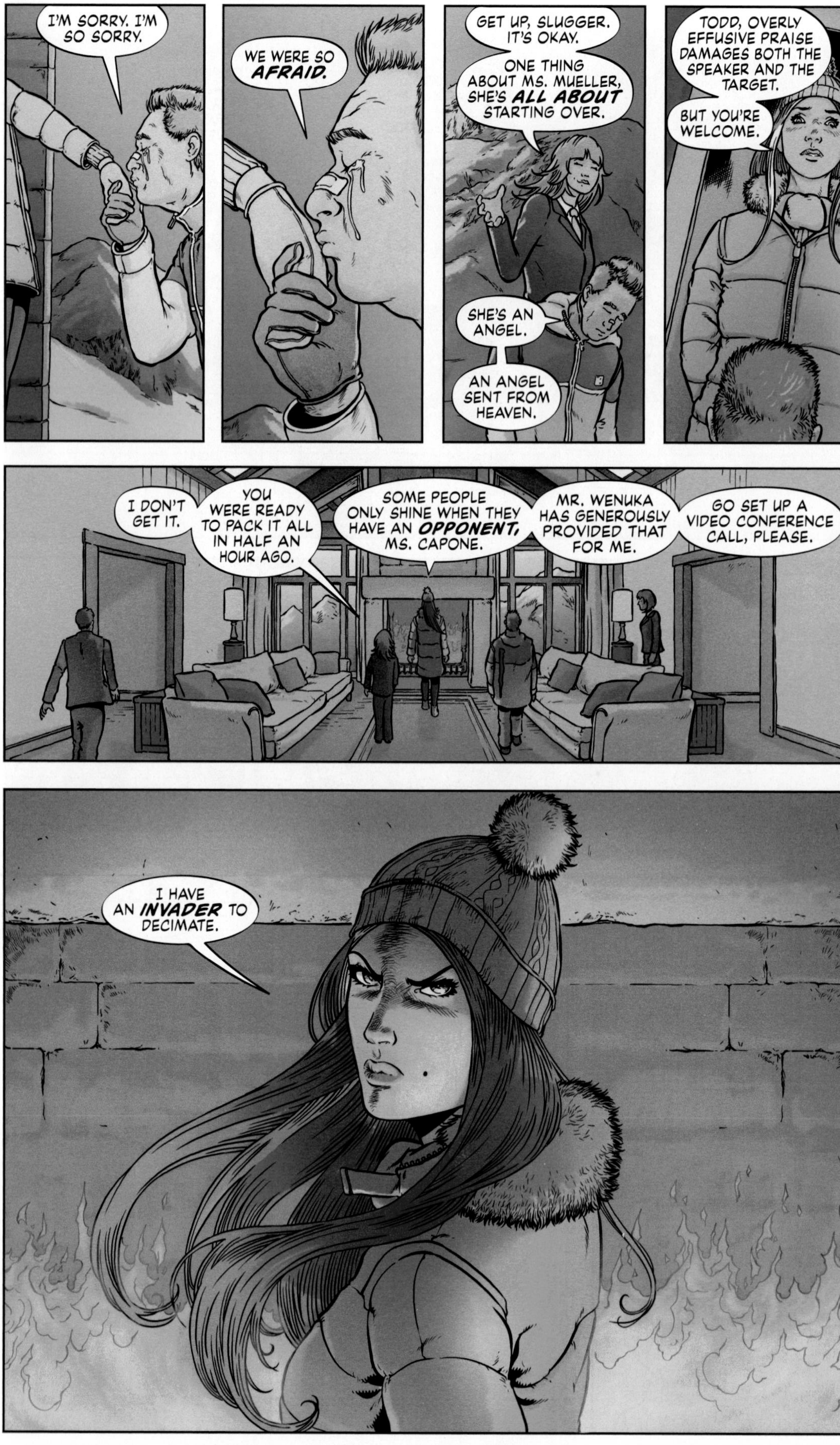
I'M SORRY. I'M SO SORRY.
WE WERE SO AFRAID.
GET UP, SLUGGER. IT'S OKAY.
ONE THING ABOUT MS. MUELLER, SHE'S ALL ABOUT STARTING OVER.
SHE'S AN ANGEL.
AN ANGEL SENT FROM HEAVEN.
TODD, OVERLY EFFUSIVE PRAISE DAMAGES BOTH THE SPEAKER AND THE TARGET.
BUT YOU'RE WELCOME.
I DON'T GET IT.
YOU WERE READY TO PACK IT ALL IN HALF AN HOUR AGO.
SOME PEOPLE ONLY SHINE WHEN THEY HAVE AN OPPONENT, MS. CAPONE.
MR. WENUKA HAS GENEROUSLY PROVIDED THAT FOR ME.
GO SET UP A VIDEO CONFERENCE CALL, PLEASE.
I HAVE AN INVADER TO DECIMATE.

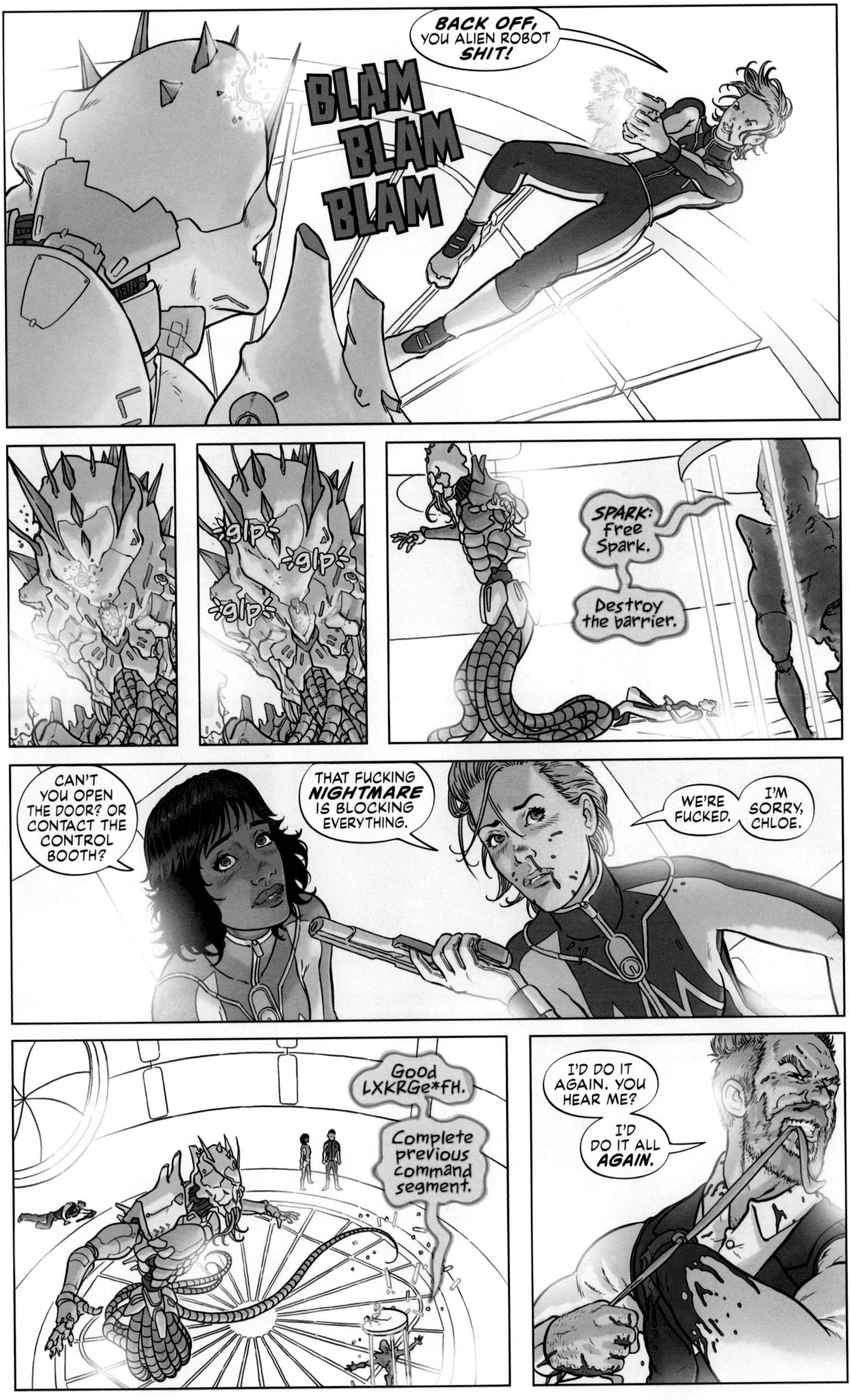
BACK OFF, YOU ALIEN ROBOT SHIT!
BLAM BLAM BLAM
glp glp glp
SPARK: Free Spark.
Destroy the barrier.
CAN'T YOU OPEN THE DOOR? OR CONTACT THE CONTROL BOOTH?
THAT FUCKING NIGHTMARE IS BLOCKING EVERYTHING.
WE'RE FUCKED.
I'M SORRY, CHLOE.
Good LXKRGe*FH.
Complete previous command segment.
I'D DO IT AGAIN. YOU HEAR ME?
I'D DO IT ALL AGAIN.

OKAY. SO BE IT, I GUESS.

A JOURNALIST. I ALWAYS WANTED TO BE A JOURNALIST.

EXCUSE ME?

MY PROFESSOR SAID YOU NEEDED TWO THINGS TO BE A JOURNALIST.

WHAT THE HOLY *FUCK* ARE YOU GOING ON ABOUT, CHLOE?

HE SAID, "YOU NEED AN EYE FOR THE OBVIOUS...

"...AND AN *EAR* FOR THE *GODDAMN TRUTH.*"

CHLOE...?

CHLOE?

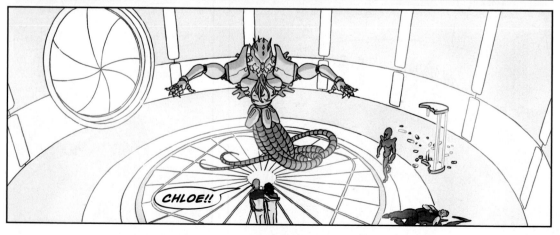

CHLOE!!

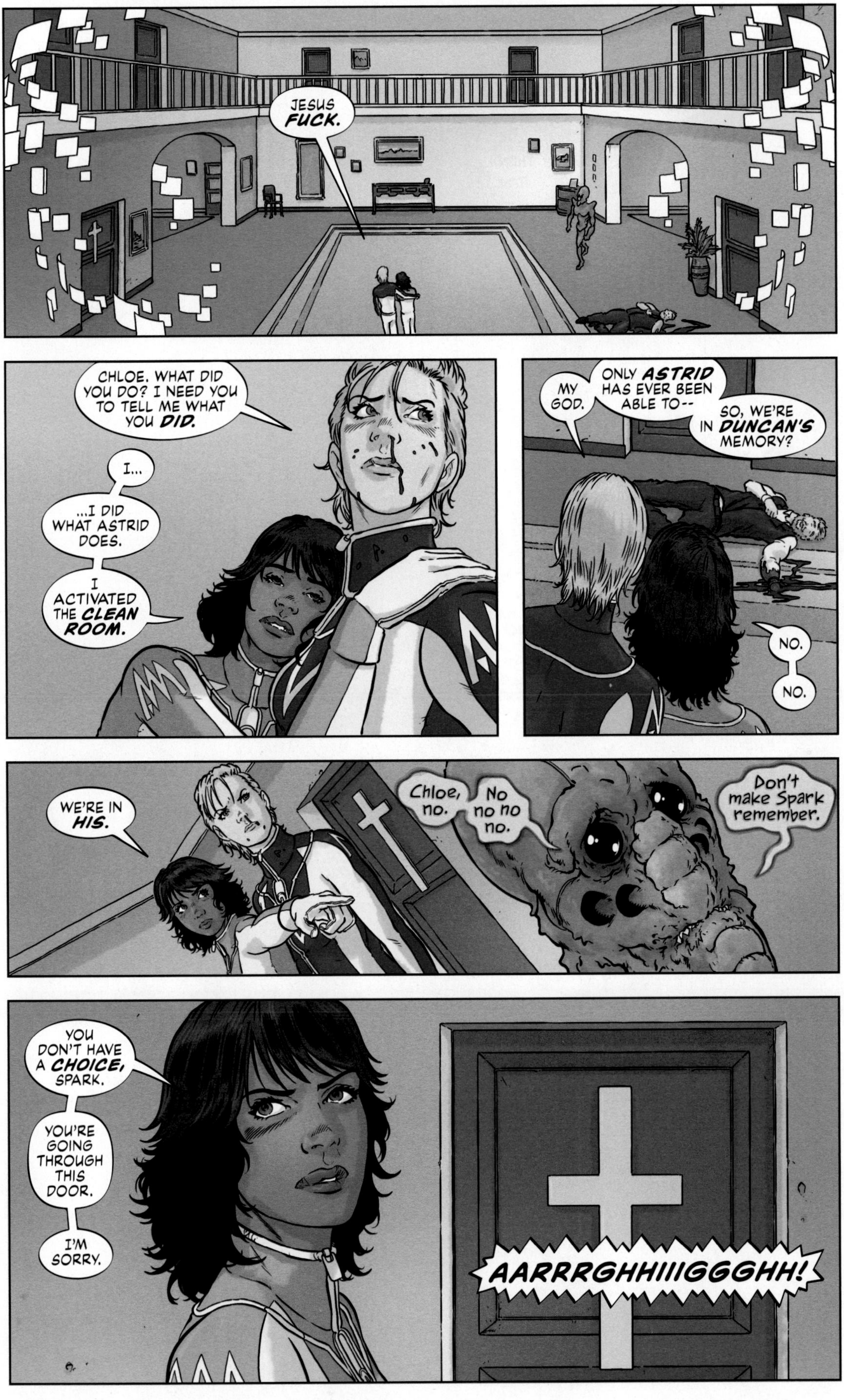
JESUS FUCK.
CHLOE. WHAT DID YOU DO? I NEED YOU TO TELL ME WHAT YOU DID.
I...
...I DID WHAT ASTRID DOES.
I ACTIVATED THE CLEAN ROOM.
MY GOD.
ONLY ASTRID HAS EVER BEEN ABLE TO--
SO, WE'RE IN DUNCAN'S MEMORY?
NO.
NO.
WE'RE IN HIS.
Chloe, no.
No no no no.
Don't make Spark remember.
YOU DON'T HAVE A CHOICE, SPARK.
YOU'RE GOING THROUGH THIS DOOR.
I'M SORRY.
AARRRGHHIIIGGGHH!

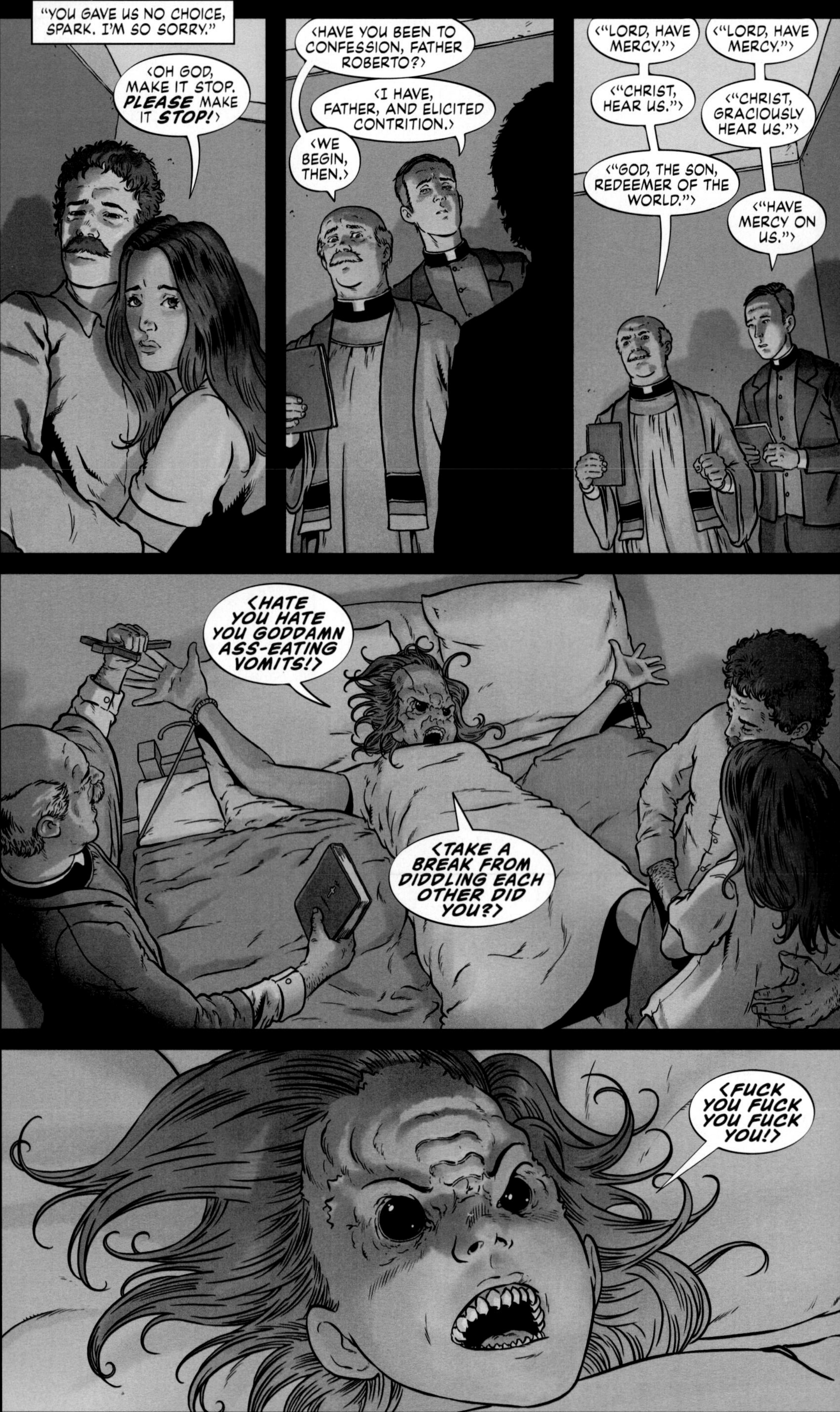
"YOU GAVE US NO CHOICE, SPARK. I'M SO SORRY."
‹OH GOD, MAKE IT STOP. *PLEASE* MAKE IT *STOP!*›
‹HAVE YOU BEEN TO CONFESSION, FATHER ROBERTO?›
‹I HAVE, FATHER, AND ELICITED CONTRITION.›
‹WE BEGIN, THEN.›
‹"LORD, HAVE MERCY."›
‹"CHRIST, HEAR US."›
‹"GOD, THE SON, REDEEMER OF THE WORLD."›
‹"LORD, HAVE MERCY."›
‹"CHRIST, GRACIOUSLY HEAR US."›
‹"HAVE MERCY ON US."›
‹HATE YOU HATE YOU GODDAMN ASS-EATING VOMITS!›
‹TAKE A BREAK FROM DIDDLING EACH OTHER DID YOU?›
‹FUCK YOU FUCK YOU FUCK YOU!›

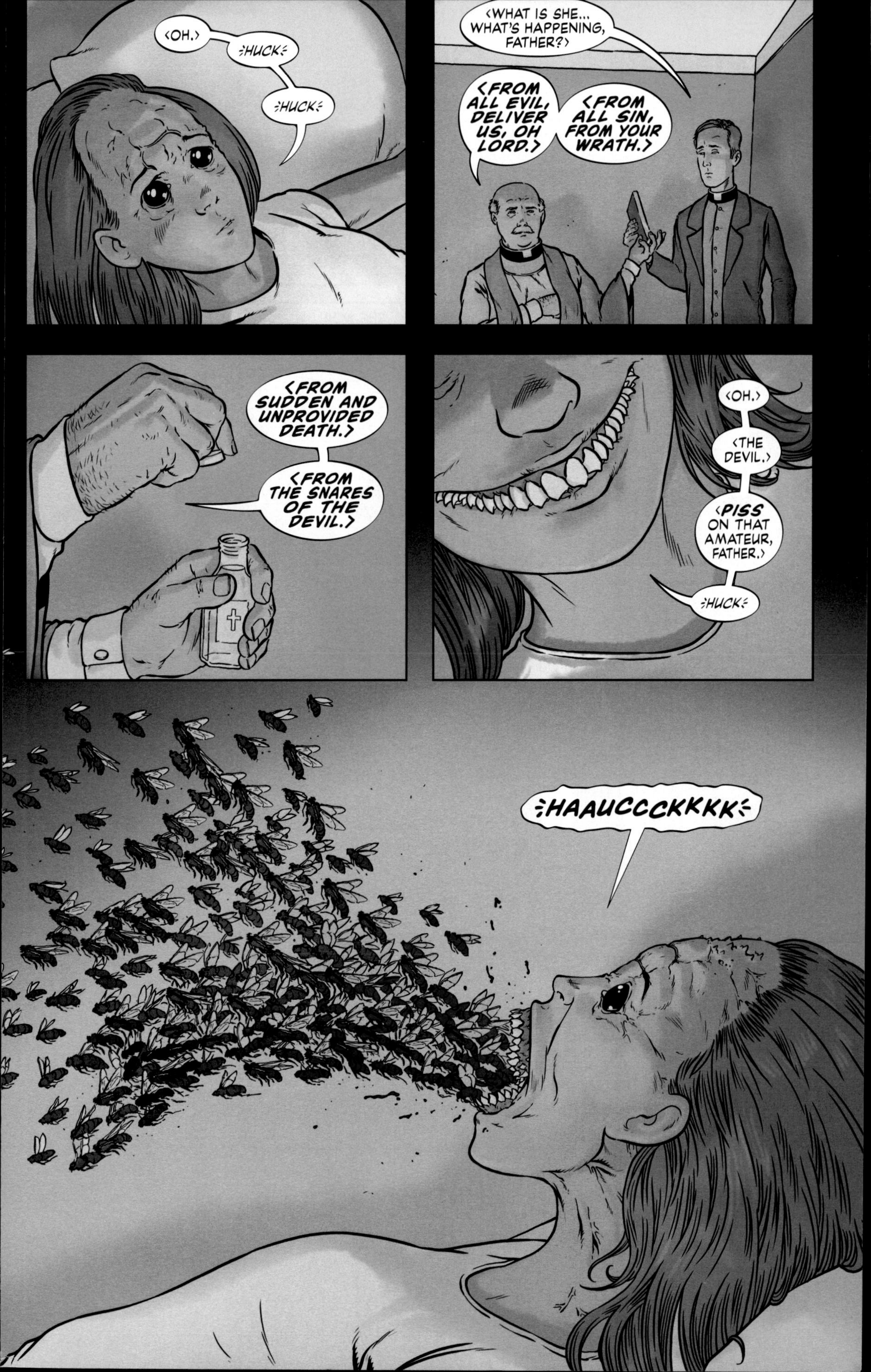

‹OH.›
HUCK
HUCK
‹WHAT IS SHE... WHAT'S HAPPENING, FATHER?›
‹FROM ALL EVIL, DELIVER US, OH LORD.›
‹FROM ALL SIN, FROM YOUR WRATH.›
‹FROM SUDDEN AND UNPROVIDED DEATH.›
‹FROM THE SNARES OF THE DEVIL.›
‹OH.›
‹THE DEVIL.›
‹PISS ON THAT AMATEUR, FATHER.›
HUCK
HAAUCCCKKKK

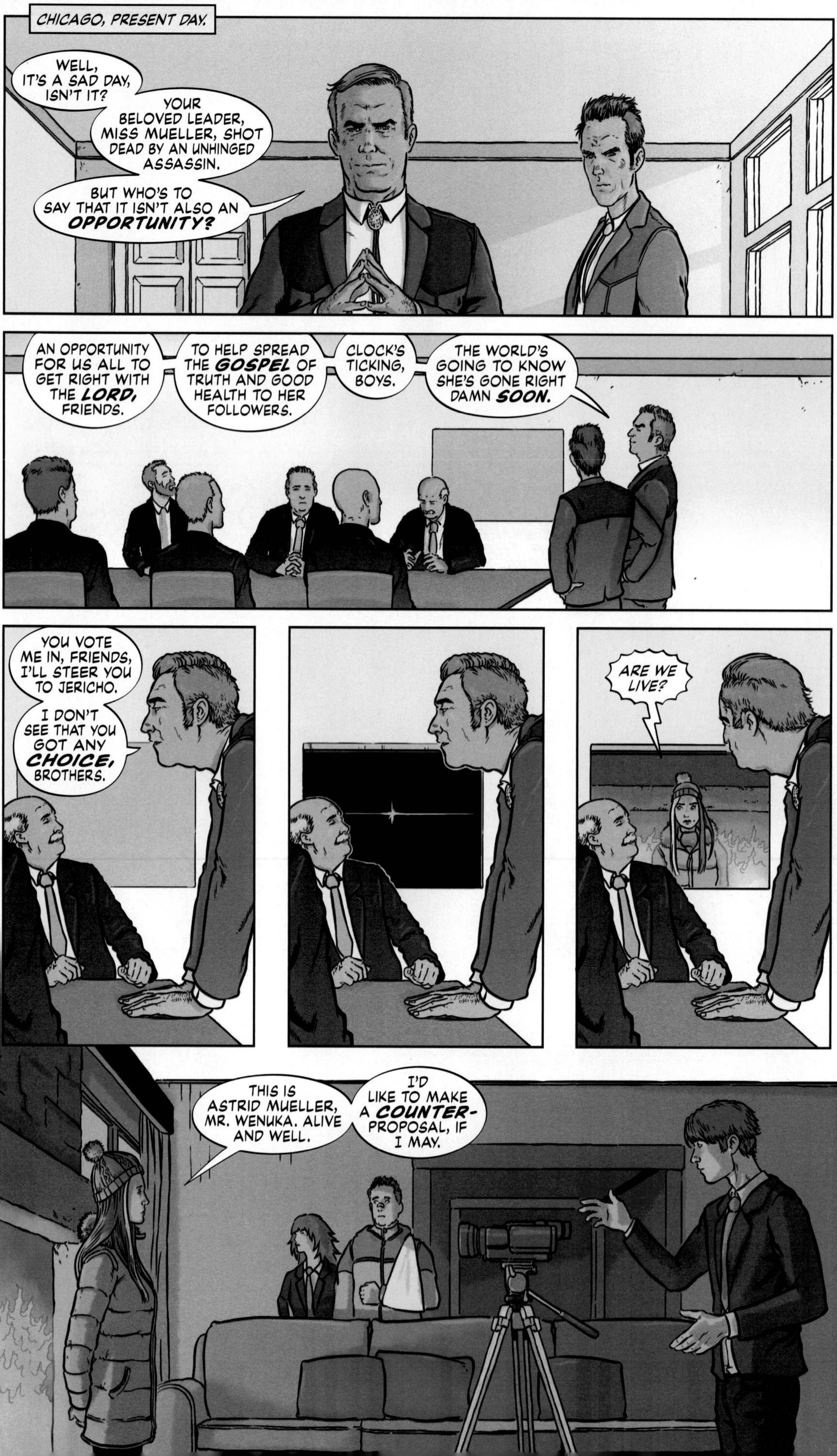
CHICAGO, PRESENT DAY.
WELL, IT'S A SAD DAY, ISN'T IT?
YOUR BELOVED LEADER, MISS MUELLER, SHOT DEAD BY AN UNHINGED ASSASSIN.
BUT WHO'S TO SAY THAT IT ISN'T ALSO AN OPPORTUNITY?
AN OPPORTUNITY FOR US ALL TO GET RIGHT WITH THE LORD, FRIENDS.
TO HELP SPREAD THE GOSPEL OF TRUTH AND GOOD HEALTH TO HER FOLLOWERS.
CLOCK'S TICKING, BOYS.
THE WORLD'S GOING TO KNOW SHE'S GONE RIGHT DAMN SOON.
YOU VOTE ME IN, FRIENDS, I'LL STEER YOU TO JERICHO.
I DON'T SEE THAT YOU GOT ANY CHOICE, BROTHERS.
ARE WE LIVE?
THIS IS ASTRID MUELLER, MR. WENUKA. ALIVE AND WELL.
I'D LIKE TO MAKE A COUNTER-PROPOSAL, IF I MAY.

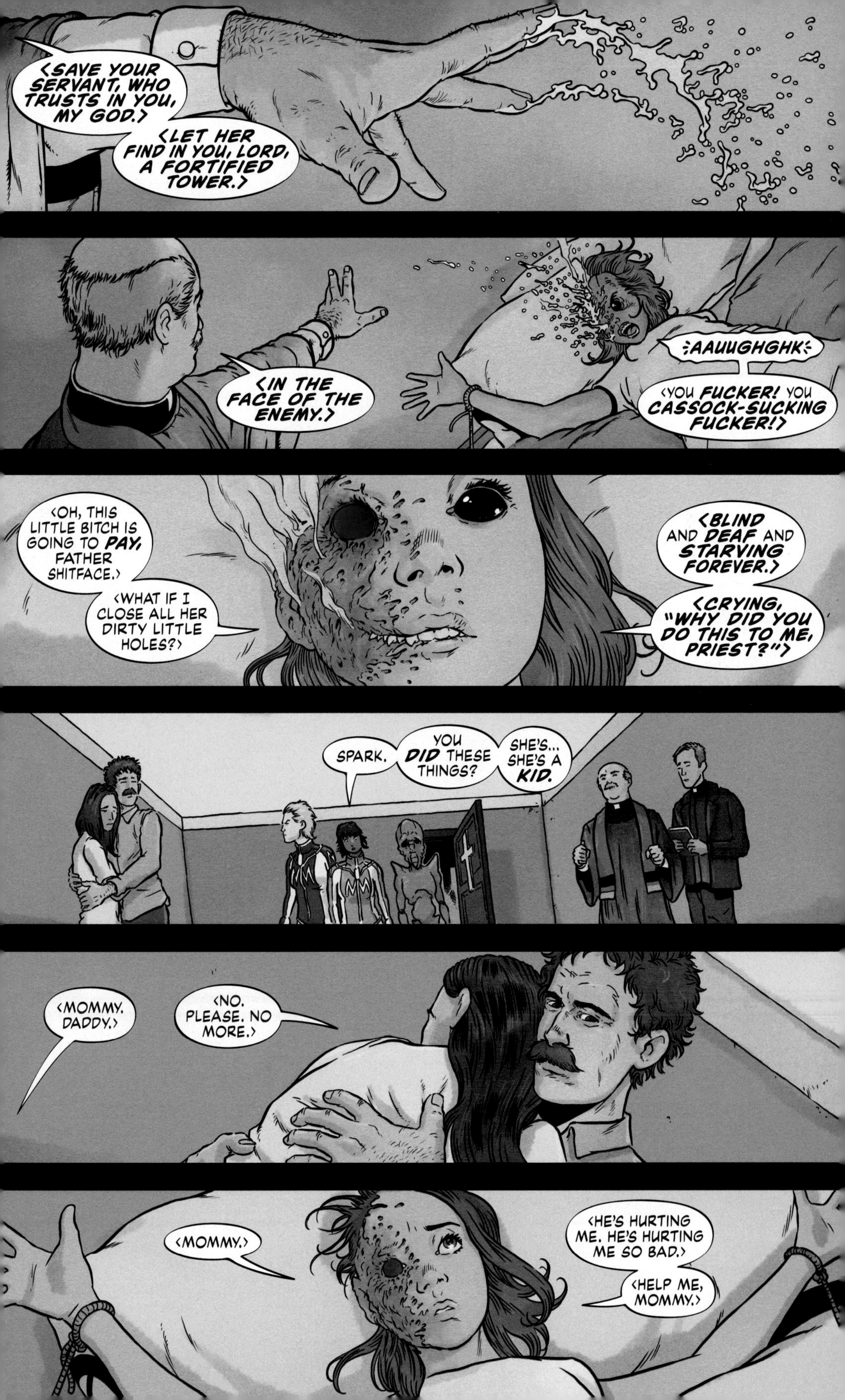
‹SAVE YOUR SERVANT, WHO TRUSTS IN YOU, MY GOD.›
‹LET HER FIND IN YOU, LORD, A FORTIFIED TOWER.›
‹IN THE FACE OF THE ENEMY.›
AAUUGHGHK
‹YOU FUCKER! YOU CASSOCK-SUCKING FUCKER!›
‹OH, THIS LITTLE BITCH IS GOING TO PAY, FATHER SHITFACE.›
‹WHAT IF I CLOSE ALL HER DIRTY LITTLE HOLES?›
‹BLIND AND DEAF AND STARVING FOREVER.›
‹CRYING, "WHY DID YOU DO THIS TO ME, PRIEST?"›
SPARK.
YOU DID THESE THINGS?
SHE'S... SHE'S A KID.
‹MOMMY. DADDY.›
‹NO. PLEASE. NO MORE.›
‹MOMMY.›
‹HE'S HURTING ME. HE'S HURTING ME SO BAD.›
‹HELP ME, MOMMY.›

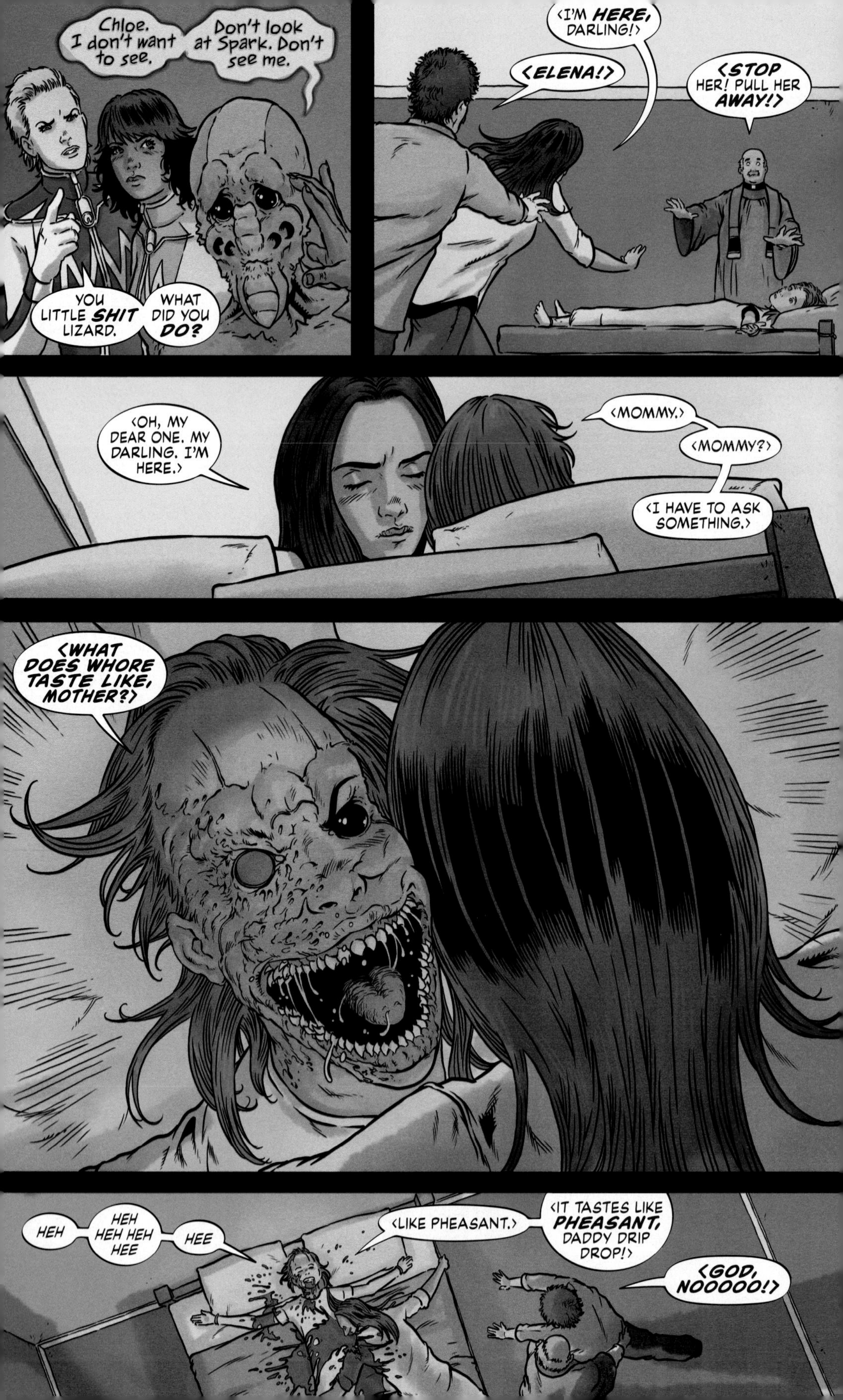

Chloe. I don't want to see.
Don't look at Spark. Don't see me.
YOU LITTLE SHIT LIZARD.
WHAT DID YOU DO?
‹ELENA!›
‹I'M HERE, DARLING!›
‹STOP HER! PULL HER AWAY!›
‹OH, MY DEAR ONE. MY DARLING. I'M HERE.›
‹MOMMY.›
‹MOMMY?›
‹I HAVE TO ASK SOMETHING.›
‹WHAT DOES WHORE TASTE LIKE, MOTHER?›
HEH
HEH HEH HEH HEE
HEE
‹LIKE PHEASANT.›
‹IT TASTES LIKE PHEASANT, DADDY DRIP DROP!›
‹GOD, NOOOOO!›

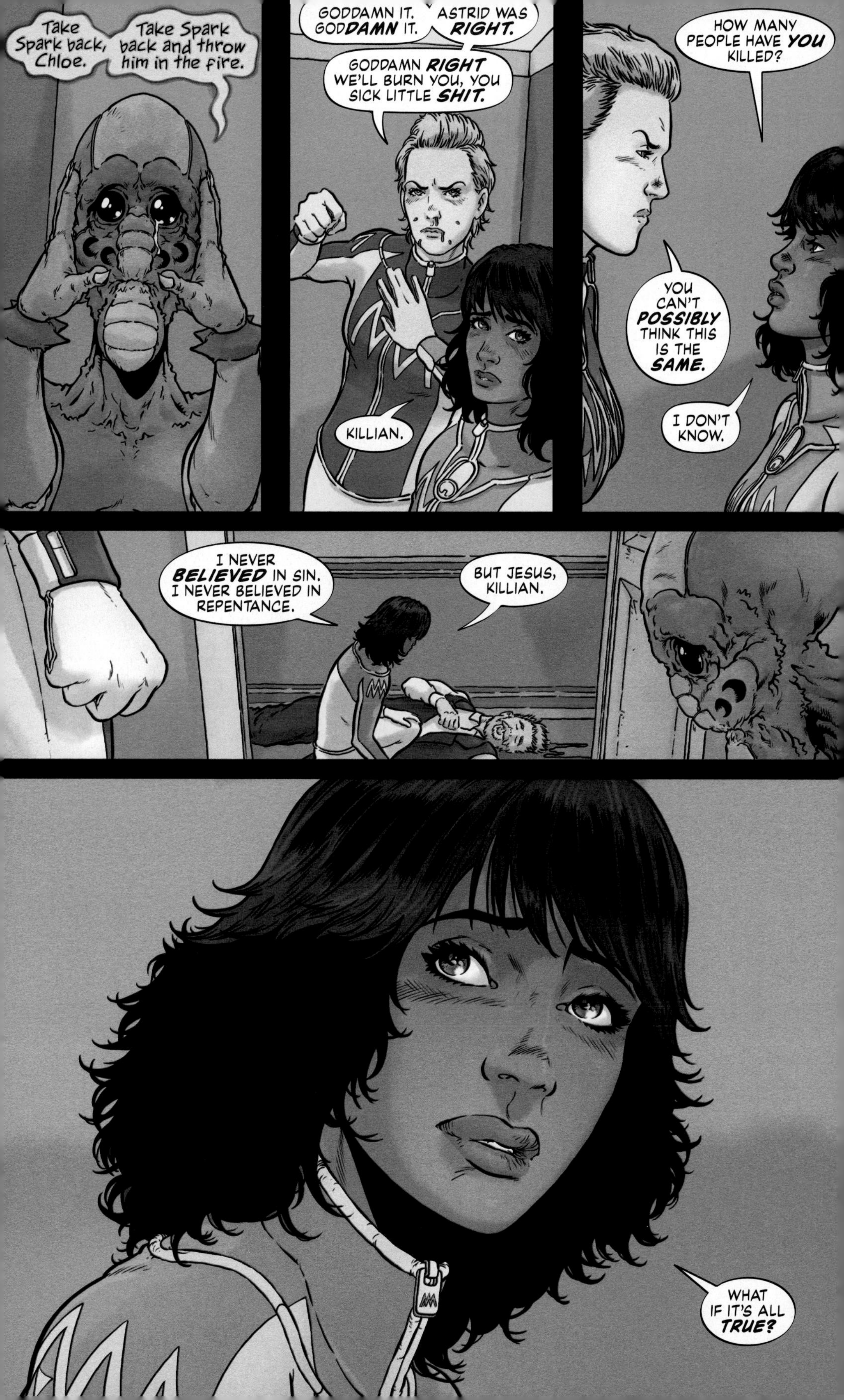
Take Spark back, Chloe.
Take Spark back and throw him in the fire.
GODDAMN IT. GODDAMN IT.
ASTRID WAS RIGHT.
GODDAMN RIGHT WE'LL BURN YOU, YOU SICK LITTLE SHIT.
KILLIAN.
HOW MANY PEOPLE HAVE YOU KILLED?
YOU CAN'T POSSIBLY THINK THIS IS THE SAME.
I DON'T KNOW.
I NEVER BELIEVED IN SIN. I NEVER BELIEVED IN REPENTANCE.
BUT JESUS, KILLIAN.
WHAT IF IT'S ALL TRUE?

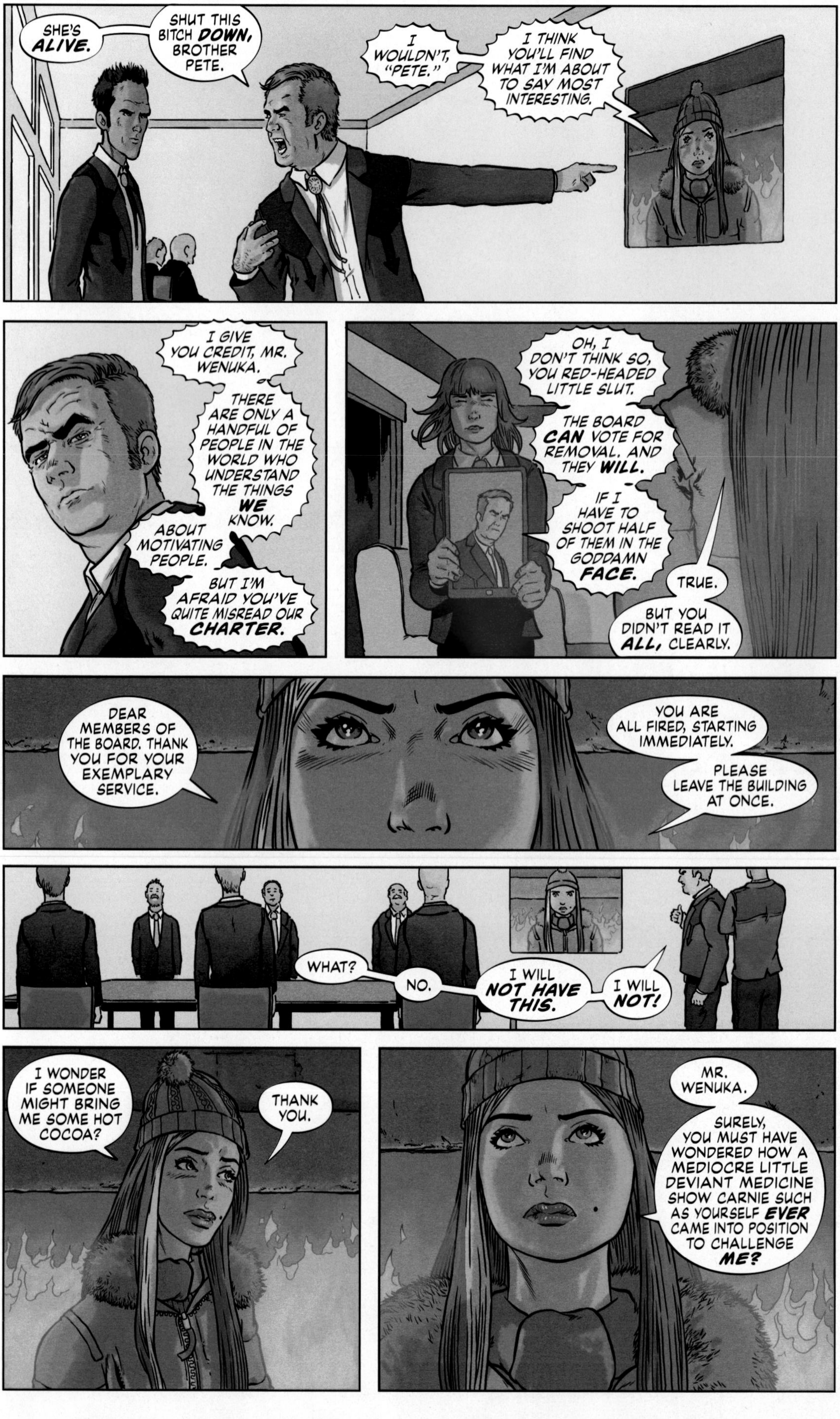
SHE'S ALIVE.
SHUT THIS BITCH DOWN, BROTHER PETE.
I WOULDN'T, "PETE."
I THINK YOU'LL FIND WHAT I'M ABOUT TO SAY MOST INTERESTING.
I GIVE YOU CREDIT, MR. WENUKA.
THERE ARE ONLY A HANDFUL OF PEOPLE IN THE WORLD WHO UNDERSTAND THE THINGS WE KNOW.
ABOUT MOTIVATING PEOPLE.
BUT I'M AFRAID YOU'VE QUITE MISREAD OUR CHARTER.
OH, I DON'T THINK SO, YOU RED-HEADED LITTLE SLUT.
THE BOARD CAN VOTE FOR REMOVAL. AND THEY WILL.
IF I HAVE TO SHOOT HALF OF THEM IN THE GODDAMN FACE.
TRUE.
BUT YOU DIDN'T READ IT ALL, CLEARLY.
DEAR MEMBERS OF THE BOARD. THANK YOU FOR YOUR EXEMPLARY SERVICE.
YOU ARE ALL FIRED, STARTING IMMEDIATELY.
PLEASE LEAVE THE BUILDING AT ONCE.
WHAT?
NO.
I WILL NOT HAVE THIS.
I WILL NOT!
I WONDER IF SOMEONE MIGHT BRING ME SOME HOT COCOA?
THANK YOU.
MR. WENUKA.
SURELY, YOU MUST HAVE WONDERED HOW A MEDIOCRE LITTLE DEVIANT MEDICINE SHOW CARNIE SUCH AS YOURSELF EVER CAME INTO POSITION TO CHALLENGE ME?

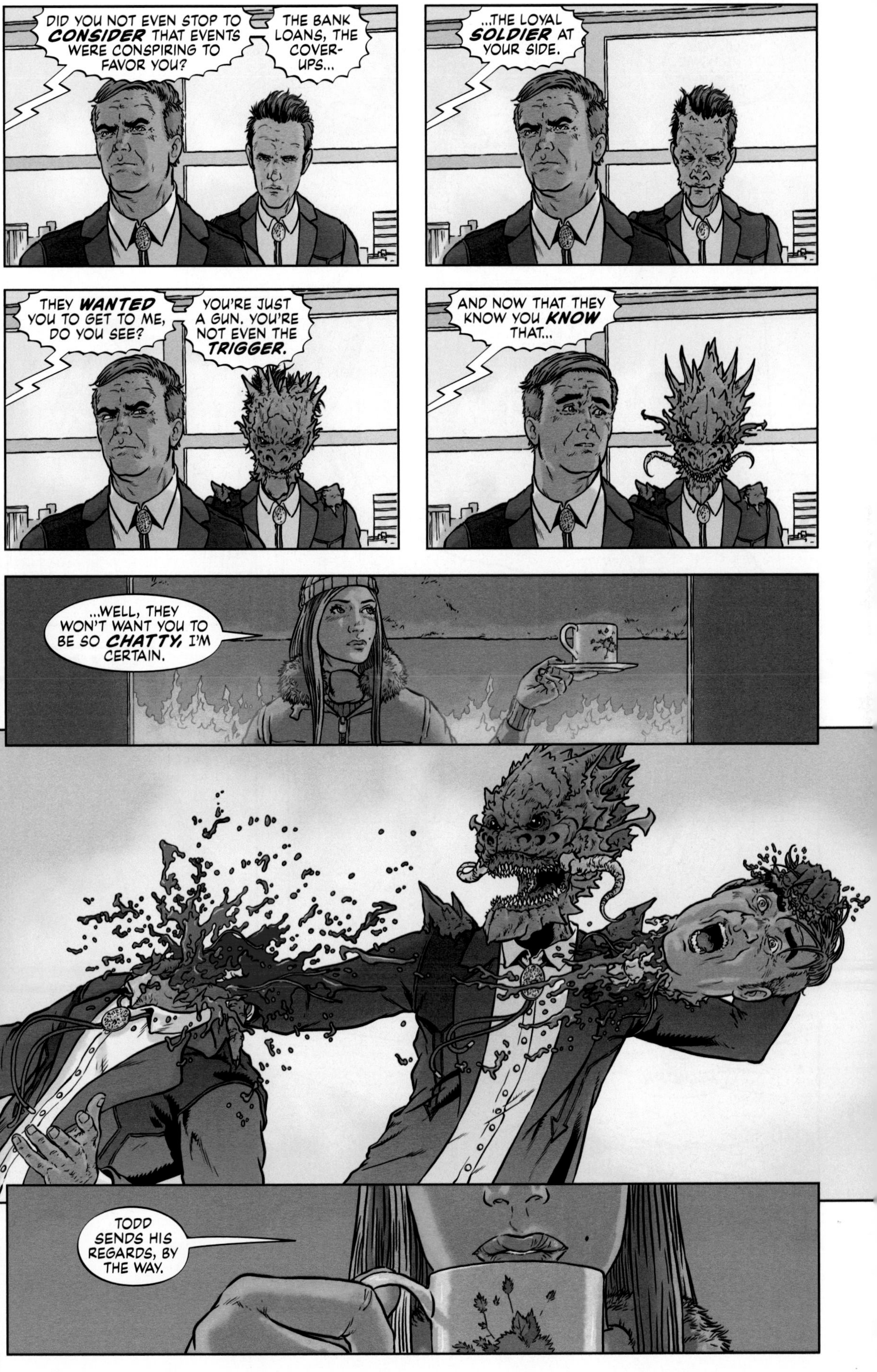
DID YOU NOT EVEN STOP TO CONSIDER THAT EVENTS WERE CONSPIRING TO FAVOR YOU?
THE BANK LOANS, THE COVER-UPS...
...THE LOYAL SOLDIER AT YOUR SIDE.
THEY WANTED YOU TO GET TO ME, DO YOU SEE?
YOU'RE JUST A GUN. YOU'RE NOT EVEN THE TRIGGER.
AND NOW THAT THEY KNOW YOU KNOW THAT...
...WELL, THEY WON'T WANT YOU TO BE SO CHATTY, I'M CERTAIN.
TODD SENDS HIS REGARDS, BY THE WAY.

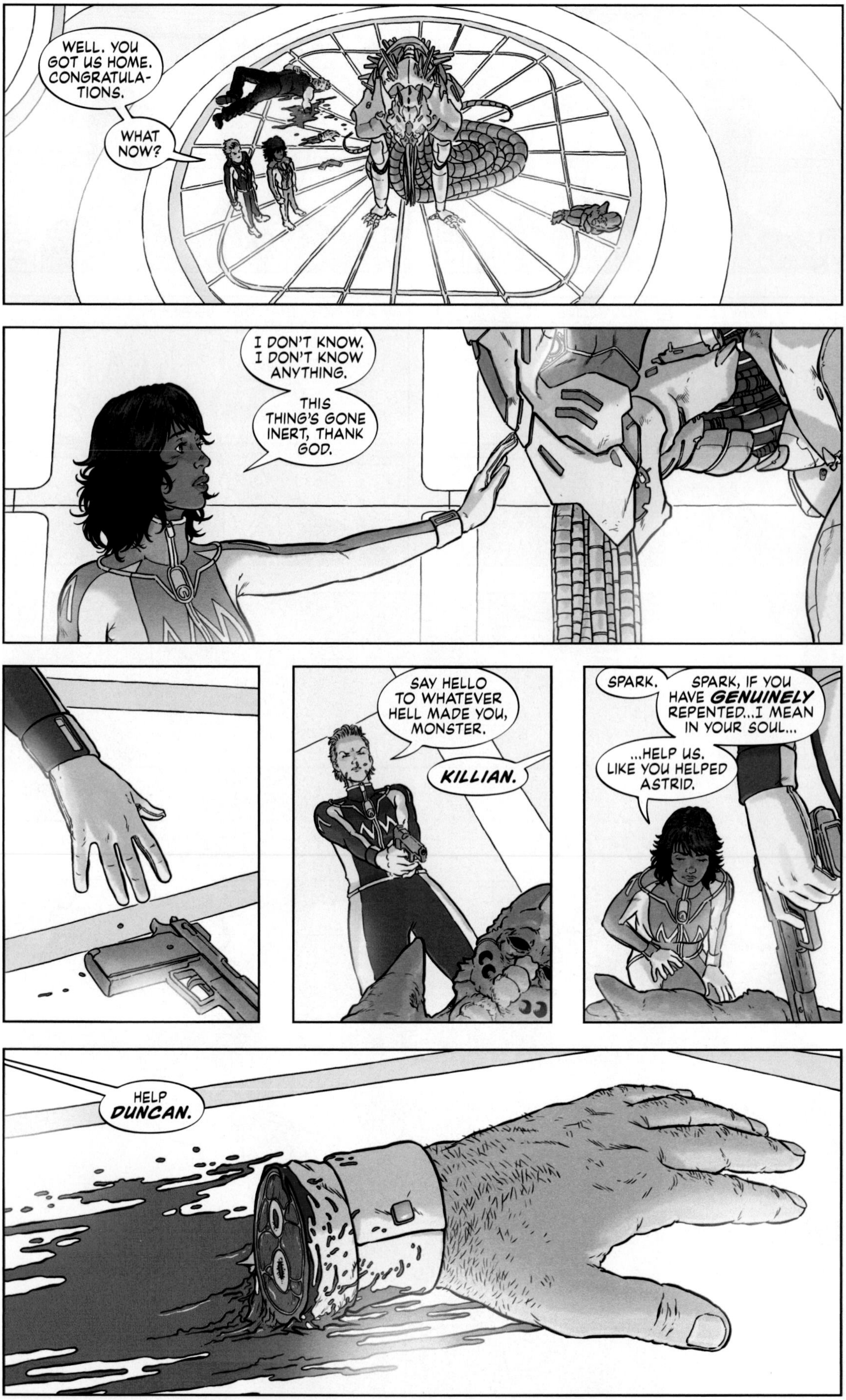
WELL. YOU GOT US HOME. CONGRATULA-TIONS.
WHAT NOW?
I DON'T KNOW. I DON'T KNOW ANYTHING.
THIS THING'S GONE INERT, THANK GOD.
SAY HELLO TO WHATEVER HELL MADE YOU, MONSTER.
KILLIAN.
SPARK.
SPARK, IF YOU HAVE GENUINELY REPENTED...I MEAN IN YOUR SOUL...
...HELP US. LIKE YOU HELPED ASTRID.
HELP DUNCAN.

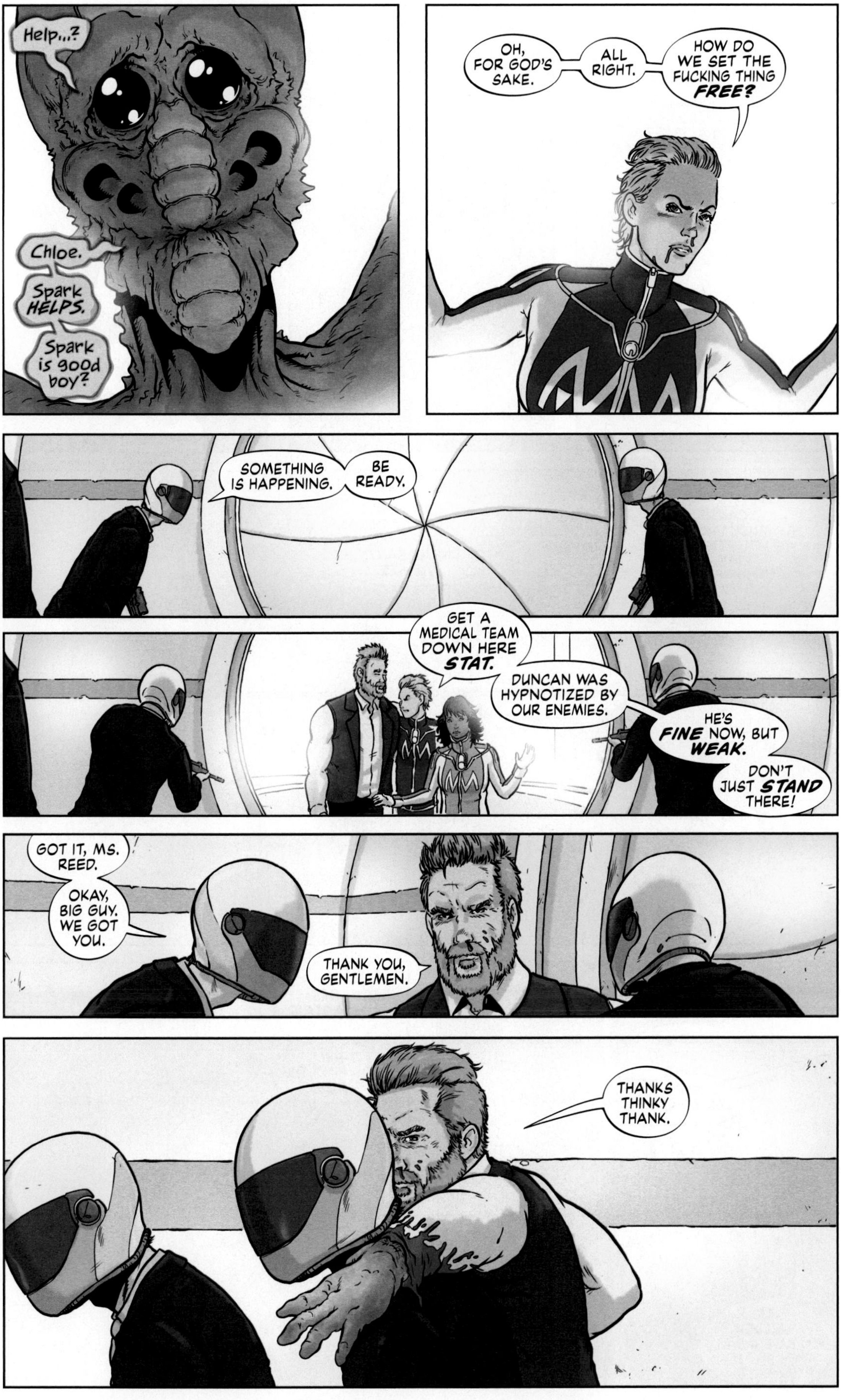

Help...?
Chloe.
Spark HELPS.
Spark is good boy?
OH, FOR GOD'S SAKE.
ALL RIGHT.
HOW DO WE SET THE FUCKING THING FREE?
SOMETHING IS HAPPENING.
BE READY.
GET A MEDICAL TEAM DOWN HERE STAT.
DUNCAN WAS HYPNOTIZED BY OUR ENEMIES.
HE'S FINE NOW, BUT WEAK.
DON'T JUST STAND THERE!
GOT IT, MS. REED.
OKAY, BIG GUY. WE GOT YOU.
THANK YOU, GENTLEMEN.
THANKS THINKY THANK.

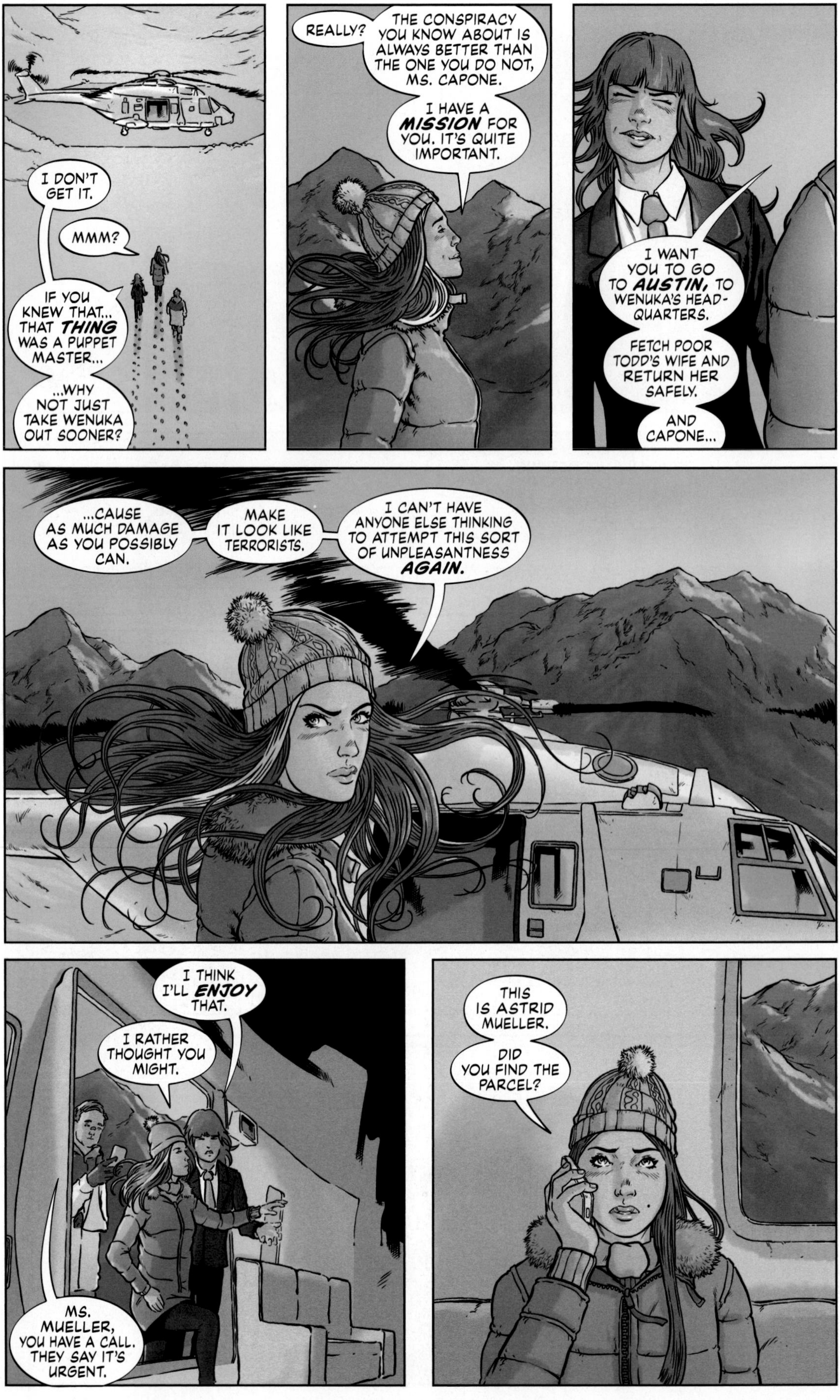
I DON'T GET IT.
MMM?
IF YOU KNEW THAT... THAT THING WAS A PUPPET MASTER...
...WHY NOT JUST TAKE WENUKA OUT SOONER?
REALLY?
THE CONSPIRACY YOU KNOW ABOUT IS ALWAYS BETTER THAN THE ONE YOU DO NOT, MS. CAPONE.
I HAVE A MISSION FOR YOU. IT'S QUITE IMPORTANT.
I WANT YOU TO GO TO AUSTIN, TO WENUKA'S HEAD-QUARTERS.
FETCH POOR TODD'S WIFE AND RETURN HER SAFELY.
AND CAPONE...
...CAUSE AS MUCH DAMAGE AS YOU POSSIBLY CAN.
MAKE IT LOOK LIKE TERRORISTS.
I CAN'T HAVE ANYONE ELSE THINKING TO ATTEMPT THIS SORT OF UNPLEASANTNESS AGAIN.
I THINK I'LL ENJOY THAT.
I RATHER THOUGHT YOU MIGHT.
MS. MUELLER, YOU HAVE A CALL. THEY SAY IT'S URGENT.
THIS IS ASTRID MUELLER.
DID YOU FIND THE PARCEL?

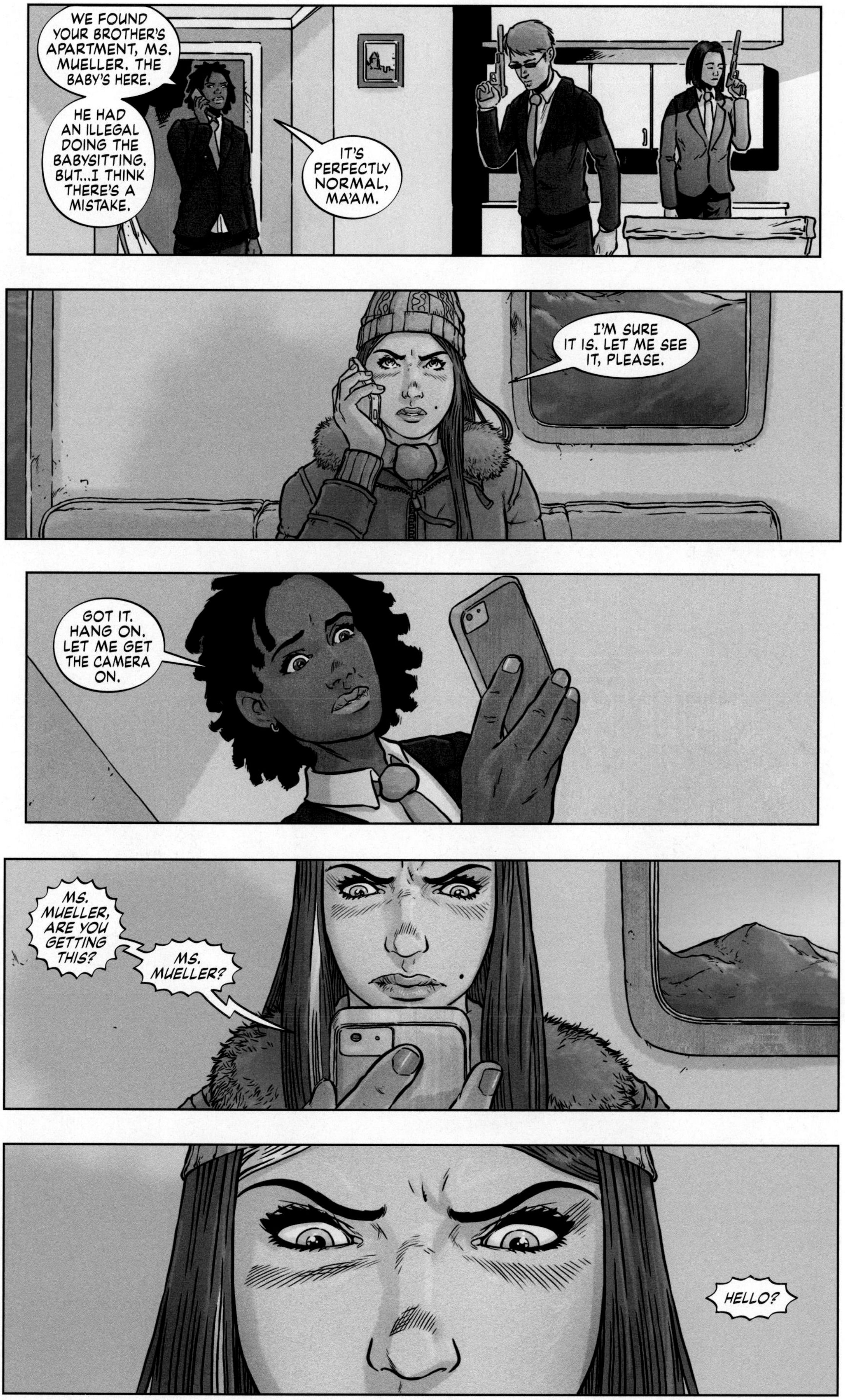
WE FOUND YOUR BROTHER'S APARTMENT, MS. MUELLER. THE BABY'S HERE.
HE HAD AN ILLEGAL DOING THE BABYSITTING. BUT...I THINK THERE'S A MISTAKE.
IT'S PERFECTLY NORMAL, MA'AM.
I'M SURE IT IS. LET ME SEE IT, PLEASE.
GOT IT. HANG ON. LET ME GET THE CAMERA ON.
MS. MUELLER, ARE YOU GETTING THIS?
MS. MUELLER?
HELLO?

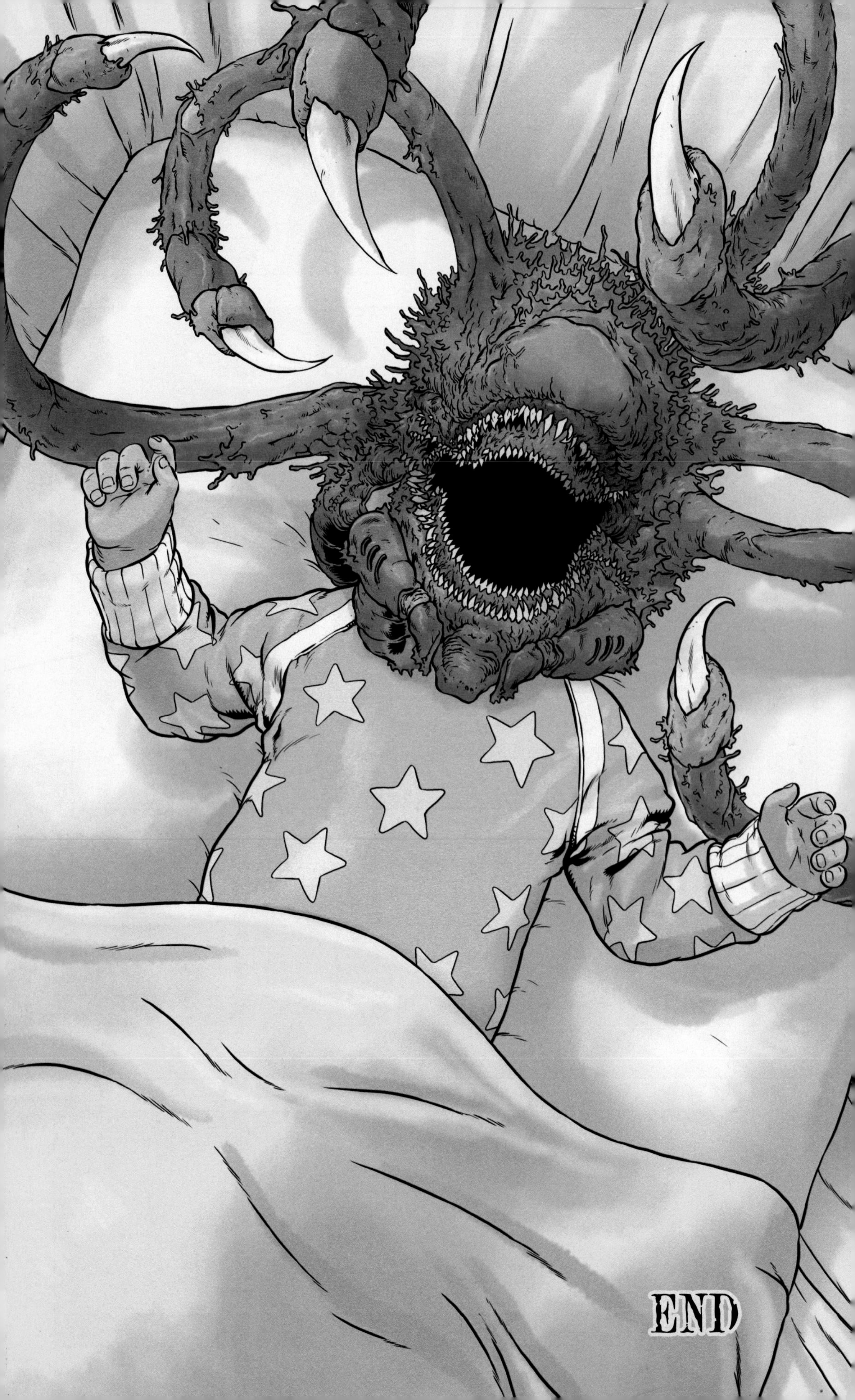
END